"Inside My Ed"

Zoe Burnett

Cover design by Danji Designs

Contents

Dedication

To my darling husband James, every time I pushed
you away, you stayed.
Every time I could not hear my rational voice, you
spoke wisdom.
Every time I found a reason to give up, you provided
a million reasons to keep going.

Thank you for being by my side every step of the way
and continuing to love and support me on this
journey.

Together, we can conquer anything.

Acknowledgements

Trying to figure out everyone I wanted to thank for helping me make this to happen, could quite easily be a book in itself. So, I have tried to keep it simple. There are so many people who have helped me get to where I am and encouraged me to pursue this. The first of course:

My wonderful publisher and editor, Taryn, who one day said, "*You should write a book*". I am sorry I laughed in your face, whilst continuing to drink my gin. Thank you for nudging me to do this, and being such a positive cheerleader, for all you have done to make this possible, for your wisdom and never-ending knowledge, and for not muting my endless emails. Also, all of her fabulous team over at the FCM group, for helping this book come to life.

The man who held my life in his hands many times, and contributor to this book. Dr Stephen Linacre. Thank you, not only for your insightful knowledge in this book, but your endless passion and determination to help all those struggling with eating disorders. Your commitment is inspiring, and I know you will continue to make a difference to so many lives, as you have done with mine.

Thank you to the rest of the amazing team at St Georges Hospital Lincoln. My incredible community support workers, who no matter what I said or did, understood with empathy and supported me wholeheartedly in my recovery. My dietician and psychiatrist, knowing exactly what is best for my body and helping my body to once again do its thing again.

Katy Baggott, Andrew Farenden and Richard Askam. My amazing managers, agents and coaches over at 3 degrees of innovation. Thank you for giving me the courage to deliver my first ever talk, taking me well and truly out of my comfort zone, but seeing something in me I never knew existed. Thank you for taking me under your wing. Not only have you given me the confidence to pursue a career as a public speaker, but you have also provided me with friendship, which I held dear to me and will continue to treasure.

Finally, but certainly not last - to all my wonderful friends, thank you for believing in me and sitting with me in my darkest moments. For allowing me to rant at you and not trying to fix me but loving me regardless. For supporting me in new projects and helping me figure out who I really am.

Foreword by 3Di

Sometimes, something extraordinary happens when you least expect it. You create a situation in which it might happen but in your heart of hearts, you don't have any weight of expectation that it will. And then it does... and the Universe is a better place as a result.

This happened when Zoe Burnett stood up to audition for her first ever speech in public, which just happened to be a TEDx talk in Lincoln in 2019.

I'd never met Zoe before this, and I can honestly say that this chance encounter has changed the course of both of our lives.

Zoe is one of the most wonderfully unassuming and natural people I have ever met, with a back story that would scare the bejeezus out of most. She has overcome this with a style and grace of someone who is wise beyond their years. Zoe knows all the words... sometimes she uses all the words... but she has some amazing words and I hope you enjoy reading them as much as I have enjoyed coaching them out of her.

Richard Askam
3Di Co-Founder and Friend of Zoe

Around 1.6 million people in the UK suffer from eating disorders, many in secret. They are of all ages, genders and backgrounds – eating disorders do not discriminate.

I first met Zoe in 2019 through a local TEDx event, her story told in her own words is profoundly moving and liberated me from the destructive belief that weight defines health.

In her book, Zoe shares with vulnerability and compassion her unique insights and a no-nonsense approach to recovery - a refreshing, encouraging and empowering read, packed full of practical help and advice for anyone living with this illness, as well as for those supporting them.

Katy Baggott
3Di Co-founder and coach

On the day that I met Zoe she was trembling; literally days out of hospital and stood before a live audience as she pitched the idea for her TEDx talk.

I find it hard to reconcile the person who stood before me two years ago to the courageous, honest and authentic advocate that invites you into her world with this book; they are simply poles apart.

Zoe's candour delivers a no-nonsense appraisal of the way that eating disorders are viewed in the UK and practical advice to recovery based on her lived experience.

The road to recovery is seldom simple or easy, but whether you are living with an eating disorder or supporting someone who is, this book is proof of the light at the end of the tunnel.

Changing the UK's attitude to weight and eating disorders will be a long road paved with the debris of a million smashed scales, one which Zoe leads the dance gracefully through barefoot.

Andy Farenden
3Di Co-founder and TEDx Curator

Introduction

About Beat

I refer to BEAT's services regularly throughout this book, they were a true ally and without them I would not be here today to share my story. So, who exactly are BEAT?

BEAT is a UK based eating disorder charity founded in 1989. They have a mission, to end the pain and suffering caused by eating disorders. They work tirelessly to support sufferers, carers, family and friends, equipping all with essential skills and advice. On their very informative website, you can find information on all types of eating disorders. There is a wide variety of inspiring blogs and stories which have been written by people living with or who have recovered from these terrible illnesses.

They provide downloadable leaflets you can take to the doctors with you, and even support for employers and teachers. As well as information, you will find a whole range of different support services, from helplines to web chat rooms. A safe space to talk through and untangle those overwhelming thoughts, or alternatively someone to talk to regarding how to help support your loved one.

They are eating disorder myth busters and work hard with professionals offering training and CPD opportunities. Please do head on over to their website to find out how they could help support you:

www.beateatingdisorders.org.uk

About The Book

You will notice each chapter of the book is based on a different component of Atypical anorexia. Each warrior is different so some elements may not match your specific symptoms.

I have explained my lived experience, how it felt for me personally and my specific behaviours. I also partner this with a recovery guide on what helped me overcome these specific behaviours and ways I coped. When reading my lived experience please note, you may find it triggering. If this is the case, put the book down and engage in some self-care, or even skip to the recovery guide. Your recovery and wellbeing come first.

The recovery guides are full of useful strategies and tips on how I personally overcame that specific area, there are other techniques out there, but I am just including my personal favourites and what I found to be helpful, in the hope it may help you. They may not always follow straight after each other but they are there.

There will be a mixture of cognitive behaviour therapy, dialectic behaviour therapy and also mindfulness techniques that I have learnt along the way. I have also included things that I have done personally, away from therapy that have helped. Please do use them and share them with others.

Throughout the book you'll see that I refer to ED – at the beginning of therapy I was asked to give the disordered voice a name, so that I could differentiate it from my rational brain, somewhat unimaginatively, I chose ED. I now recognise his voice and what drives it, having a name made this easier to visualise.

There is a section at the end of each chapter which offers a summary and key points, take a look at these to see if you're in the right mindset to read the chapter.

It is my hope that this book does not just reach out to those suffering, but also parents, loved ones and those trying to support someone through this illness. You can learn the science behind the disorder whilst reading how it looks from a sufferer's point of view, and then use the strategies and try and suggest or implement them into your homes.

Also, I truly hope that health care professionals use this as well, to broaden their views on eating disorders and realise that, yes, I may be a healthy weight, but by reading about my lived experiences, will see that a healthy BMI does not mean a healthy body or mind.

Please note, eating disorders are a very dangerous psychiatric disorder, if you, or a loved one is suffering, or struggling to recover properly, professional help is required, with a proper treatment team who understand eating disorders. This book is not designed to be used instead of professional help.

Professional Information - Dr Stephen Linacre

I have been asked by Zoe to write this chapter about Eating Disorders and in particular, Other Specified Feeding/Eating Disorders (OSFED) or what can be referred to as "Atypical Anorexia Nervosa."

As a Clinical Psychologist, having worked in Eating Disorder Services for several years and having recovered from my own eating disorder, I know the pain that eating disorders cause and how difficult recovery can be.

However, I know that many people do get better and like the author and I, this is fully possible. It requires the team around the person to work together in a way that allows for "joined up" care. Eating disorders are a dangerous mental health condition and no matter what your weight is, gender, age, background, sexuality or any other characteristic, they can cause serious problems for your health and relationships; we know that at least 25% of all cases of eating disorders are in males (4).

Eating Disorders are not a "phase" or a choice and over time, they become debilitating and rule your life. Sadly, in some situations, they can lead to death. Approximately, 5% of cases who have Anorexia Nervosa can result in death, either from physical health complications or suicide (1). Research evidence indicates that the sooner a person obtains help for an eating disorder the more likely a good prognosis will occur. However, people can often feel shame and denial and unfortunately at times, service barriers can occur in slowing down the ability to get the specialist help; we know that eating disorders are much more common in society than people acknowledge.

Estimates are that 1.6 million people have eating disorders (2) but this figure is likely to be significantly underestimated. It has become clear over the last year that the COVID-19 pandemic has led to more people struggling with eating difficulties. During the pandemic, people's coping strategies have been restricted and people have often felt anxious and out of control. Sometimes eating disorders can start in a positive way (i.e. an attempt to lose a bit of weight or to be healthier) but in time, it can start to take over your life. It can become obsessional and people can feel that they need to engage in compulsive behaviours (e.g. restriction, body checking, label monitoring, excessive exercise, vomiting or laxative abuse just to name a few). Eating disorders are often also co-morbid with other mental health difficulties such as Anxiety Disorders, Obsessive Compulsive Disorder, Depression, PTSD and Emotional Unstable Personality Disorder (EUPD).

Atypical Anorexia has all the features of Anorexia Nervosa but the person's weight may not be below a body mass index (BMI) of 17.5; a healthy BMI is considered to be between 20 to 25, however this also has its problems as people can be slightly higher and lower depending on other physiological factors. Some evidence suggests that a healthy BMI in modern day society is 27 (3).

When the person's presentation is not overtly emaciated, this can allow the eating disorder to remain unidentified by others and allows it to become stronger and get a further grip on the individual's life. Although Atypical Anorexia can present differently in people, the two common features of the presentation are a "preoccupation with body image, weight and shape" and an "unhealthy relationship with food". A third component, that is not necessarily stipulated, in the DSM V but appears to be relevant across all eating disorders is that the individual has significant low self-esteem. We know that as the eating disorder psychopathology develops and behaviour changes, this can maintain the eating disorder as it can provide the person with a sense of achievement and a perceived boost to their self-esteem.

Atypical Anorexia is as dangerous as any other eating disorder, because even though the person's weight does not appear to be extreme, the impact on the body can be severe. Digestive issues are common, and this can lead to pain and problems with the organs associated with the digestive tract. We also know that the lack of nutrition can influence the person's hormones and affect a person's fertility. It also can affect the functioning of the heart and particularly in those who engage in self-induced vomiting.

A lack of nutrition can also affect blood glucose levels which can be extremely dangerous. Furthermore, the lack of particular nutrients such as calcium in their intake and excessive exercise can affect bone density, increase fractures and lead to serious conditions like osteoporosis. Whilst it may seem outwardly, that a person is healthy, they may be going through cycles of restricting, bingeing, vomiting and exercising. All of these have a serious impact on the body and the mind.

The psychological treatments for Atypical Anorexia or OSFED are the same as Anorexia Nervosa or Bulimia Nervosa. NICE guidelines stipulate what evidenced based treatments should be considered (5). However; the last published guidelines for eating disorders (Eating Disorders: Recognition and Treatment) was produced in 2017 and encouraging psychological therapies are forever developing (e.g. Cognitive Remediation Therapy, Compassion Focused Therapy – Eating Disorders and Radically Open Dialectal Behaviour Therapy). Although they may not have the strongest level of evidence base yet (i.e. Randomised Controlled Trials), further research is warranted.

The most evidenced based therapies include Cognitive Behaviour Therapy-Enhanced (CBT-E) which is a transdiagnostic psychological therapy designed by Christopher Fairburn's team in Oxford. This focuses on the maintaining factors of the eating disorder (e.g. negative automatic thoughts, unhelpful compensatory behaviours, dietary restraint, body image issues and reinforcing behaviours, clinical perfectionism, low self-esteem and interpersonal problems). The Maudsley Anorexia Nervosa Treatment for Adults (MANTRA) has also obtained a reasonable evidence base and Specialist Supportive Clinical Management (SSCM) is also utilised with some patients. Focal Psychodynamic Therapy (FPT) can also be considered if one of the above has been ineffective. As we know, no one therapy works for everyone and often the team working with the person will need to be integrative and receptive to the person's needs.

Although Family Therapy for children and young people has a good evidence base for younger people with eating disorders, it is not considered as a front-line treatment for adults. However, adults with eating disorders often have family members and friends who want to help and as we know that all eating disorders require a systemic approach it is important that they are involved. Interventions like Carer Skills Workshops based on the Maudsley approach have shown to have a positive growing evidence base that can support "carers" with their own psychological wellbeing and promote the person with the eating disorder to move towards recovery. Although psychological therapy is one component of an effective treatment plan, it often involves a full multidisciplinary team (MDT) approach as the author describes in the book.

Atypical Anorexia patients present with significant hatred of their bodies and strive to lose weight in the hope that they will feel better about themselves. Psychologically, it is often linked with a fear of negative judgement and rejection from others.

Patients can have significant anxiety about what others think of them and may also have difficulty in trusting others. The negative automatic thoughts (NATs) that arise tend to be what are called "mindreading", whereby they think they know what others think about them. Sometimes there has been developmental incidents that have shaped the person's view of themselves, others, and the world, in a negative way and therefore they strive to have control over some aspect of their lives. Restrictive eating disorders in particular, also have the effect on numbing emotions (which can be viewed by some as a positive) and often what patients need to learn are adaptive emotion regulation skills and emotional intelligence to help them to cope with the demands and responsibilities of life. Some patients may have experienced trauma (e.g. sexual abuse, bereavements, negative life transitions) that they have not processed. In some cases, this needs to be addressed in therapy as they may maintain what keeps the eating disorder going.

Although the emergence of an eating disorder is a coming together of multiple factors (e.g. genetics, biology and environment), social media can play a part in the growth of an eating disorder mindset. The Western culture that "thin is best" can certainly enhance the likelihood that an eating disorder may develop. It has been identified that eating disorders are more prevalent in Western societies compared to non-Western societies (6). Although social media can be something that can help people stay connected and provide support, there are websites whereby harmful tips and strategies to lose weight are sought and shared (e.g. pro-ana websites). Research has shown the risks of these websites, despite them operating under the guise of "support", they can reinforce eating disorder behaviour and prevent professional help being sought (8).

The "eating disorder voice" is not like hallucinatory "voices" in psychosis but is an internal commentary that is critical and shaming of the individual that can make them feel compelled to act in certain ways (e.g., miss meals, increase their exercise, engage in vomiting, withdraw from others). Experience and evidence demonstrate that the "voice" can be stronger to challenge if a person is emaciated, however it can remain a significant issue in people with eating disorders who are not underweight. Feelings of entrapment and defeat are associated with the "eating disorder voice" (7), however, some individuals value it, as they perceive that it helps them to stay motivated with their striving (i.e. to lose weight and be a better person).

Being able to recognise the "voice" and challenge it through interpersonal interactions can help the person to change their unhelpful behaviours that keep the eating disorder going. Although some people who are recovered can occasionally experience the "eating disorder voice", over time this does not affect them at an emotional level, and they can refocus and get on with life and their valued activities.

The extreme negative view of the body that people with Atypical Anorexia (and many other eating disorders) experience, often leads to either (or both) a preoccupation of checking behaviours (e.g. excessive mirror use, skin pinching, various ways of measuring body parts and feeling for bones) or a total avoidance of seeing the body (avoiding reflections, withdrawing self, wearing baggy clothes and changing clothes in total darkness). The former causes the person into a viscous cycle of over scrutiny and hours can be spent in front of a mirror and can lead to extreme levels of disgust and anxiety.

A mindset of "compare and despair" NATs (that everyone else looks better than them) consequently lower's the person's self-esteem. The latter (body avoidance) can also lead to a sense of hopelessness, depression and withdrawal from society. Body image work in psychotherapy is an important part of recovery, but often this is only completed when a person is at a healthy weight. Coming to accept your body is difficult and it is common in society to have some mild dissatisfaction with some aspect of the body. Helping the person to recognise that their self-perception can be distorted is useful. Other therapeutic work around understanding the cultural influence on body image, valuing the function of body parts, reducing checking behaviours and being more aware that individual differences and flaws are ok can be part of the process. Furthermore, assisting the person to have a better understanding of their core values can also assist in reducing the obsession of trying to make the body perfect.

In most people with Atypical Anorexia they are either obsessive with weight monitoring or they become weight avoidant as they become too scared to know the number. In clinic, I have often seen people shake with anxiety as I ask them to step on the scales. I recall myself (many years ago when I was ill) getting a boost when the weight dropped and this alongside other "perceived achievements" (e.g. reducing my calorie intake), gave my insecure self-worth a boost. In research, people with eating disorders can report positives with having an eating disorder such as, having a purpose, feeling they can do something others cannot, feeling "high" from malnourishment and receiving more support or attention from others (9).

This can be why some people are so reluctant to let the eating disorder go. A key maintaining factor to an eating disorder is obsessive self-weighing. The results from the scales will be inaccurate and weight does vary naturally during the day due to fluid, hormones and other biological processes. Total avoidance of weighing also does not help the person to reduce their fear of weight. Therefore, in treatment it advises that patients are weighed once per week so that risks can be monitored but also the person can habituate to the fear of a weight reading.

Clinical perfectionism is often observed in many people with eating disorders, particularly those with Anorexia Nervosa and Atypical Anorexia. It can often be perceived as a good thing as it strives to improve themselves. However, it can also maintain their belief "I'm not good enough" and lead them to re-evaluate their inflexible standards to a higher level becoming increasingly impossible, thus increasing their levels of anxiety and reducing their self-esteem. Clinical perfectionism can also lead to procrastination which can also maintain their belief "*I'm not good enough*" and lead to a sense of worthlessness and increase levels of depression. Clinical perfectionism in eating disorders is predominantly around weight, shape and control, however it often leads to many other areas of life, including relationships, athleticism, academia and work performance. At it's extreme, it can debilitate a person so that nothing else becomes important and they must strive to improve. This must be challenged in psychotherapy, helping the patient to see that they can reduce their standards, still achieve and be successful, and this will not lead them to be judged or rejected by others. People with restrictive eating disorders are frequently high achievers and when perfectionism is reduced to a healthier level it can lead to successful life goals, like the author has done with writing this book!

"Carers" (family, friends, colleagues and whoever wants you to be well) are an important part of recovery. In past research literature from the 1970/80s, it suggested that parents and particularly mothers, were part of the cause of an eating disorder. This is utter rubbish! What society now understands is that "carers" are a crucial part of the recovery process. We know that "carers" can support someone to get better by learning to understand the eating disorder, being empathic with their loved one, adapting their communication style and how they respond to eating disorder demands and statements. Research has demonstrated that "carers" who attend Carers Skills Workshops can feel more equipped to support someone with an eating disorder, feel less burden, feel less isolation, reduce conflict and arguments and increase their relationship with the person. We also know the importance of "carers" looking after themselves. Fifty percent of "carers" looking after someone with an eating disorder can develop clinical levels of depression and/or anxiety and this is a higher percentage of "carers" compared to those caring for people with other conditions (10). As "carers" can be a role model for people with eating disorders it is therefore important that "carers" demonstrate effective coping strategies to deal with their emotions.

In summary, all eating disorders are serious mental health conditions, however "Atypical Anorexia" can have the added complication in that it may not be picked up by others and can remain untreated for longer. People with eating disorders often can and do get better (both the author and I are evidence of this), but this can take time, and ongoing support from the team around the person is vital. I believe that despite there still being stigma around mental health, the more we discuss it, the more people will realise that mental health conditions are not just "crazy people" they can be you, your family member or your friend, colleague or doctor. No-one is exempt! Managing your emotions in helpful and adaptive ways will ensure that you can navigate the challenges that everyone will experience in life.

About Stephen

Dr Stephen Linacre is a Highly Specialist Clinical Psychologist currently working with children, young people and their families with eating disorders in an NHS specialist CAMHS Eating Disorder Service in Derbyshire.

He qualified as a Clinical Psychologist at the University of Leeds in 2011 and wrote his thesis on "*The Wellbeing of Carers of People with Severe and Enduring Eating Disorders*".

He has written several peer reviewed journal articles on eating disorders and presented at conferences, spoken on TV and radio about the subject. He specialises in the support for parents and carers to help them understand and support loved ones move towards recovery, as well as promoting the paramount importance of parent/carer self-care.

He is also the Chair of the Trustees Board for the charity Freed Beeches Eating Disorder Services, in the past worked closely with the national eating disorders charity (Beat).

He is passionate about mental health being talked about more and is an advocate for increased funding from the Government to recognise the severity of eating disorders and how services, particularly in Primary Care (e.g. schools, GPs, Social Care and first contact services) need more resources and training.

He openly shares his personal experiences of recovering from an eating disorder, contributing to the In2gr8mentalhealth message about clinicians being open with their mental health experiences.

He wants people to be more open about their thoughts, feelings and behaviours so that this can reduce stigma and contribute the fight against eating disorders.

References

1.   van Hoeken, D., & Hoek, H. W. (2020). Review of the burden of eating disorders: mortality, disability, costs, quality of life, and family burden. Current opinion in psychiatry, 33(6), 521–527.
https://doi.org/10.1097/YCO.0000000000000641
2.   Sweeting, H., Walker, L., MacLean, A., Patterson, C., Räisänen, U., & Hunt, K. (2015). Prevalence of eating disorders in males: a review of rates reported in academic research and UK mass media. International journal of men's health, 14(2), 10.3149/jmh.1402.86.
https://doi.org/10.3149/jmh.1402.86
3.   Afzal S, Tybjærg-Hansen A, Jensen GB, Nordestgaard BG. Change in Body Mass Index Associated with Lowest Mortality in Denmark, 1976-2013. JAMA. 2016;315(18):1989–1996. doi:10.1001/jama.2016.4666 Change in Body Mass Index Associated With Lowest Mortality in Denmark, 1976-2013 | Cardiology | JAMA | JAMA Network
4.   Sweeting, H., Walker, L., MacLean, A., Patterson, C., Räisänen, U., & Hunt, K. (2015). Prevalence of eating disorders in males: a review of rates reported in academic research and UK mass media. International journal of men's health, 14(2), 10.3149/jmh.1402.86.
https://doi.org/10.3149/jmh.1402.86
5.   Eating disorders: Recognition and treatment. Full guideline [Internet]. 2017 [cited 15.05.21]. Available from:
https://www.nice.org.uk/guidance/ng69/evidence/full-guideline-pdf-161214767896.
6.   Makino, M., Tsuboi, K., & Dennerstein, L. (2004). Prevalence of eating disorders: a comparison of Western and non-Western countries. MedGenMed : Medscape general medicine, 6(3), 49.

7.   Viviana Aya, Kubra Ulusoy & Valentina Cardi (2019) A systematic review of the 'eating disorder voice' experience, International Review of Psychiatry, 31:4, 347-366, DOI: 10.1080/09540261.2019.1593112

8.   Rouleau, C. R., & von Ranson, K. M. (2011). Potential risks of pro-eating disorder websites. Clinical Psychology Review, 31(4), 525-531.

9.   Nordbø, R. H., Espeset, E. M., Gulliksen, K. S., Skårderud, F., Geller, J., & Holte, A. (2012). Reluctance to recover in anorexia nervosa. European Eating Disorders Review, 20(1), 60-67.

10.   Linacre, S., Heywood-Everett, S., Sharma, V. and Hill, A.J. (2015), "Comparing carer wellbeing: implications for eating disorders", Mental Health Review Journal, Vol. 20 No. 2, pp. 105-118. https://doi.org/10.1108/MHRJ-12-2014-0046

Chapter 1
Who Am I?

As I am sat here trying to figure out the answer to that unnerving question, *'Who am I?'*, I find myself somewhat reflecting. I guess the easiest way to describe myself would be a Mental Health Warrior. I have struggled with ***Atypical Anorexia*** for over fifteen years, alongside PTSD, anxiety and depression. I was born in the beautiful county of Lincolnshire in England and still live locally, with no intension of moving. I adore Lincoln, with the charm of independent shops and wonder of the magnificent cathedral, to the friendliness and warmth of the general public.

I grew up alongside an older sibling, my sister. My dad worked as a machinist and Mum was unable to work due to being disabled. This meant she was always there after school, always making playdough with us or teaching us to bake, which is a skill I treasure now.

Throughout our lives we watched her battle with rheumatoid arthritis, she developed this disease as a teenager and over the years it has taken over her whole body. She has had every joint possible replaced, many twice, full of scars, which I call battle scars, attacking this illness. Eventually the strength of all of the medication throughout the years left her with severe lung disease and she was fitted with a Percutaneous Endoscopic Gastrostomy (PEG), which is a procedure to place a feeding tube through your skin and into your stomach to give you the nutrients and fluids you need.

Combatting many operations a year, being unable to walk some days, and now being unable to eat or drink again, never bothered her. It never even appeared to phase her, she is a remarkable woman and always has a *'just get on with it'* attitude.

I always admired this and tried to enforce this attitude with myself, a chin up, keep calm and carry-on attitude. My sister and I both learned how to help Mum around the house from an early age, and it gave me a strong work ethic. We were able to help care for her when she had another operation and were always happy to help her, as she did so much for us. She never needed long to recover from an operation; she was determined to be back on her feet as soon as possible and never wanted to be cared for. She hated fuss and still, to this day, refuses to ask for help when it is needed. She was and still is an inspiration, wonder woman, my mum.

I lived in a small village south of Lincoln. Attended a small Church of England primary school, where I learnt to play guitar and sing. I continued to develop a love of music and was fortunate enough to go on to university to study Music and Education studies, in the hope to one day teach my passion of music to others. I loved my time at university, of course I was faced with many stresses of a typical student however, I had the most incredible course leader. I learnt how to play the steel and Taiko drums, we delivered workshops around the country spreading our love of music and teaching the importance of music within the curriculum.

After graduating though, I was quite unwell, mentally I was broken, so unable to go on to do my PGCE, I worked as a supply teacher for a while before discovering my passion for the early years. I then started working in a nursery and was able to use my creativity and love for music in day-to-day activities, helping young children to grow and scaffold their learning to suit their individual needs.

Since recovery though, I have developed another passion which I never knew existed. I hate the idea that there are others out there like myself, too afraid to reach out for treatment due to the belief that they are not "ill enough" or believing that they are "too fat" for an eating disorder. I decided that as I was finishing treatment, I wanted to do something about this.

I started to speak out more about my experience and discovered there was a local TEDx group within my city, I applied to do a TEDx talk and I was fortunate enough for my application to be approved and before I knew it, I was on a stage in front of a room full of people and a camera facing me. Something my inner critic would never have allowed me to do, but I was determined. I named my talk, Healthy Weight, Unhealthy Mind: Embracing Your Set Point (please do go and check it out on YouTube). I wanted to share my recovery journey with others that may have 'Other Specified Feeding and Eating Disorders' (OSFED) and try and change people's stereotypical views on eating disorders.

Since doing my TEDx talk, I find myself engaging in other public speaking engagements, alongside my nursery practitioner role. I am fortunate enough to be able to travel both nationally and internationally (virus permitting!) delivering talks on my experience of having atypical anorexia, the barriers I faced with treatment, and the way I was often spoken to by health care providers. Things were said to me that actually discouraged my recovery, such as, "*you don't look like you have an eating disorder*". I am fortunate enough to talk to, not just members of the public and fellow eating disorder warriors, but health care professionals, medical students and anyone with an interest in eating disorders.

Ensuring my message is spread everywhere, as well as talking about eating disorders, I now also deliver workshops and talk on body image. I encourage people to review how we look at ourselves and teach the techniques I have learnt and practiced myself, showing it is possible to go from hating every bone in your body, to actually accepting your body and then learning to love it for all the wonderful things it can do.

Throughout my recovery journey I have battled with a severely low and distorted view of myself, I am very honoured to help others use the techniques that I have found helpful.

My recovery journey has certainly been a rollercoaster of self-hatred, emotional outbursts and battles. However, I want to spread hope to others, recovery is possible, with the right support, treatment team and a lot of determination; you can fully recover from this dreadful illness.

I am not fully recovered. Yet.

But I will be.

Chapter 2
Trauma

Unfortunately, everyone faces trauma in their lives, some of us may experience more than others, and I feel it is safe to say, I was dealt a very difficult hand. Any type of trauma you may encounter from death, bullying, abuse or a time where you may fear for your life can be classed as a traumatic event; and leave you with severe Post Traumatic Stress Disorder (PTSD) symptoms. Along with my eating disorder, I do struggle with PTSD. Mainly from one key event which I encountered in my teenage years.

Sadly, due to safeguarding rules and legal complications, I am unable to disclose the full details of what happened in this book, but I can cover some basic details, leaving out locations, specific times and obviously names. But know this, it was this series of terrifyingly abusive events, which left me fearing for my life and is one of the roots which formed my eating disorder.

Going back to secondary school, I was bullied, very badly. I mean I played flute, had braces, wore glasses, hormones made me very spotty and to top it off I was a Goth. Looking back I had no chance really, the worst episodes of my bullying were on the bus back home from school, from a group of boys. I always tried to put on my mask and show my brave face.

My parents had always told me to ignore bullies and that they would get bored eventually, but with these particular ones, it only seemed to add fuel to the fire, and made it so much worse. The constant body shaming, calling me fat, to teasing me for playing the flute, for trying to express myself through my choices of clothing, they would find any way they could, to tease me daily. They used to steal my belongings and empty out my things onto the floor, kicking them around, laughing at me, tormenting me, pulling my hair and even putting gum in my hair. One day I snapped and shouted back, they had taken the one thing very dear to me, and started smashing it up, throwing it around kicking it. They had taken my flute.

My only escape from the world, the thing I cared most about. I was struggling, and the constant abuse was getting too much I stood up and pushed one of them over, away from me, off the seat next to me and screamed "enough!" The whole bus fell silent, and I remember one of the girls who always sat on the back seat say, "I thought she was going to hit him."

But truth was, I wouldn't hurt a fly, I did not have it in me. I could not and would not stoop to their level. I was so ashamed that I nearly snapped. I stopped getting the bus and started using my lunch money to get public transport home, or, trying to sneak onto one of the other busses that went to my school from my village.

I was ashamed of my outburst, and distraught that they had broken my flute. I did not want people to think I was like that, I was not a thug like them so I decided to open up a little, I tried to tell my form tutor, I did not want to be known as a 'tell-tale', but I could not go on like this either. I waited behind after registration one day and asked him if he had a moment.

A tear rolled down my cheek as I started to explain what had happened, what had been going on and the constant torment I was receiving every day. I also told him about the other bullying I was experiencing from people throughout the day, the constant fat jokes, the name calling, being threatened and made to feel completely worthless, getting told I was a waste of space and that the world would be better off without me. I was miserable, struggling to cope and I had started to self-harm.

I kept a razor blade in my top pocket and every day when the bullying peaked, I would cut myself, at the time it was a release, a release from the tension, a way of punishing myself almost. I deserved the pain. Once I started to talk, I found that it all started to pour out, I could not stop. After I had told my tutor everything, I looked up expecting a response, something, some hope that this constant torment would stop. He had taken a few notes and said the names back to me and said, *"These do joke around a lot, boys will be boys, are you sure it is not just that you are being a bit sensitive? I do not believe that they are doing it maliciously at all."*

I was told to learn to take a joke, it was banter. So, I learnt how to wear my mask, and wear it well. I carried on, but something was now very different, the people had been spoken to about the bullying and that only made things worse; as it was just seen as a little warning, nothing was done, and they could continue to do what they liked.

The bullying started to follow me everywhere; it was no longer just in school but online too. One of them had got my number and passed it around, so now I was receiving texts too, and a few had noticed I had started wearing loads of bracelets and had spotted my cuts along my wrist.

I remember being in a P.E. lesson one day, I had always hated P.E. anyway and this day we had athletics. I had to take my bracelets off as they were unsafe to wear during lessons. I got changed and headed to the field with everyone else. My best friend was in the lesson with me, he was extremely camp and could always make me laugh no matter how rubbish I was feeling; he was also very badly bullied, but seemed to handle it better than I did, he took it all in his stride. I admired him for it, I loved William, we really did have such a good giggle.

We were split into groups and Will and I were separated, I was gutted, but did as I was told and went to line up by the long jump area with a group of others. It was a group of girls that normally tormented me and there they were, in front of me. When they realised I was behind them, straight away they started to say, *"can you hear that, I think an elephant is approaching?"* I was so used to comments like this that by now, they no longer bothered me, but one of them noticed something, the marks on my wrist. She turned to her friends whispering and they all turned around, I hid my arms, but it was too late, I had been found out.

They asked me, what the point was, and reminded me I was ugly enough without even more ugly scars, I was unlovable and messed up in the head. No empathy, no remorse for what they were doing, not realising it was because of them that I had begun this unhealthy trend. I was constantly reminded of how alone I was, and it felt like I did not deserve happiness. I was indeed just a fat waste of space. And from that day on, I was known as an emo kid.

When I was in my teens, I met someone, a boy. Popular, fit and he seemed to show interest in me. I had no self-esteem, I hated myself, I truly believed I was fat and worthless, years of bullying and torment had left me broken, so when he showed interest, I felt so lucky, so amazed, I was so blinded.

I did not see the danger I was in. This boyfriend was a few years older than me and I felt the luckiest girl in the world. When the emotional abuse started, I saw nothing wrong with it, this had become normal for me, the name calling, fat shaming, calling me worthless, waste of space and so on. I had heard it all before. I was numb to it. I wanted to impress him, so I tried to diet and change my shape to please him, I started exercising more and restricting heavily at mealtimes when I could.

I did of course lose weight, but the abuse still happened. I was still called names and pulled down, eventually the physical abuse followed. The first time he hurt me was in his room, we were playing a video game and eating a bag of sharing crisps, he reminded me I was fat and did not need them. I laughed it off and took another in a joking teasing way, he then stood up, grabbed me by the dress pulling me to my feet and threw me on the floor, like a rag doll and said to me, "*I told you, you've had enough, fatty.*" I felt hot, ashamed that my behaviour had driven this amazing boyfriend to do this, it was my fault, I should be trying to please him, not make him upset with me.

He straight away apologised lifted me up and wrapped me in a blanket, we stopped playing the video game and watched a film instead. I was then afraid to eat anything around him, unless he had given me permission, and upped my efforts to try and make myself good enough for him. I thought nothing of his behaviours. This was what I deserved. But then following the physical abuse, finally the sexual abuse started, and this 'boyfriend' raped me.

Everyone thought my boyfriend was lovely, kind and so caring towards me, I was lucky to have him, he would treat me like a queen when we were around others, it was only when we were on our own the vile comments would appear. He reminded me constantly what everyone would say, reminding me how lucky I was to have him, how I was worthless, and I should be thankful someone was paying any attention to me at all.

He pressured me into starting a sexual relationship. I was desperate to make him happy so agreed. I was of course nervous and scared, as he roughly stripped me off and pushed me onto the bed. He had an animal look in his eyes, but I had to do this, I had to prove I was worthy of his affection. He grabbed me extremely hard by the wrists and pinned my body down onto the bed, I asked him to go gentle as it was my first time, but he ignored me, continuing to get what he wanted that was all that seemed to matter. I asked him to stop as I was in pain, again he ignored me, and carried on. I started to try and struggle to get free, begging him to please stop, I was in pain and did not want this, but he ignored me and just carried on, regardless of me pleading with him. Eventually he stopped, finally finished with me, I grabbed the bedding and covered myself up, feeling ashamed and disgusted in myself, as I pulled the sheet around me covering myself up, we both noticed something on the bed, a stain, I was bleeding, he seemed a little shocked and then noticed the marks he had made on my wrists, he said he was sorry and he had just got carried away, so I thought nothing of it. He showed me lots of love and affection afterwards, saying I had made him happy, un-use to such compliments I took them all in, and found myself completely under his control.

The weeks went by and the verbal, emotional and physical abuse continued. I was blind, as he was loving and kind and seemed to care one minute, but in the next pointing out my body flaws, especially my legs and stomach area, teasing me for being fat. He kept suggesting ways to improve my appearance, telling me what exercise I should be doing and also reminding me how worthless I was and how lucky I was to have him. Tearing into my already shattered self-esteem.

We were watching a film one Sunday afternoon and he turned to me with a familiar look, I knew what he wanted, but I really could not go through that again, he started to tug at my clothes and leaned in kissing me, I told him, not today. I still hurt from last time, and the trauma of it was still raw.

He called me pathetic, weak for letting it bother me, reminded me he did not have to be with me and telling me I was unlovable. He ignored my requests to stop again, and continued, his hands running all over my body, I wanted to run, I knew what was coming but I had completely frozen, I could not move, I was literally frozen with fright. He tore my clothes off me once again and I found some strength to push him off and shout, "no!"

He fell to the floor I told him this was not what I wanted, and begged him to stop. But this outburst of mine seemed to only anger him, he was outraged I had disobeyed him, that I had fought back.

He grabbed me once again by the wrists with one hand, gripping them tight and with his other hand grabbed me by the throat. He was a lot taller and stronger than I was and once again I found myself defenceless and unable to comprehend what was happening. He ignored my pleas; my begging only spurred him on. Choking me hard, I was struggling to catch a breath, and, in that moment, I really thought I was going to die.

I was gasping for breath and unable to break free. I could do nothing. He eventually finished with me and once again I was 'gifted' with love and affection, given chocolate and told how incredible I was. It was followed up by him telling me how lucky I was I had someone love me. I was confused, hurt and so warped; I did not know what to believe anymore.

But this was not love, nothing about this was love. I was in pain, humiliated, and worst of all, I had been made to feel as if this was all my fault. I should have seen the patterns of abuse and left the relationship sooner, I deserved it. I was no longer living my life, I was so scared, and when I did cry, show emotion and plead with him, I found that the physical abuse became worse. If I said no, he would do it anyway but with force, and he laughed and teased me if I cried. I had learnt it was a weakness to cry. I became numb from my emotions, unable to feel anything.

Eventually I managed to get out of the relationship. I can't tell you what gave me the strength, but one day after again being forced into sex and once again hurt, I managed to dig deep and find some willpower.

I got dressed and left.

I just walked away, then I started to run, running faster and faster away from him, away from the abuse, away from everything. I have no idea where I ended up and I seemed to have been running for hours. My feet hurt, I had blood on my top as my nose was bleeding from being struck, my eyes were puffy from crying and my make-up smudged. I was a mess; I found my way to the train station, sat down and started to cry. All of these un-wanted emotions flooding my brain, all the feelings and self-hatred were filling my body.

A stranger asked if I was ok and handed me a tissue and suggested I visited the ladies to get sorted, so I did. I caught the train home and never looked back.

I threatened him with police and blocked him on all media platforms, I refused to speak about him, and he seemed to get bored of pursuing me and eventually did leave me alone. I felt like it was my fault, my body's fault, if I had been fitter, more attractive, maybe just maybe, it would not have happened. Not just this abusive relationship, but the bullying and constant teasing I was faced with at school and at home too.

The damage had been done, the torment, trauma and abuse had led to me developing this life changing illness, the illness that controlled me for years, this illness that saw me fighting for my life.

I had developed an eating disorder.

Chapter 3
Emotional Avoidance

The abuse I had encountered haunted me, and from that moment on, every time I felt anxious, scared or any negative emotion, it would catapult me back to the relationship. I did not want to be reminded of these events, so in an attempt to numb out negative emotions I tried a variety of methods. I blocked out what had happened, refused to think of it and refused to acknowledge the trauma. I pushed it all away to the back of my mind and kept ignoring any reminder of the traumas.

This worked in the short-term but was very un-successful when it came to healing the inner cause of all my problems. I started to do this with everything, every other trauma I encountered every death (I'll talk about those later). I did not want to feel weak, so instead I put on a brave face and carried on as though nothing was happening, refusing to let my mask slip. I originally did try drugs to numb the pain, I wanted to get rid of the memories, forget them, the problem with drugs is they wear off quite quickly, I needed something stronger, something to numb the pain longer, so I turned to controlling my food.

I had no control over what had happened, but I could control this, and I found that restricting and obsessing over my weight, numbed out the painful experience better than any drug. What is more interesting, is it was a lot more addictive than any drug. I found myself dipping in and out of disordered eating for fourteen years before eventually everything I was running from caught up with me.

After school, my eating disorder seemed to settle a little, the stress of GCSE's was behind me and I was in 6th form, doing well. I had the most wonderful friends, and what was more amazing is all the bullies had left school and gone to college. I was free from torment, I was in a healthy relationship with James, we had started seeing each other in the later stages of year nine and have been together ever since.

Slowly my eating habits started to return to normal. And remained somewhat 'normal' for a few years. I still had severe body image issues, and still kept trying new diets and exercise regimes, but found that my studies took over. I was studying music, something that I adored, and I wanted to go to university to do Music and Education Studies. Playing helped sooth those eating disorder thoughts, and the fact I was playing constantly, always practicing and was pretty much living in the music block, were my only saving graces. I had managed to bury and somehow lock out what had happened, and never thought or talked about it.

I was over the moon when I was accepted into university and truly adored studying for my degree, we had the most incredible lecturer, she was kind, supportive and never let us struggle. In my third year, I had however, started to find it really hard. The stress of my degree was getting on top of me and I was constantly running around everywhere trying to get interviews and quotes for my two dissertations. I felt completely out of control and anxious, which of course opened up that little box in the back of my mind I was so desperate to keep shut.

So, I turned back to disordered ways, I started to monitor what I was eating again and upped my exercise regime; I joined the gym at the university and found myself either constantly studying or exercising. It seemed to do the job of numbing me from how stressed I was and gave me a sense of control. Yet by the time we had finished university, I had become unwell. I graduated with a 2:1 Hons Degree in Music and Education and I knew deep down I was not well enough to go on to do my teacher training. I was exhausted and found myself snowballing back to my disordered ways. So instead, I decided to take some time and find a job for a year or two before returning to do my teaching qualification.

I then entered the world of unemployment and very quickly felt like a burden on society. I was claiming job seekers allowance and working voluntary in two local primary schools to gain experience. I found I could not get a job because I did not have experience, but I could never get that experience because of my lack of previous jobs. It was a cruel loop. I continued to exercise and became more engrossed in my disorder, but strangely, I had found my disorder had flipped; instead of restricting, I had episodes of binging instead. I found the days where I had to go to the Job Centre I could not stop eating, it was a different way of numbing the emotions but still extremely disordered. I then became so ashamed about what I was doing that I soon found myself struggling with depression. This of course, brought back those negative emotions I was running from, which, in turn, made ED worse.

As soon as I had enough experience, I was able to join an agency, I worked as a supply teacher and loved it, I was sent to different schools across Lincolnshire and was able to proudly walk into a classroom and use my skills from university to take charge and lead a lesson from only vague plans I had been left. One day my agency rang me and asked if I would be willing to try nursery work, I had focused my degree on the early years curriculum so jumped at the opportunity. I was sent to a very large nursery and seemed to just slot right in, by the end of the week I knew all the staff well and felt like part of the team. From that moment on, I never left.

Eventually I was offered a permanent job, and once again I was settled and happy and found my strange eating habits settled. I still kept trying to diet, trying to manipulate my shape and was still dissatisfied with my body, my disorder was still very much there, but I did not recognise it.

My weight continued to yo-yo throughout my early twenties. I was still engaging in unhealthy behaviours and found myself often having binging episodes when I had a bad day at work but was convinced everyone had more to eat when they were stressed. This might be true, but not everyone was doing it to try and change their emotions, I wanted to block out the strong negative feelings that I was still running from and had still not dealt with effectively. I was getting married to my amazing partner, we both had jobs and had bought our first home together. But then tragedy hit us.

We received news my Uncle Clive had suffered with a heart attack, and was very poorly in hospital, to avoid negative emotions and stop them from taking over me, I resorted back to my disordered ways. If only to have a sense of control and to numb me from what was going on. I had always adored my uncle, he was blind but had the most incredible ears, meaning he was musically talented. He would enjoy hearing me practice when he visited my mum, and we could discuss different composers and artists. I had such a soft spot for him, he had the most incredible sense of humour and would often make really inappropriate jokes about his own disability. Jokes you really should not laugh at but couldn't help, I guess that was his way of coping. To find out this amazing man was fighting for his life in the intensive care unit struck our family hard.

However, what made it more difficult was the fact that my godmother Pat, was also in the ICU at the same time. An incredible lady and my mum's best friend. I felt so sorry for my mum, not only was she losing her brother, but she was also losing her best friend to cancer. My 'Aunty' Pat was always full of life, her laughter cheered up the darkest of rooms, and she helped care for me when mum was poorly. She let me paint her nails badly whenever she visited, she always managed to make my mum smile and be there for her; she really was a rock to many. Seeing her slowly deteriorate, losing her love of life, and suffer in the cruellest way possible was heart breaking.

Both Clive and Pat lost their lives within weeks of each other. I, of course, worked through the heartache and hit the gym and focused on losing weight as a way of coping and I know, I keep going back to this, but a way of having some control. I just used the excuse it was a wedding diet, and no one was concerned as it is perceived to be a normal thing to do.

James and I got married and on my wedding night, I remember my best friend Charlotte pulling James onto the dance floor, and dancing with him. At the end of the song, she said to him, *"Now James, you better look after my Zoe, she is very special to me and one in a million, if you hurt her, I will hurt you!"* I could not believe what she had done, and I found myself in fits of laughter.

However, she was moving to Cyprus after my wedding, we were broken when she told us, but we promised to come and visit her. I had flights booked to go and stay with her in the summer, we would Skype and when her husband was posted back, we could pick up where we left off. We worked at the same nursery and in the same room and always seemed to pair up when the room split into two. We were unstoppable together and made an amazing team. Work was never stressful when she was around, when we were getting stressed or agitated, she was able to diffuse the situation and have us all in absolute stitches. Work had become so much fun and we loved working together. We had the best team in the nursery, team Tornados.

There were five of us in the team, our room leader Debbie, our second lead Sarah and then Charlotte and me. There was also a support worker named Sian, who would come in for a few days a week to work as a one to one. Together we were always in a bundle of laughter. Charlotte could see I was hurting, I wanted to grieve for the loss of my loved ones but couldn't, I did not know how to cry, the abuse had taught me that crying showed weakness. She was also aware of my disordered habits and when I started to lose weight for my wedding, she knew more was going on. She knew I was struggling, and she took me to the side and held me one day, letting me cry, for both my uncle and my godmother. Thanks to this moment I started to increase my intake.

Then what seemed like a normal day at work, turned into a nightmare, I was in the staff room on my break, ten minutes to go before I started work again when my manager, Pam came into the staff room and explained she needed a word with me. I was racking my brains, thinking "*Oh my goodness, what have I done?*", but I knew I had done nothing wrong. My work was flawless, and I always tried my absolute best. She pulled me into the talk time room upstairs and I noticed she was crying, I asked her what on earth was going on and if everything was okay, she looked at me and said,

"*Oh, Zoe I do not know how to tell you, it's Charlotte*", I replied with,

"*Oh god what has she done now, causing mayhem in Cyprus already?*"

She shook her head and just said two words. Two simple words that shook me to the core.

"*She's dead*".

"*What!?*" I replied in a moment of panic and heartache.

My fun, full of life Charlotte, was gone. How and why did this happen! Pam explained that she did not know what had happened they were waiting for an inquest, but it was a suspected heart attack. I was in such denial, there was no way I could have lost one of my closest friends. After all, I was talking to her only days ago and she was fine, drunk as usual, loving life and living it to the fullest. Yet, she really was gone. I wanted to completely break down and cry, but I couldn't, instead I just fell to the floor in disbelief. There had to have been a mistake, there was no way this could be happening.

I tried to pull myself together as quickly as possible and return to work, I would put on my happy face for the children, and by the end of the day when parents were collecting them, the news had spread about Charlotte's death. I agreed to answer any questions they might have had about the situation. There weren't many questions, yet I still found myself struggling to answer them. I went home that night and I was broken, again I wanted to cry and let out all of the emotion I had built up throughout this awful day, but I found I couldn't. I was feeling selfish now, this was the third loss in as many months, and I was hurting.

A few months passed and Christmas was just around the corner, my beautiful niece had been born and I was slowly starting to come to terms with the deaths of my loved ones. I was even allowing myself to begin the grieving process. This was until one evening in December when I received a phone call from my mum explaining how Amy, my new-born niece, had been rushed to hospital with suspected bronchitis. She was being transferred to Queen's Medical Hospital in Nottingham straight away and was currently fighting for her life. I thought to myself *"how can this be happening again, has my family not suffered enough?"*

My sister was really strong, and she had her husband by her side. My other niece was staying with me and my parents, so we tried our best to shield her a little from what was going on. Every day we were anxious, tense and afraid. After a few days had past, we were allowed to the hospital to see her, I remember seeing her hooked up to loads of machines and ventilators and I could hear her chest rattling as she tried to breath. Still, she seemed peaceful, she was such a precious miracle, and I could not believe that she was going through this pain. I really did not know what to do, I couldn't help my little niece, the staff were doing an amazing job and it was out of my hands, so I tried my hardest to look after my sister and brother-in-law. We brought them food every day and helped look after their other child, Ava. We eventually took Ava up to the hospital with us to see her mum and dad and helped to explain that Amy was just a little poorly, so Mummy and Daddy needed to be with her at the minute.

Every time my phone rang, I feared the worst. Christmas Day arrived and we received news that Amy was well enough to be transferred back to Lincoln, she was doing well, and they kept lowering her oxygen support a little bit at a time. We went up to see her the evening of Christmas day and were thankful, to all the incredible nurses and doctors that had helped save her life. On New Year's Eve she was discharged, we celebrated our Christmas day on New Year's Day, together as a family.

I learnt a lot about myself during this time, I found myself in my normal caring role, being the support for my whole family during this torrid time. I was the one who needed to be strong throughout all of this, acting with reason and really trying to bring everyone together in hope for this poor little girl. The only problem with trying to carry on and pushing every bad situation to the back of your mind is that eventually, your glass starts to get full, then it starts to leak and then it overflows. It all comes out, I found everything I was running from, the trauma, the bullying, the deaths, nearly losing Amy, Mum being so unwell and every other trauma I still was yet to talk through.

I was working overtime and stressed out at work. All of it flooded out and I was unable to control my emotions anymore. This time when I had turned to my disorder for comfort after Christmas, I couldn't stop. I couldn't run anymore. I couldn't cope with everything that had happened in my life, this time when I turned to my disordered ways, I was trapped. It slowly started to consume me, as I was still adamant, I would run away from everything, and not acknowledge the emotions, not even allowing myself to cry.

Thinking Styles

As well as trauma and emotional avoidance, ways of thinking can leave you vulnerable to an eating disorder.

There are so many different styles of thinking, and when the negative styles of thinking were explained to me for the first time, I remember sitting there thinking, *"oh my goodness, this is me, I do this all the time."* I talk about these in Chapter 6 but here are the ones that resonated the most with me.

Catastrophising

The first thinking style I remember seeing and thinking I could completely relate to, was catastrophising. I always assumed the worst would happen. This I now understand was due to the trauma and abuse. I feared the worst because for me, if I could prepare for the worst, I could handle it better and be prepared. However, I found it interfering with my whole life, for example, when I was at university, if I found myself struggling on a module, I was convinced it was because I was rubbish and that I should not be at university, or that I was going to fail. Luckily, like I have previously mentioned, we had an amazing tutor who recognised when her students were struggling and was able to help, but actually asking for help made this style of thinking worse. I assumed my lecturer would realise I should not be on the course, and I would be humiliated and get thrown out.

This of course, never happened, but this constant way of thinking certainly held me back and was exhausting to try and live with. Constantly assuming I was going to fail at everything I tried to do, even writing this book!

Thoughts like, *"Zoe what are you doing, you cannot write a book, you are not capable, this is stupid, and you will fail and embarrass yourself."* I found myself seeking lots of reassurance, but I was well encouraged and supported. I also managed to catastrophise recovery, and entering treatment. I doubted many times if I was strong enough to recover, what was the point in trying? Surely, I was just wasting everyone's time? How wrong I was. As I soon learnt, recovery is possible and I could do it.

Mind Reading

Another key thinking style I found myself being drawn to when discussing them in therapy, was mind reading. I always assumed I knew what others were thinking about me, I always presumed people were judging me and secretly laughing at me behind my back. This is something admittedly, I am still working on.

Whenever I meet new people, I find myself wondering what they thought of me, I end up analysing everything I may have said to make sure I have not offended them, and I would always assume they thought I was an idiot. No matter what I did I assumed people thought the worst of me.

I remember the first time I met James. We were young and he was sat next to me in Geography; back at school, I was not the most well-behaved student, and I lashed out often. My friend was sat across the room from me, and each week we would attempt to move closer to each other throughout the lesson without getting found out. We both adored the band *My Chemical Romance* and I was always singing one of their songs. I remember one day the shy lad next to me said, "I like that band too", and he started a conversation with me, something about him was different, I hadn't been out of the abusive relationship for long and still found it hard to trust people, but for some reason I trusted him. I actually quite liked him. The weeks went on and I found we had a little crush on each other.

However, for some reason I found every time we spoke, I assumed he actually hated me, when I was being a little silly with my friend and found him looking over, I assumed he was thinking I was an idiot, or just a silly, ugly teenage girl. You can imagine the shock when I realised, he was actually quite attracted to me. He later admitted every time he was looking over it was because he thought I was a funny and bubbly young girl who was different from everyone else.

The mind reading approach I have, has stopped me making many friends and actually encouraged me to keep people at arm's length so to speak. I struggle to let people in and trust them, and always assume they are scheming behind my back. I feel, I can trust no one initially.

All Or Nothing

My life has either been wonderful or terrible, no in between, I have either had a good day or bad day. It seems impossible for me to have a good day with a few hiccups, or a few moments that haven't gone well; if one thing goes wrong during the day, that's it, the whole day is now terrible. If I made a mistake at work for example, it would lead to me thinking, "*see I am rubbish at my job*", not, "oh we all make the odd mistake, and we are only human". I am automatically a failure. This very much links into my perfectionism personality trait, if something is not completely perfect, in my eyes I had failed. I found this way of thinking very prominent again when in recovery.

Every time I fell or wobbled, I found myself saying things like, "*I am never going to recover*". Instead of acknowledging the fact that, of course, wobbles happen.

Also, when I was eating meals if I was struggling or finding something difficult, which in recovery happens extremely often, again I would resort back to, "*I should be able to do this, I am rubbish I cannot recover.*"

This was also apparent in my recitals during university. I could play a whole piece perfectly but if I went wrong once, played one note incorrectly, that was it, I was rubbish and a failure, it was not perfect and I was an imposter being at university. I now realise I was actually just terrified of making mistakes and just had an unhelpful way of thinking.

Key points to take away

- It's not your fault! Bullying and abuse is wrong, and you should never believe that you are to blame for their actions. They are in the wrong, not you.
- If something feels wrong, chances are it is, trust your gut.
- Past events and trauma leave us with lasting scars. Try not to bottle them up or use unhealthy methods as a form of control.
- Please do not downplay your own trauma by thinking, "well others have it worse, I should manage." What others have been through is irrelevant, if you feel something has been traumatic, then you deserve help.
- Not all traumatic events will lead to PTSD, however if you are unsure and start displaying PTSD symptoms, please speak to your doctor.
- Anyone can develop PTSD from trauma, not just soldiers.
- Your trauma is valid.
- Unfortunately, you cannot change the past, you cannot change what happened. Focus on what you can do to heal.
- Learn to please yourself not others.
- There are different thinking styles. If you learn what they are, you can recognise what is happening and why you're doing the things you do.
- Avoiding emotions may feel strong, but in the end they will all come flooding out. There is nothing strong about not crying, often letting out these emotions is the bravest thing of all.
- Not all abuse is physical, the mental scars from emotional abuse can hurt just as much.

Chapter 4
Diagnosis

Let me take you back to June 2018, by now I was twenty-six. I was in A & E after collapsing at work, which was slowly becoming a more common occurrence. I was sat on a green coloured, medical couch covered in blue roll, in a small room just off the main accident and emergency treatment area.

My husband had met me there, I had to have an IV of fluids as I had become severely dehydrated due to restriction, over exercising and laxative abuse. My body was struggling and starting to shut down, the doctor explained that they were really concerned about my heart rate, it was far too low; it should be around sixty beats per minute, mine had dropped to thirty-five beats per minute, even with the fluids.

They wanted to admit me and were finding me a bed on a ward. I needed more tests to see what was going on and why my body was fighting so hard. This could have been life threatening.

But I was not listening, all I was thinking about at the time was, *"I wonder how many calories are in this bag of fluids, is this going to make me gain weight, what can I do to burn this off?"* Regardless of the fact that it was this train of thought, this pattern of behaviour, which had put me in this situation in the first place.

The doctor left the room and I immediately took out my phone to Google what was in this bag of fluids, to start working out what I needed to do. I looked over at my husband, who I had been with for over thirteen years, and had never seen cry. He was a broken man. He snatched my phone out of my hand, sat next to me, held my hand and sobbed. He said,

"Zoe do you not see what you are doing to yourself, can you really not see that this is going to kill you?"

In that moment, looking at my broken husband, I started to recognise my thought patterns and recognise maybe, just maybe, I needed help for this.

Doctors Visit

However, accessing treatment was not easy. I was still fighting a war with myself, still fighting with my inner voice which was adamant I was not slim enough to have this illness. I did not fit the stereotype. I was too fat to have an eating disorder. That said, I could not ignore the fact that my body was struggling, my heart was fighting, I was experiencing crippling chest pains and palpitations daily, my periods had stopped, my muscles constantly ached from the over exercise, my stomach hurt due to laxative abuse and I was collapsing often.

I finally realised maybe this latest diet was not such a good idea, but I couldn't stop, and my checking behaviours (I'll define these later) were becoming worse. I decided enough was enough and I went to visit the doctor.

I booked an appointment and when I entered the room, I broke down, deep down I knew something was not right. I poured my heart out to this doctor, explained everything I was doing, explained the thoughts I was having and my behaviours and explained what was going on with my body. At first the doctor seemed quite empathic, he straight away said the words "eating disorder" and I felt like everything started to make sense, he then asked to do my Body Mass Index (BMI), so he knew where to go. I agreed and allowed him to weigh and measure me, and then his whole attitude changed.

I was told I was not slim enough to have an eating disorder, I did not fit into the Anorexia category. He then went on to tell me to *"just drink a full fat can of Coke a day."*

This was to keep my blood sugars up and stop me from collapsing. At this point I was broken even more inside, because what he was asking me to do was too much, I knew the calorie content in that drink and I could not possibly do that!

He then said there was nothing he could do for me and asked me to leave.

All I took away from that appointment was that I was not slim enough, which my inner voice twisted into "*I was not good enough.*"

I was too fat.

I went home and really upped my efforts to lose more weight. I spiralled more and more into my disorder. That doctor caused me to lose what little control I had left, but what was more dangerous, was that he normalised everything that I was doing.

Getting A Referral

Adamant I did not have a problem I continued my path of self-destruction. My husband is a very logical man and knew what the doctor had said was not right, but I was in no frame of mind to be argued with. I had a comeback, an excuse for everything. James then did a little research and found the UK's leading eating disorder charity BEAT. From there he found that there were many more eating disorders than we had realised and found loads of information on their site, about Other Specified Feeding and Eating Disorders (OSFED). James read them aloud and he quickly realised that this was me, but, having the information and knowing what to do with it, were two different things. Luckily, he delved deeper and found the support section and within minutes he'd acted. James rang BEAT and soon spoke to an advisor, they confirmed that you did not need to be underweight to have an eating disorder. James went on to explain what had happened at the doctors surgery, and how we had been to A&E many times, but no one had realised or even thought I could be struggling, because my weight was normal. Regardless of the fact that I had lost a severe amount of weight in a very short amount of time.

The advisor tracked down what treatment options were available in my area and gave James the email address and number to my local adult eating disorders unit. He emailed them straight away, again explaining what had happened at the doctors. He explained all my habits and my rapid weight loss, he explained all of my checking behaviours and how my personality had changed.

James expressed his concerns about my physical health and the service responded very quickly to the email and offered to speak with him on the phone. James then had a telephone conversation with an eating disorder specialist, who agreed I needed help. They gave him all the details we needed in order to get a referral, including her name to quote and contact again if needed. BEAT also sent us a leaflet that we were able to print off at home and take back to the doctors with us explaining a little more about OSFED, and atypical anorexia.

Time for round two. I was very reluctant, but James marched me to the doctors. I was adamant that nothing would come of it, we were wasting time and I was too fat for an eating disorder, but I went along to get my husband off my back and to make him happy. Also, I figured that if he heard it from the doctor's mouth, he might believe my inner voice too.

We saw a different doctor this time, James told him everything that had happened up to this point. He went through my behaviours, my health in general and what the other doctor had said, he then presented the leaflet from BEAT and the details of ED service and refused to leave until I had a referral to this specialist team.

This doctor had a very different interest and attitude, he admitted he had not come across this type of disorder before but agreed from what had been said that I needed specialist help. He then went onto the BEAT's website there and then. He looked at the information on their website and decided to refer me with no more questions asked.

This sent me into utter turmoil because now I had all these people telling me I had an issue, but how could I? I was just dieting, just being healthy. My thoughts were so tangled, and I was so confused.

I decided to contact BEAT myself. They have a web chat page and I was able to speak to an advisor who helped me challenge the core belief I held, which was that I was too fat to have an eating disorder. Every day, from that moment up until entering treatment, I spoke to an advisor at BEAT and I felt validated, I felt heard, and I did not feel so lost.

First Appointment

The first appointment I had at the specialist unit was an assessment. I waited very nervously in a small, but homely waiting area, my anxiety was through the roof and I kept thinking to myself; *"I'm just wasting these professionals' time. I don't have a problem, what am I doing here?"* I then tried to argue with myself and remember the evidence from BEAT, reminding myself that my body was struggling, and that my behaviours were not normal. The negative voice was so intense and strong, I just wanted to leave, I wanted to run. At the point I was about to leave, I was greeted by two professionals; they had the warmest and kindest smiles and so I decided to stay and see what they had to say.

I had my assessment with a psychologist who later went on to become my one to one and had the seemingly impossible task of untangling my thoughts. I also had a nurse who was an eating disorder specialist. I found myself during that first appointment, downplaying everything, I was not completely honest with the two professionals and when I look back, I realise how foolish that was.

Deep down I was embarrassed, ashamed of how many behaviours I was engaging in and despite everything, I still wanted to lose weight. The thought that they were either going to dismiss me or make me fat were spinning around my head. I laughed and joked throughout the whole of my appointment, refusing to tell them things about my past and traumas which could have led me to developing this illness. My mask was on and I did not want them to see how vulnerable I really felt.

To me being vulnerable meant being weak, this ironically, turns out to be my biggest weakness!

Coming up to the end of my first appointment they decided to check my BMI, *"here we go again"* I thought, *"time to be told I am too fat to have an eating disorder and told off for time wasting, at least James will leave me alone now"*. But to my astonishment they didn't say this, not at all. They told me that yes, my BMI was in the healthy range, but the speed I was losing weight, my behaviours and physical and mental health, showed that I needed help.

The psychologist in the room told me that I had Atypical Anorexia, which meant I was engaging in all the habits typically associated with anorexia, but my weight for now was in the healthy category.

To me this mixed up a whole host of emotions. I had a problem, it was official. I had an eating disorder.

However, again that eating disorder voice twisted it into, *"yeah but not a serious one, you are too fat for anorexia."* I somehow felt like I had failed at having an eating disorder. I completely ignored the fact that atypical anorexia is just as dangerous as any other eating disorder, completely disregarding how much damage I was doing to my body and ignoring the warnings from my heart. I had an issue, but it wasn't that bad, not that serious.

Key points to take away

- If the inner voice in your head is telling you to restrict, over exercise or giving you negative thoughts about yourself, it is not your friend.
- You don't have to be a low weight to have an eating disorder.
- Certain stereotypes we have surrounding eating disorders are harmful. They do not discriminate, anyone can struggle regardless of weight, gender, ethnicity and race.
- There are more than one kind of eating disorder and often doctors aren't aware of them.
- There are resources on BEAT's website you can take to the doctors when seeking support. Use them if you don't feel confident explaining what you are going through.
- Eating disorders are a mental illness. If your days are being ruled by thoughts around food shape and weight, and it's having a negative impact on your health and life, you deserve help.
- Nice guidelines state: "Do not use single measures such as BMI or duration of illness to determine whether to offer treatment for an eating disorder." If you get turned away and a referral is denied due to BMI, quote these guidelines. Please keep fighting. Contact charities and seek assistance on appealing the decision.
- Seeking help and taking the first step can be extremely daunting. If possible, take someone with you for support.
- Do not wait. If you think, "I will be fine, I can keep going a little bit more" stop and remember, eating disorders kill.
- You deserve help.
- You can heal from an eating disorder with the right help and support.

Chapter 5
Acceptance

Accepting Help

I am a strong independent woman! I do not need any help! This was something I said way too many times. A friend once said to me,

"Zoe you are a super woman, but you are not Superwoman and asking for help when needed, is the bravest thing you can ever do."

Thanks Chris. This has stuck with me. I always thought it was weak to seek support, again the stigma of seeing a therapist was overwhelming and I had a strong '*get on with it*' attitude. However, there had come a point where I had to admit that I needed help.

Coming To Terms With My Diagnosis

I had a massive issue accepting the fact I had an eating disorder. I was classed as healthy, my BMI was healthy and the thought of it being an eating disorder seemed ludicrous. I started accusing people of overreacting, I was just dieting, it is just another diet, defending and protecting my habits and my eating disorder. However, if I had kept up the speed I was losing the weight, I would have ended up becoming underweight eventually. That is if my heart had not given up before. I truly believe my heart would have packed in before I reached a weight where I 'looked' ill. The amount of exercise and the stress I was putting my body under was dangerous. I needed to accept this was the cause and accept that eating disorders DO come in all shapes and sizes.

The thought of having all these tests on my heart to find out what damage I had done was truly a wakeup call. The thought that I may never be able to carry a child because of my dieting habits, were breaking my heart. I needed to accept this was more than a diet and accept I had a problem. The fact I had a diagnosis from a professional did help, as I realised, they would not diagnose and help me with treatment, and invest their time in me if they did not feel it was necessary.

I researched a lot into eating disorders when I was given my diagnosis. This provided me with evidence and resources that helped me to see that this was as serious as any other type of eating disorder. All eating disorders can kill, and there are so many different types of eating disorder, not just the one that effects young woman and leaves them all skin and bone.

I will hold my hands up and say that this was what I used to believe, I had in my mind what an eating disorder "looked" like. Now I can accept I was extremely wrong and this very thinking did delay me from reaching out for help.

Eating disorders do not have a 'look'. Everyone I have met along my journey, every other eating disorder warrior out there, looks different and not one of them matches the stereotypical image I had in my head.

Big shout out to all the men out there! It has been a massive eye opener seeing how many men are affected with this illness too. I have come across other people struggling with atypical anorexia that have been classed as obese, people of all ages, helping me see it is not a teenage girl illness. I have met people of all races effected by these terrible illnesses. It has been such an eye opener for me, and I keep pushing this message forward to everyone and anyone I meet to help raise awareness that eating disorders can affect anyone and does not have a certain look.

By talking to fellow sufferers, I have found atypical anorexia just as dangerous. I suffered all the same side effects as someone with anorexia, all the same thought patterns and all the same behaviours. The only difference was my disorder was hidden, masked by the dieting culture in which we live in. It is guarded and instead of people raising concern about my habits, I was praised. I highly recommend you read all the information found on BEAT's website about OSFED, it really did help me realise there is no 'look' for an eating disorder, I had it all wrong.

I took a long hard look at myself after receiving my diagnosis and learning that my stereotypical image of eating disorders was all wrong. I looked at my overall physical health. I was cold all the time, worn out, tired, irritable, weak, I had constant brain fog, every bone and muscle in my body was hurting from exercising, I had chest pains and a low heart rate, my menstruation had ceased, constant thoughts of food, calorie obsession, checking behaviours, the hours spent obsessing over the scales and sizes.

This was just a few of the symptoms I had been experiencing, there were so many more but does this sound healthy? Do any of these things suggest a healthy lifestyle? I realised that just because that BMI chart told me I was healthy, I was far from healthy, physically and mentally. When I started to take this seriously and recognise it could kill me, I was able to engage properly in treatment. Health is not measured on a chart, being healthy means so much more than what a number on the scale tells me.

Chapter 6
Diagnosis and Entering Treatment

Working With The Team

I found myself being somewhat bombarded by a whole host of different professionals, but each one played such a vital role in my journey.

I started off by entering a day treatment programme, which consisted of me attending the centre three days a week. Here we would have a group session and together we could learn more about eating disorders and learn strategies and ways to deal with that eating disorder voice.

The group was run by two community support workers, both with lived experience of eating disorders, which I adored. For me, this meant that they would understand more about what I was feeling.

I also attended appointments with an eating disorder specialist dietician. The dietician devised a meal plan for me and bit by bit we increased it into a more realistic daily allowance.

I saw a psychiatrist who helped me with medication and finally, I saw a psychologist one day a week for Cognitive Behavioural Therapy, but specially designed for those suffering with eating disorders.

It was in these one to ones that we got to the bottom of why I had developed this illness, we worked on my self-esteem and past traumas that I was so afraid of.

I feel that I was incredibly lucky to have each one of these professionals, as each and every one of them made me feel heard. Nothing I said sounded silly, they really were the most remarkable and patient people I have ever come across.

All of a sudden, I was surrounded by an incredible amount of support, I had a whole team of specialists around me and I was also still using BEAT's support network. Of course, I had my husband as well who was very keen for me to recover whatever it took.

I had all of these people assuring me that my problems were real, they wanted to help and support me in the best way possible. It truly felt like I had people fighting in my corner for the first time in my life.

But again, that voice, that annoying eating disorder voice, was adamant that I did not need to be there, I was wasting time, and I was not sick enough for help. The voice was very much screaming, but part of me wanted help. I knew something was not right and knew that there had to be more to life than what I was doing.

First Group Session

On the first day of day the programme, I was ridiculously early and again my anxiety was off the charts. The voice was adamant I did not have a problem and everyone would laugh at me because I did not look like I had an eating disorder.

I waited nervously and was greeted by an incredibly tall gentleman who ran the day programme, who was also a community support worker. He straight away reassured me, telling me that if I felt uncomfortable at any time, I could just go into the side room and either himself or the other member of staff would talk to me. He also said that if at any point I wanted to ask anything, I was not to be afraid to speak up or pull him to the side and ask. He took me into the room and showed me the kitchen, dining and seating area where we would do our sessions. Straight away I felt at ease, he had this warming natural empathy that made me actually relax a little. The fact he had lived experience too enabled me to open up a little more than what I had expected. I was actually able to express my concerns, and voiced what my eating disorder was telling me - that I was too fat and concerned about wasting time.

He smiled warmly at me and was able to shut down that voice almost instantly. He reminded me, I would not be here, not have been accepted into treatment, if I did not have a problem. He continued to explain that this was just the ED voice, it was trying to keep me trapped by feeding me these lies.

I decided again to go ahead with the day programme and waited nervously in the seated area whilst the other community support worker and leader of the day programme, went to collect the other patients from the waiting area. The other staff member working in the day programme was also extremely welcoming and made me feel at ease.

The other patients all joined me and were all so welcoming and friendly, but straight away that voice piped up, *"you are too fat"*. All I focused on to begin with was the fact that all of the other patients were smaller than I was, and I felt back at square one. *"Surely, I could not have an eating disorder, look at the size of me."* However, as the session progressed, I realised, just because we looked different, our behaviours and thoughts were exactly the same. The checking of behaviours, the way we felt about ourselves, the fact we all shared similar fears. We were all incredibly similar.

We had to have snacks and lunch at the day programme, and we were encouraged to voice what we were feeling, and again as I listened to the other patients, I realised how much they sounded like me. I felt validated, listened to and most importantly accepted. The leader asked me at the end of the session how I felt, and I replied with, *"I have an eating disorder, I am ready to accept this and ready to recover"*. Acceptance of my disorder was a huge step for me and my recovery. I'm incredibly happy I had my husband to push me, to get the help I needed and at this time, it felt like I was repaying him and making him proud of the steps I had taken to recover.

So, now I had a treatment team, every member of that team was important; I needed to listen to each and every one of them in order to recover properly from this.

First Dietician Appointment

I handed over my book to the dietician who wanted to know what my intake was currently like. I had started to get used to being a little more open and honest, so I just accepted that she needed to know. I kept a diary of my daily intake and exercise. She looked through it but was not surprised, she took a few notes and then started to educate me on what my body needed to actually function. I was completely shocked and amazed all at the same time.

She told me about my resting metabolic rate and that my body needed fuel in order to function. She was able to explain my dizziness, lack of periods and also explain why my heart was struggling. I told her the sort of food I liked and the sort of things I had enjoyed in the past and she developed a meal plan for me to follow for the next few weeks, with different options and ideas.

This was a minimum, any extras would be a bonus. I looked down at this meal plan and felt overwhelmed, I could not believe how much I was expected to eat, I don't think I had ever eaten this much, surely this woman was just trying to make me fat, just saying this to get me to eat.

My eating disorder voice had woken and was strong. I was looking at the meal plan and trying to find safer foods and replace bits and pick ideas I knew had less calories. However, she had the proof, the science, facts and research to back up what she was saying. The voice was screaming, trying to pick faults in the logic trying to argue with every piece of evidence, every fact that was in front of me, but my rational voice was empowered. I started to believe her.

Again I knew if I wanted to recover, if I wanted to get truly better, I would have to follow her meal plans and listen to what she was saying.

The main arguments I had were with my dietician, the amount of food she was suggesting seemed ridiculous, and surely she was wrong. With help from my psychologist, I recognised my dietician was not wrong, and it was just years of discorded eating and being trapped in the dieting circle that had messed with my brain. What I perceived as normal was very different to what I should have been eating. It was my disorder that was wrong, not the dietician.

First Psychologist Appointment

Mask on, guard up. I did not want to be judged, I did not want this man to know too much about me. However, my body language gave away just how nervous and anxious I was. My feet were bouncing up and down and I could not physically sit still.

I felt like I was going to be sick and once again, my anxiety levels were through the roof. I was lucky to have the most compassionate psychologist I could have asked for. When I expressed my concerns about not being slim enough, not being ill enough, he reminded me what he had said in my assessment appointment; that yes, my BMI might have said healthy, but my mind and physical health was not.

I had an eating disorder and I deserved help. He assisted me in feeling a little more at ease, so I could engage in the appointment. My first appointment was more about educating me about my diagnosis. He did of course ask me a few questions and looking back I am kicking myself for not being completely honest in the first place and instead waiting to tell him everything that had happened in my life bit by bit later on in my treatment. We could have saved so much time.

However, I struggle to trust people, so I liked having some say over what I was going to tell him, and trust needed to be built. We talked a lot about my core beliefs and the way I saw myself. Very quickly it was obvious I had no self-esteem, which was one of the issues which had led to me developing this illness.

We spoke in great detail about the voice and I felt reassured that I was not going insane and that it was this voice that was driving my behaviours. We decided to try naming the voice, and from that moment on I referred to it as ED; not very imaginative I know, but all of a sudden, I was able to start separating my thoughts. I was able to challenge what was an ED thought and what were my own thoughts. I was able to understand how it had driven me for such a long time and how each behaviour I was engaging in only made that voice stronger.

We discussed what behaviours I was doing and decided which ones to tackle first. We needed to get more of a balance between my restriction and exercise, and cut down on my checking behaviours, and also find other coping strategies when I felt I had no control.

I had no idea my disorder was focused so much on me trying to control aspects of my life, but it all made sense. He somehow untangled some of my feelings and again made me feel at peace with my diagnosis, made me feel validated and importantly, feel safe.

My psychologist played the biggest part in helping me to heal; however, it took me ages to take my mask off and let him in. I had spent so many years building up my wall, my defence, perfecting my poker face.

As much as it pains me to admit, if I had been completely honest with him in the first place, it would have saved so much time and effort on both parts. On the days where I said I was "fine" instead of spending most of the session trying to get me to admit to him and myself that everything was not "fine", we could have actually spent the session helping me to solve whatever it was bothering me. Please do not repeat my mistakes. I also cringe when I think back to my initial assessment; I was not honest at all about the extent of my behaviours, thoughts and feelings. I hid from what had happened and lied about what had caused my eating disorder. Once again, if I had been honest from the beginning it would have made things so much easier. The second I opened up about my life, fully, was the day the real work started.

I had to trust my psychologist for this to work. I urge you to find a therapist you are comfortable with, as once I realised this man could be trusted and really did want to help me, that was when my mask started to slip. I learnt I could trust him to help me make the right decisions and he would listen and advise accordingly. My life was in his hands several times, and I had complete faith that he would help me recover from this journey. It took me a while admittedly to allow this to happen. It's just the way I am, I do not trust people easily, but I needed to learn to if this was going to work.

First Psychiatrist Appointment

My psychologist recognised that my low moods needed a little more intervention. I was honest in the survey I had to fill in that, yes, I had felt suicidal at times, due to not understanding what was going on.

I automatically thought I was going to be judged, and told I was being a drama queen for feeling depressed and to just get on with it. For some reason I had associated being depressed and feeling suicidal with being taken instantly to a hospital in a white jacket (very dramatic and not true, but my mind works in funny ways).

I was terrified of telling this professional the truth and was convinced that I'd be looked down upon for struggling.

I also associated being on medication for depression as weak and unnecessary.

I had heard so many horror stories about how they had turned people into motionless zombies, unable to feel anything. I did want the pain to stop but I did not want to be on medication. I could not be seen taking anti-depressants, I just couldn't take them.

Again, the empathy I received from this professional was outstanding but not enough to break down the mask I had worked so hard on. I found myself saying that I was fine, and now I had treatment I felt better within myself and I did not need medication.

I spoke a little about my self-harm habits, but again played them down and shrugged them off as they were not a big deal. I laughed and joked my way through the appointment and it was decided I did not need medication. I appeared to not be struggling with depression, and even though I had struggled in the past I was now in a better place and doing well.

Fast forward a few months later, my psychologist finally managed to break down my wall and I opened up to him, so I found myself with another appointment with the psychiatrist. Once again, I found that I was kicking myself for wasting time and not being completely honest in the first place. I was ashamed for some reason that I had to take anti-depressants, ashamed that I was struggling. I was strong and always happy and bubbly, but underneath that bright, cheerful exterior, I was at war with myself. I started taking the medication and they did help to begin with. They balanced out my moods and made them more stable and manageable.

Similar to taking pills, why is there a stigma about needing help for mental health? Going to see a psychologist or psychiatrist should be as normal to talk about as going to see a doctor. It should not be a taboo, and I feel the more we talk openly about our problems, encourage others to seek help, the more the stigma is being stamped out.

Once again, trust came down to me accepting the right support with the psychologist. Not being honest on my first appointment, resulted in me having to have another appointment to reassess later on. Similarly, looking back at the first few appointments, I am kicking myself for not being straight forward from the beginning.

Community Support

As well as all the support mentioned, I was also incredibly lucky to receive community support appointments to deal with some of those beliefs I had around my eating disorder. I would use my community support appointments to tackle certain fears that seemed too scary and too much to try and manage on my own. My support appointments ranged from meeting in restaurants and ordering things that were not in the low-calorie sections, supporting me in the home and cooking a meal from scratch and eating it outside my safe times, to meeting in coffee shops for a snack and a drink. But many of my community support appointments were based in supermarkets, trying to do a normal weekly shop without buying all 'safe' foods. Making sure I had enough to eat and choosing items that did not have the low-fat sticker splattered on them. I had a meal plan to follow at this stage, so I knew what I needed thanks to my dietician.

I met my support worker outside a supermarket. Already my anxiety had started to show, my heart was racing and my chest was very tight, it felt as if the fear was trying to paralyse me, to stop me from getting better. Straight away they made me laugh to put me at ease, we had a small talk just to settle the nerves a little and then entered the supermarket.

I had a shopping list and the first thing on it was cereal. We headed to the breakfast aisle and I was overwhelmed with choices. I wanted Weetabix, they were safe to me, I went straight for them, but my support worker stopped me in my tracks and asked me what I liked, not what ED liked.

I had to think, what did I like? I had no idea; I couldn't remember buying any other cereal but Weetabix. My community worker told me the sort of things she enjoyed and I agreed with a lot of them. I would probably like them too, but they had a red 'traffic light' on the front of the box - red means bad, red means no.

We then worked together to challenge these thoughts - what was a better way of looking at it? Would choosing a safe food help or hinder my recovery? What was more important, getting a cereal I liked and wanted and challenging the thoughts, or sticking with my safe food and never getting better? Eventually I found some nut clusters that I liked the look of. I remember feeling a rush of emotions as I placed these in my basket. Excited to try something different, nervous as it was not safe, but most of all I felt like a bit of a rebel.

I had rebelled against that voice and although it was screaming at me, I felt good for disobeying it. We continued with our shopping trip, challenging the thoughts as we went around, choosing things I may not have normally picked and I felt 100% supported through all decisions.

Then we reached the last thing on the list, yoghurts. I was not allowed to buy any yoghurts that were considered low fat. This is impossible; every yoghurt I looked at seemed to say low calories, low in fat, which made it so hard to decide if I wanted it or if ED wanted me to choose it because it was safer. I kept hearing the voice reminding me I was a normal weight, I needed to watch what I was eating, I needed low fat yogurts, surely a few safe foods would not hurt right?

After about 15 minutes I remember turning to my support worker almost in tears, and saying, "*I give up, this is stupid it's impossible*". She then agreed that yes, the diet culture makes it very difficult to recover as everything is all low fat etc. She then pointed towards a big tub of Greek yoghurt, full fat, no low calories splattered on the label. She suggested I get this and add different fruits I like to change the flavour.

I had never thought of that, and that would also mean challenging the voice to make sure I dished out a proper serving. Another trial I could do, whilst adding different berries and nuts, that I liked. I looked up and stopped sulking for a moment. I wanted to give her the biggest hug, but that was obviously not allowed. By just suggesting different ideas and helping me to challenge that voice, she had made such a difference. Without her, in that moment, I would have chosen all safe foods.

We then had another appointment meeting at a supermarket a few weeks later. In between the appointments I went on my own, but something was different. Yes, I still got overwhelmed and may have made a few safe options, but I had my support worker's voice in my head as I was walking around, talking me through the whole experience. I had remembered what she had said and what to do if I was feeling flushed.

I was able to pause and take deep breaths when the ED thoughts were getting too loud and, more importantly, I was able to make a few different choices and purchase unsafe foods.

The next time we met I had improved so much; I was able to navigate through my list without getting too flustered. I challenged the voice more and actually somewhat enjoyed having options. Going to the supermarket no longer brought me crippling anxiety.

For some reason I trusted the community workers from the very beginning, I was able to talk to them as I would a friend. I was so fortunate to have two people that had both been through and recovered from eating disorders, so I felt an instant connection to them, and no matter what I said I knew they would understand.

Admittedly the irritating belief kept popping into my thoughts saying "*I did not need treatment, I was a healthy weight, I was fine, I was not sick enough*". However, I learnt that every time I had one of these thoughts, when I voiced them, whichever member of the team I was with at the time was able to remind me that I was sick enough, eating disorders do not have a look, and I would never be ill enough in the eyes of ED.

I remember feeling selfish for having community support appointments, as surely other people in the service needed them more than me? But once again, I had to remind myself atypical anorexia can still kill, it's still dangerous and my eating disorder is valid.

I realise I was very fortunate to have a treatment team that were very dedicated to their work and did work tirelessly and extremely hard to help me get to where I am today.

I am saddened that this is not the case everywhere and realise truly how fortunate I was. For anyone struggling with eating disorders, finding the right support is vital. You cannot overcome this on your own. Having a treatment team that you can trust and be honest with is key, and please do not do what I did. Be honest from the start and it really will save so much time.

Speaking Up – Not Sick Enough

I will not lie, I faced a huge amount of stigma around my diagnosis. Atypical anorexia is something I had never heard of, let alone anyone else. When explaining to loved ones what was going on, I was greeted with the damaging phrase of "*you do not look like you have an eating disorder*." I remember talking to a colleague when handing in my sick note, I explained what had happened and that I needed to take time off so I could take part in a three day a week recovery day programme. Also, that by the time I had attended other medical appointments, and then had weekly therapy session on top of everything else, it would be impossible to work. I remember being greeted with that phrase, one that still sends chills down my spine, and I felt humiliated. Was I overreacting? I did not look ill, but then I had to remind myself of my own thoughts, I had also once believed that eating disorders had a certain look.

Instead of getting upset with the comment, I educated her, I explained a little about atypical anorexia and how it was just as dangerous as other eating disorders. She was shocked and could not believe it was a thing. She actually thanked me for opening her eyes and then when I had left work for a while, I knew that everyone would understand my diagnosis. I also signposted a lot of people to BEAT's website, my manager wanted to know more about what it was, I explained the best I could but at the end of the day I was still learning too. There are brilliant resources for employers on the BEAT website, and instead of me trying to explain to everyone what atypical anorexia was, I was able to send them a link instead.

Even health care professionals I have come across have not heard of atypical anorexia, once again making me feel invalidated. However, again instead of letting those thoughts take over, and running with them, I pause and educate instead. Explaining what it is, describing that eating disorders do not have a 'look', and trying to raise awareness every time I am questioned. It does infuriate me, yes. However, I refuse to let it bother me, and simply remind myself, that I was like them once, and still would be if I had not entered treatment and gotten the help that was needed. I still do find it triggering and exhausting to deal with. Be that as it may, that is why I raise awareness and I am trying to do something about it, so others do not feel they are not 'sick enough' or they do not 'look' like they have an eating disorder. This way of thinking and delaying treatment can kill.

Please accept the help that is offered to you, be honest with your treatment team from day one so they can fully understand the extent of your behaviours. I was embarrassed by mine, however soon realised they had heard it all before. Nothing surprised them; they were professionals simply trying to help. Being sick enough is absolute rubbish, if you are struggling that is a valid reason to seek help. Eating disorders do not have a look, and again even though I was healthy I had to accept that my behaviours, thoughts and body were far from healthy.

If you find yourself in a similar situation to myself, in the fact that the GP would not refer me as my BMI was not low enough, please do point them towards BEAT's website. There is a leaflet on there you can print out and take to the GP with you, and if you are still struggling after that, contact your nearest treatment team and ask them for advice. They will be able to help you get a referral. I have accepted that it was not my doctor's fault, he also had the same belief as I did and held onto that stereotypical image of an eating disorder. This is why taking in information with you and signposting towards BEAT can actually help them too, and then next time they come across a patient who may not be aware they have an issue, then the GP may remember and be able to help others.

For everyone struggling with atypical anorexia, OSFED or any eating disorder - I hear you! Your disorder is valid and despite what your mind is telling you, you deserve help and support.

Key points to take away

- BEAT states that the earlier someone receives help for an eating disorder, the better their chances of making a full recovery. What was I waiting for? For it to kill me? Then it would have been too late. I kept delaying getting help because I was a healthy weight and size, that is what mattered surely?
- Getting help for an eating disorder is an act of bravery, admitting you need help is one of the most courageous things you can do. Accepting the help is also incredibly brave, it does not make you weak, and no one will think less of you for trying to improve your health and wellbeing. I admitted I was not Superwoman and accepted help. It was the hardest thing to admit. I had dealt with everything on my own, or so I had thought, but I could not deal with this on my own, and that was okay.
- If you're getting treatment – be honest from the start. They will not judge you, nor are they there to make you feel worse.
- Chances are anything you say and do, the staff treating you would have heard and seen before. Never be embarrassed to share your whole story. They can help.
- A key piece of advice is to keep all the information and notes given to you from the dietician, any piece of evidence about how our bodies work. I wrote key points down and referred back to them so often when I was fighting with the ED voice. The evidence from the professional helped me to find my rational voice when the inner voice was screaming back. Do not just read through them once and file them away, keep them handy.
- My meal plans looked huge, again because of that disordered way of thinking. I learnt to trust my dietician

and worked closely with her to develop an increasing meal plan to get me back to regular eating. Re-feeding syndrome was an issue, as my body had been starved for so long, going from eating nothing to trying to eat three meals a day with snacks would have been dangerous. Which is why I suggest you seek a proper dietician's advice during recovery, to ensure your body is getting the nutrients it needs and a gradual approach is provided.

- The diet industry will not make this easy on you. Learning to not buy the 'safe' foods is key to helping you recover.

Chapter 7
Trauma Recovery

One of the best analogies I have heard describing trauma is that it's like a balloon, every time you avoid talking about it and every time you try and push it away, it adds air to the balloon, until eventually it bursts. This is exactly what happened with me, for years I tried to push away trauma, bury the truth and hide from it, until it finally popped.

For me, the only way to stop this cycle and stop my balloon from popping over and over was to talk. I was unable to open up fully about the abusive relationship from my teenage years to begin with, so instead I wrote it down. That was fine, it was a start and it allowed the conversations to start.

It does not matter how you start that conversation, some people I have spoken to find it is easier just to blurt it out, like ripping off a plaster, others have said they spoke a little about it each therapy session until the whole scene was set and all was told. Another example I have heard is describing it like a play, saying it or writing it out in the third person so it involves characters, not yourself. This is an incredibly personal thing to do, and I must stress this: ***do whatever you are comfortable with and do what is right for you***.

The absolute worst thing I ever did was try and bottle up the traumas that had happened, like I said, it just adds to that balloon. These conversations may be challenging. They may be difficult and uncomfortable, but the effects it can leave you with if the conversations are not had, can be worse. I developed post-traumatic stress disorder as a result from not having those conversations sooner. Prior to this I had been successful in burying my feelings but that wasn't a good thing as it resulted in eating disorder behaviours. I did open up to my psychologist about the events. The first thing I needed to do was accept what had happened. I kept trying to play down the trauma, tell myself people had been through worse, that my experience was not that bad. Trauma is trauma, end of. Yes, people may experience different traumas, but everyone's trauma is valid. Accepting this was the first big step.

What had made it harder was that I never really got what I thought was justice. There was not enough evidence by the time I reported it and so he was merely (in my opinion) left with a black mark against his name.

This in turn led me to believing it was my actions that had caused it, defending what had happened, blaming myself, when the truth is, it was not my fault.

No matter how much my brain put up a fight and tried to defend the situation, I was a young vulnerable teenager; there was no excuse for his behaviour. I needed to recognise that this was abuse and admitting this out loud was incredibly difficult.

However now, it is not the case, it does not have power anymore as I have acknowledged it and stopped hiding from it. I have accepted I was abused, accepted it was not my fault. No one deserves to be treated in such a negative manner. I found the emotional abuse just as difficult as the physical and sexual abuse. The constant cycle, telling me one thing one minute then pulling me down the next, the mind games, the control - this was harder to understand and harder to accept. I was completely manipulated and was gripped by his every word. Every type of abuse is still abuse and can still lead to maladaptive coping strategies.

Once accepting what had happened, we could then work hard on easing these intense flashbacks I had been having. We purposely exposed me to things that triggered my flashbacks and worked on grounding techniques. The idea of purposely causing flashbacks but in a safe and monitored environment was extremely helpful, as I learnt how to ground myself and prevent them. This needed to be done in a safe environment though, as I had a tendency to scream and shout and sometimes lash out as I thought I was in danger. Doing this does require proper intervention and a therapist who is trained in trauma.

I used to be obsessed with a certain soft drink, it was all I would drink, and it had unfortunately become one of my triggers for a flash back. I remember him smelling of it and I could taste it on his breath as he forced my mouth open with his. I had avoided the drink since walking away, completely avoided it, and I would not even look at it in supermarkets, as even the sight of the bottle caused very strong emotions. After discussing this, it was decided that the next session, my psychologist would expose me to the sight and smell of this drink, and we would practice the grounding techniques to help me deal with the flashbacks.

At first I remember laughing, "*are you for real? You want me to actually purposely trigger myself? No, not doing it, not a chance.*" However, what choice did I actually have? He pointed out that there was potential for someone to drink it around me and that I was unable to avoid it, how would I then cope? We needed to work on how I could handle it. Of course, he was once again right.

The next session I was prepared, I knew what we were going to do and I felt sick to my stomach. I wanted to call in sick, miss my appointment and run. Anything to avoid this session, but I knew we had to do it eventually, so if I delayed it, it would only add to my anxiety and stretch out the uncomfortable feeling.

We sat down in the normal therapy room we were in. I was comfortable, I felt safe there and more importantly, I knew I was in safe hands, which was extremely important. We discussed what we were about to do and went through the grounding techniques we had been practicing. I prepared myself and was already taking deep breaths as we went through the strategies.

The first thing we went through was safe imagery work. When I felt myself dissociate, I would imagine a time and particular place where I felt truly happy and at peace; for me, this was on my honeymoon.

A trip to the Caribbean coast, a once in a lifetime holiday to Mexico, I could picture the beautiful white sandy beach, feeling the warm soft sand in between my toes. I could easily hear the waves gently sweeping onto the shore and smell a hint of salt in the air. I could also still taste the freshly squeezed orange juice with a hint of champagne in that we were greeted with every morning on the beach (take me back right now! It really was bliss). This particular memory was a treat for all my senses and I also felt safe being in my husband's company, celebrating being together, celebrating how happy we are and being married.

This also worked when I was struggling with ED. When I was getting stressed and worked up I used this technique to calm me, as it engaged all of my senses and distracted the unwanted thoughts.

Another grounding technique we recapped on was a breathing exercise, breathing in through your nose for five seconds, holding it for five and exhaling out your mouth for five. And finally, a technique to bring myself in the present moment, as a result from the PTSD I would think I was back to being fourteen, back in the danger and I would freeze, I was taught the five to one technique, which means to - *Look around you and name 5 things you can see, 4 things you can touch, 3 things you can hear, 2 things you can smell, and 1 thing you can taste*. The idea being that it brings you to the present moment.

Again, these two techniques are not just helpful for trauma work, I used these techniques all the time throughout my eating disorder recovery. When I felt myself getting stressed and my anxiety peaking, I used these grounding techniques to help ease the anxiety and bring me back to the present moment, and temporarily muting the ED voice, as I was engaging my senses and thoughts elsewhere.

After going through the grounding techniques and reminding myself I was safe, I was at St George's Hospital, Lincoln and it was 2018; it was time to do the exposure work.

My psychologist carefully opened the bottle, but it resulted in the liquid fizzing everywhere, and I could not help but giggle. This completely broke the tension and seriousness of the situation, but as it did so I caught the smell of it.

Straight away I was catapulted back to the memory, I could hear my psychologist remind me of the date and time, bringing me back to the present moment, and it worked, but my mind was racing, heart pumping and I was convinced I was in danger. He then poured some into a glass and encouraged me to smell it again and then to actually taste it by taking a small sip, reminding me it was only a drink and it could not hurt me. I was extremely reluctant, taking deep breaths, concentrating on my breathing, reminding myself the year and where I was. I took one final breath and took a small sip.

Instantly, I could feel his hands around my wrists, I could feel his breath and I could taste it now as well. I could hear my psychologist talking in the background, but it was blurred, everything was blurry as I was fighting a flashback.

I opened my eyes and heard my psychologist say, what are 5 things you can see? I forced myself to look around, heart racing as I was reliving the memory, what could I see?

A painting on the wall, I noticed the colours, the chair I had been sat on, suddenly aware I was pacing the room. Unable to remember that I had at some point stood, I could see the trees outside the window, I could see the door handle shining in the light and finally the cabinet behind my psychologist. Four things I could touch, one being my clothes, the fabric I noticed was soft. I was holding a stress ball, I could feel the textures, I could feel my heart beating out of my chest and finally, my feet on the floor; I had also managed to lose my shoes in this process. Three things I could hear, I could hear the wind outside rustling in the trees, I could hear my breath slowing and I could hear the radiators working away. Two things I could smell, I could still smell the soft drink, but it was just a drink, it couldn't hurt me, I could smell my perfume. Finally, one thing I could taste; the drink, but I was in the here and now, I was safe.

We then explored the mental imagery work after being exposed to the smell and taste, and grounding me, just to make sure my anxiety levels were eased, and to calm my racing heart further.

We talked about the honeymoon and the sounds I could hear. I imagined I was in that happy safe place, again engaging all my senses. I had done it though, exposed myself to a trigger; yes - I was having unwanted images flashing in my mind, and was convinced a few times I was in danger - but I was able to ground myself and bring myself back to the present moment. I was safe.

I learnt by doing this that the drink really was only a drink and it could not hurt me. But doing this once was not enough; I needed to keep exposing myself to the trigger to bring the intensity down further.

I then decided I would keep some in the house, so I would see it and be exposed to it most days. It was simply left out on the side, James was encouraged to drink it, as I felt safe with him. I was able to keep reminding myself it was just a drink, one that caused unwanted memories, yet that is all it was, a memory and it could not hurt me now.

One by one we recognised what my triggers were, and I worked through them, exposing myself to them over and over again until they no longer caused such strong emotions.

Constantly reminding myself that yes, they gave me memories, but that is all they were, memories.

I was safe.

The grounding techniques described do not just help with trauma, they really did come in useful when challenging the ED thoughts. When I recognised the voice was strong and taking charge and I was unable to provide counter arguments, the 5-1 technique reset me, allowed me to refocus, once I had calmed and then try again.

We also did a technique called re-scripting, where we would rewrite the ending to what happened, re-scripting it. However, for me personally, it was not enough; the therapy and trauma exposure work was simply not enough. Even though my flashbacks had calmed, my nightmares were still intense.

I spoke a lot about this in sessions. It seemed every time I was getting somewhere with my eating disorder, something would trigger a nightmare and my PTSD became stronger and more difficult to handle. Therefore, as a way of coping with the trauma, I would once again return to ED as a way of control. I felt like I was just not progressing.

As we continued to work through the trauma and were doing the exposure work, I found myself constantly thinking of the trauma, exposing myself frequently and grounding myself. It was exhausting, emotionally and physically draining. I needed to rest, I needed sleep, however the trauma followed me to sleep. Every time I closed my eyes and tried to sleep, I would awake screaming, drenched in sweat and tossing and turning replaying it. I became afraid to sleep, and the fact I was so worked up about sleeping meant I could not fall asleep naturally. It was decided that I needed a sleep hygiene routine to help me sleep, making sure I was not worrying or in a heightened sense of anxiety when trying to get to sleep, as this only increased my nightmares.

I followed these tips:

- Ensure my sleeping environment was relaxing, was it dark enough and the right temperature?
- Making sure I had my evening snack and a small drink before bed, so I was not going to sleep hungry.
- Avoiding stimulants before bedtime, this included alcohol, nicotine and caffeine.
- Putting phones and laptops down 30 minutes before I planned on going to bed, avoiding any types of screen when settling down.
- Avoiding napping during the day. I was exhausted but needed proper rest, not a power nap.
- Establishing a bedtime routine. For me this included, a set bedtime and doing a sleep meditation or a mindfulness practice before bed to help calm those racing thoughts.
- Avoiding high intensity workouts before bedtime, exercise can stimulate your brain and produces the hormone cortisol which keeps your brain alert.
- Writing down any worries, parking what is keeping your mind racing. There is nothing you can do at that moment in time. By writing it down I was acknowledging it and could deal with it the next day.

I kept making sure I did all of these things, and I was starting to sleep a little better. However, I still had an issue awakening from nightmares and then struggling to settle back down again. So, between myself and my psychologist, we also developed a nightmare management plan, that I could do when awakening from a nightmare, instead of getting up and therefore only having a few hours of sleep each night. I got into the habit of getting up and cleaning or even baking after a nightmare. I was too afraid to go back to sleep.

This was my nightmare management plan:

1. Prompt myself to breathe in a controlled manor, practice taking deep breaths to calm myself.

2. Ground myself to the present place and moment (utilise the senses – e.g. what can I see, feel, smell, touch, and even taste, the 5-1 technique)

3. State out loud the date, time and that I was safe.

4. Do an activity that was calming and relaxing.

5. Do not fear sleeping again; tell myself it is a nightmare and that it was understandable considering what had happened.

6. Engage in the sleep hygiene principles that we have previously covered. I downloaded a sleep app on my mobile and participated in guided meditations, to enable me to drift back off to sleep once calmed.

I needed rest. Battling an eating disorder requires a tremendous amount of strength and getting a good night's sleep is crucial. Despite all of this hard work - the sleep hygiene tips, nightmare management plans - the trauma was still there and still bothering me. The only way I could finally let this rest and be free from the living nightmare and recover once and for all, was to report it. I needed to go to the police.

Taking that first step was utterly terrifying, I won't lie. But the nightmares were literally keeping me awake, the flashbacks becoming too much to bear and I could not recover properly from my eating disorder whilst I was still living in a heightened state of anxiety. The police specialist centre (Spring Lodge) do look after you. They have a team who go through the process with you and enable you to speak out. I decided to go down the anonymous intelligence route, which meant I could give evidence and a statement against the abuser but remain anonymous.

For some reason I was still frightened of him. He still had power over me, so this way it enabled me to feel safe, but also to do the right thing. I urge anyone who has been through anything similar to report it, not just for justice for what has happened to you, but to also protect others. It was this that haunted me, in the back of my mind I was constantly thinking, *"what if he has done this to others? What if someone else is struggling under his power and I have not done something to help them?"* This was my main motivation to finally take that step and report it. Not just to ease my PTSD symptoms and finally heal, but also, I felt it was my duty. It was my responsibility to speak up, so others did not suffer.

Something incredible happened once I had finally dealt with this trauma and I had realised that the bullies were just ignorant children; their words may have been vile but could not physically harm me. I truly started to heal. I was no longer running from my past but had dealt with it. I was no longer haunted by the nightmares and flashbacks.

Yes, I still get occasional nightmares from time to time, however I am much more equipped and able to deal with them now. I finally realised that facing the trauma and responding to it, took massive courage and catapulted me forward in my recovery journey.

My heightened anxiety had eased, PTSD symptoms relaxed, and I was no longer living in fear. Once the past was dealt with properly, I could then work towards my future.

Emotional Avoidance

Not only was ED used as a way to deal with trauma but it also numbed me from negative emotions, gave me something else to focus on so I did not have to deal with being upset and hurt.

It was a distraction however; it was not a healthy way to deal with things. I started to deal with every trauma I had buried, including the death of my friend, which I had not properly dealt with. I decided to set some time aside on the anniversary of her death and actually mourn, properly, allowing myself to cry. I had always seen crying as a weakness and this was something we explored in therapy. What was so wrong with crying? Where did the idea of crying being a negative thing come from? There is a saying that goes, *"even the clouds rain when they get heavy"*.

I needed to see it was not a terrible thing, that crying was actually okay, and sadness is just an emotion. So, I was set an unusual task, I was told to ask a few of my friends if crying meant I was weak, I asked them a simple question:

"Is it good to cry?" These were their answers:

Male:

Matthew – *"Yes, it is natural, it helps deal with a large spectrum of emotions, such as joy, sadness and anger, it should never be treated as a weakness."*

Nicky – *"Yes, I'd say it is good personally, just means so much is being stored inside and it has to come out."*

Ryan - *"Yes, it makes me feel better, I sometimes feel silly afterwards, but it helps."*

Sam – *"Yes, it is healthier to let your emotions out, having a cry makes me feel better."*

Jonty – *"Yes, let it out, all out at least I know what people are really feeling instead of guessing."*

Female:

Gemma – *"It depends, it lets out the emotion that is being bottled up but hate it when people get to me that much, I feel that crying is the only way to calm down."*

Becky – *"No, absolutely not, just get on with it, crying isn't going to do anything."*

Ellie – *"Yes, good for your heart and your soul, bottling it up will eat you up. Happy tears are good too."*

Jess – *"Depends, there is a time and a place, but it helps release the emotion."*

Kirstie – *"Yes it's good, if you keep it all in it will get worse until something snaps, it is a relief."*

Debbie – *"Depends, I cry when I am angry which makes me feel weak, however it always makes me feel relieved afterwards, no matter what I am feeling in the moment. Crying with laughter is the best, as it's being in a happy place with people who can make you laugh like yourself."*

I had proof, it was just me that felt crying was such a terrible thing, I had all of these people both male and female telling me otherwise. Reassuring me that actually crying helps, bottling up emotion and pretending I was okay was not healthy. I also had a discussion with James about crying and he told me he wished I would more; that way he could actually tell what I was feeling instead of guessing, getting it wrong and not helping when I need him.

I had learnt how to wear my mask so well and not allow others to see what I was dealing with. I had mastered my mask, it showed I was brave and that nothing fazed me. However, the bravest thing I did was take the mask off and admit my real feelings. I was not okay, far from it, and that is okay.

I had forgotten how to feel emotions, ED completely blanked them, one of the hardest things I had to learn was allowing myself to feel emotions again and not be afraid of them. The main one was anxiety; yet, ED caused a lot of anxiety itself which was kind of ironic. The thing hiding my anxiety and masking it was causing more anxiety. I was anxious around mealtimes, anxious about breaking my rules, so to avoid feeling anxious I would avoid eating. Not helpful, however, I was once given the best piece of advice ever regarding emotions, and it has stuck with me.

Your anxiety is just an emotion, an unpleasant one, yes, but it cannot hurt you, your eating disorder can.

This rang true to me, I was avoiding unpleasant feelings, especially when it came to challenging ED, but they were indeed just emotions, just feelings.

It is human of us to feel these things; it is normal, and they cannot physically hurt us. However, trying to mask these feelings, hide them and run from them, using ED as a way to numb these emotions or avoiding dealing with the disorder because of anxiety, that can hurt us, in fact it could even kill us.

So, I had to ask myself again, is crying and embracing emotions really such a bad thing?

ED did not just conceal the negative emotions though, it numbed me completely from all emotions and left me with nothing but emptiness and depression instead. I could feel happiness yes, but not the extreme delight that everyone else feels, and I was aware it would not last and would plateau. Once I realised that ED was also numbing me from all the great feelings, I started to work on getting in touch with my emotions again.

I was, yet again, set another task (honestly the amount of homework I received from my CBT sessions was madness, it was a full-time job recovering, but worth investing the time in). I was set the task of pausing every hour and asking myself what I was feeling. I set myself an alarm on my phone and for the week, gave it my all. When my alarm went off, I took a deep breath and asked myself, *"Okay Zoe what are you feeling?"* I was able to really think for a minute about what my body was trying to tell me. Quite often I noticed I was in pain across my shoulders because I was tense, which was telling me I felt anxious. Other times I felt a little calm and recognised my breathing was slow, eyes relaxed and that meant I was relaxed. By doing this every hour for a full week, I was able to explore my emotions, get back in touch with them and think about them a little more.

Also, by doing this I was able to ask myself what I could do to make it better and ease the unpleasantness without using the disorder. For example, if I was tense, I could do some deep breathing and relax my shoulders to take away that tension and anxiety.

After the week I had explored so many different emotions, not just how I felt but also what I physically felt and where I could feel it. For example, for me when I am feeling anxious, I recognise that my body temperature rises, I am able to tell my heart beats quickly and I tense my jaw. I can pair the physical sensation to the emotion. What is my body trying to tell me? Tuning into where I hold tension and thinking why and what could this mean? If I am unable to identify the emotion, I can simply scan my body instead and pinpoint what my body is feeling as an alternative.

When I am now dealing with a particularly difficult time, or experiencing a strong emotion, instead of hiding from it, I own it. For example, if I am having one of those weeks at work, where I feel tense and stressed, I admit that is how I am feeling, recognise that I have strong negative emotions and instead of masking them, I do something about it.

Masking and running from the emotions may work short term, but similar to the trauma balloon, eventually it will build up and will cause you to pop.

More Thinking Styles

I had developed many unhelpful and unhealthy thinking styles over the years, some of which I have already explained. I had to start challenging those automatic negative thoughts if I was to overcome them. They were a driving factor for my eating disorder and made me believe I was the worst person in the world. I always felt as if I wasn't good enough and the constant belief that I was nothing but a failure, tore me apart inside. The only way I could improve the way I thought about myself was to try and improve my self-esteem. This sounds easy, but when you have spent years tearing yourself down and belittling your own achievements, it really isn't. However, I knew by doing this, ED would have less power over me.

I started logging the thoughts when I recognised I was having them, writing down every single negative thought and automatic response. All of the, "*I am stupid, they hate me*", just to raise self-awareness. By doing this I was able to quickly pick up on how often I was tearing myself to shreds. Once I had become more aware of them, I was then able to start challenging them.

First, I wrote down the situation; what was going on around me? I then logged the automatic response, what were my automatic thoughts? I then asked myself, If I believed this thought, how would it affect my feelings and also what were my feelings? Then after recognising how hurtful I was being towards me personally, I would then ask myself, "*what would I say to a friend who was saying these things about themselves?*"

How else could I look at this situation, before finally counterbalancing the two, to a more realistic approach? I made it into a little grid and laminated it, so I could quickly work through my automatic responses, and by doing this, eventually, I was able to do it on the spot, without working through it. Here is an example of one of my automatic negative thoughts:

<u>Situation</u> – Trying to cook tea, mind wondering to calories, as I had forgotten to weigh out a few of my ingredients.

Negative automatic thoughts (NAT) – "*You are so stupid, you are now going to get fat, and you cannot eat this without knowing what to burn.*"

- *Feelings and what would happen if I believed this?* – Feeling anxious, stressed, heart beating quickly and I am upset with myself. I know if I believe this I will not eat and therefore my eating disorder wins.
- *What would you say to a friend?* – Your body needs fuel, you do not need to weigh every single thing out, enjoy the meal, you will not get fat from eating this one meal. Knowing the exact calories in a meal isn't necessary.
- *Realistic approach* – Okay so I did not follow ED rule, this is okay and actually a good thing as I can challenge it. I will not automatically get fat from this one meal just because I do not know the calorie content. Does anybody else weigh out every ingredient to their meals? No. I feel anxious yes, but that is okay. It is just a feeling and emotion, my emotions cannot hurt me, but letting my eating disorder voice win will.

I did this constantly, not just for ED but in day-to-day life, making myself aware when I was being critical to myself and automatically jumping to conclusions and negative thinking styles, let me give you another example:

Situation – Work meeting, we were all asked if we had any ideas regarding parent collaboration and partnership.

Negative automatic thought (NAT) – *"Everyone will laugh at you if you speak up, your suggestion is stupid, your opinion does not matter, it will fail and your boss will think you are stupid."*

- **Feelings and what would happen if I believed this?** – I would never allow myself to give suggestions; I may have a really good idea that is never brought forward out of fear.

- **What would you say to a friend?** – You do not know if you do not try, it might be a good suggestion and shine light on how creative you can be. If they do not like the idea, it does not matter, at least you tried and contributed to the meeting.

- **Realistic approach** – Okay speak up, say what you are really thinking, if they do not agree with your idea that is okay, but at least you gave a suggestion and your opinion is just as valid.

I am such a strong believer of talking to myself like I would a friend; admittedly this took a lot of practice. Now I can make a counter argument against those negative thoughts and when I recognise them, I literally cut myself off mid-sentence. *"Zoe we don't have time for this type of negative thinking, what would you say to a friend right now? Treat yourself like you would a friend, have some self-compassion."*

Sometimes the negative voices are stronger and coming up with that self-compassionate voice, as well as a counter argument can be extremely difficult. In these moments it's completely okay to pause and take some time for self-care, soothing yourself and letting those intense feelings settle a little before trying to argue against it. The one thing I can guarantee is, the more you challenge those NATs, the easier it is to become your own best friend and give yourself the same compassion as you so freely give to others.

Key points to take away

- Emotions are not weakness. It's okay to cry and to let people see how you feel. You can only get stronger by recognising and owning your emotions.
- Emotions and feelings cannot hurt you, they are not physical.
- Emotions are temporary, they do pass. They will feel painful and difficult at the time but ride the wave.
- This is one of the bravest things you may ever do. Please, after exposure work or talking about traumas, rest afterwards and engage in self-care.
- Finding a therapist that you trust is such a big factor in this process. Do not be afraid to seek different support if it does not feel right for you.
- Exposure work can be dangerous if not carried out correctly. Again make sure the therapist is trained and you talk through grounding techniques and safe place imagery beforehand.
- Face your fears. Exorcise your demons, even if it means reliving trauma that started your eating disorder.
- Letting go of the past is the way to build your future.
- You do not need to forgive someone that has wronged you, often forgive and forget can be harmful. Allow yourself to feel the emotions attached to it, you do not owe anyone anything. You do however owe it to yourself to heal in a way that works for you.
- Finding your compassionate self can be extremely tricky. Learn to talk to yourself like you would a friend. Give yourself the same love and compassion that you give to others.
- Just because an automatic negative thought appears does not mean it is true, take time to evaluate it, explore what is going on.

Chapter 8
Personality Traits

Certain personality traits can feed an eating disorder, being able to recognise them in yourself can help you to manage certain behaviours.

Perfectionist

This is something I never knew was in me, as I always felt far from perfect and no matter what I did, I was never good enough.

However, looking back I realise how much of my life and how many elements of my behaviours were me being a perfectionist. Not just with ED but all aspects of my life.

I am a baker. I adore making cakes and spend many hours in the kitchen creating new recipes, in particular cupcakes. I enjoy decorating them extremely delicately and I love making things with fondant icing and the intricate, detailed work and high level of concentration it requires plays into my perfectionist traits extremely well.

The number of times I have thrown a cake away or started again because it was not good enough, or I had made the slightest error in my piping and it was not perfect, was to be fair, ridiculous. It drove me insane at times; it would reduce me to tears and often screams of frustration.

What could have easily been a simple job, a nice easy task, turned into hours of work because it had to be just right. My husband never seemed to mind as he got all my misfits, and the ones that were not one hundred percent that I could not give out - how could I if they were not perfect? Even when it went well, when everything went to plan and whatever I was baking or decorating looked okay, I would find a way to criticise it. It would never be absolutely perfect.

I could never be perfect.

I struggled with perfectionism all the way through school and university as well. Looking back, I always worked really hard to get good grades, often until I burned out, and then I would not get the grades because I had exhausted myself. So then I would work harder, trying to get better grades, until again I would become exhausted. It was a vicious circle I was unknowingly trapped in.

It continued into University, I adored playing the flute and would practice many hours a day to again, try and do well in exams and get good grades. The practices that didn't go well, I found I struggled to handle. I would question my abilities and assume that the piece should be perfect by now and it was my fault that it wasn't. Recitals always went well, however, never perfectly. I struggled with anxiety and nerves, which is not the best when trying to perform. Whenever I had finished, again, I pulled myself down, ignoring everything that went right and obsessed purely on the few things that went wrong. If it was not perfect, I was going to fail surely.

Every year all my friends come together for 'friendsmas' It's basically a Christmas Eve, followed by our own Christmas Day with our closest friends. Friendmas Eve we will play games, have a few drinks, have party food. Then Friendsmas Day, we would wake up and sit around the Christmas tree; opening presents from each other, cook a Christmas dinner and then again play a few games.

It was a tradition that started when we were at university and has now become embedded in our lives and is a yearly routine which we all absolutely adore. We have the most room at home, so we always host the occasion. The day before, I would wake up ridiculously early, I'd start to clean the house from top to bottom, a ritual I always used to do when I knew I had people coming over. My house had to look perfect, clean and immaculate. After hours of scrubbing, and cleaning every inch of the house, it would be time to bake. Every year I'd handmake loads of pastries and sweet treats for everyone to enjoy over the coming days. I would always bake way too much. I'd spend the whole day in the kitchen, baking and cooking a variety of things so I could ensure everyone had something they liked. By the next day I'd be exhausted, but keen to make our Friendsmas as perfect as I could. I'd put out the treats on a cake stand and play the perfect host all evening, constantly making sure everyone's glass was full, making sure everything was still tidy and ensuring everyone had everything they wanted.

My friends often just walk into my house and help themselves to drinks or whatever is in the cake tins, there is no need for me to constantly ensure they are okay. If they wanted anything they would ask, but I did not want anyone to have to ask, it was my job.

The next day we'd all help in the kitchen after opening our presents, we'd have a lot of fun and while everything was cooking, I would be back to fretting and trying to make sure everything was just right. I'd have already set the table first thing, but would fiddle with it, adding extra touches. Everyone else would be playing a game but I'd miss out because I was too obsessed with everything being perfect.

I doubt now my friends noticed the extra details, they were too busy enjoying each other's company! Throughout the whole day I'd obsess over everything, making sure everyone had enough to eat and drink, making sure everything remained somewhat tidy and playing the perfect host. I'd be so busy doing this, I'd miss half of the day.

Things have changed and I try and obsess less over things being perfect and try and focus more on being present, however I still find my perfectionist traits overwhelming at times.

This trait manifested into my eating disorder, and the perfectionist trait that had always been there, seemed to really take over. I have always been quite particular over my appearance, paranoid that everyone was laughing at me, I needed to make sure I looked good enough, however as I have previously mentioned, it was never perfect and that would play on my mind.

I always thought that if I lost weight, I would achieve the perfect body. If I worked out more and concentrated on my figure, I would achieve perfection. However, the perfect body does not exist. No matter what I did, how hard I worked, there were always other parts of my body to criticise. But I kept trying.

I found perfect bodies on the internet and had the images handy on my phone for inspiration, these women looked perfect, the perfect legs, the perfect hair. I focused so much of my time trying to look like someone else, I slowly lost who I was, but continued trying to achieve something that was never really possible. I also kept setting myself goal weights, I had an idea what my perfect weight would be. If I could get to this weight, I would be perfect but again, when I reached that weight, it was somehow not good enough.

Whenever I went out anywhere, I would always make sure my make-up looked perfect, and I would obsess for ages if it looked okay. Again I would tear myself to shreds for not being perfect. It slowly took over.

It also manifested during recovery. At the beginning of treatment I was so worried about opening up and talking, because I wanted to be an easy patient, I did not want to make a lot of work or be a cause for concern. Is there even such a thing as a perfect patient? If I was perfect, I would not even be a patient. I wanted to appear that I had a perfect life, and it was just a diet that got out of control.

I was always very particular and fretted over homework and tasks that were set. I had to do them and I had to do them well. I am very creative and part of me did enjoy getting creative and doing the tasks in my own unique way, although it took so much time.

I was never able to do work sheets, I would always find a way to make them look nicer, redesign them. Worksheets just bored me, I could not seem to help it! Armed with glitter and different colour pens each week, a task that would have taken minutes, took me hours. I look back and question, how much of this was down to me just being creative and doing things my own way, and how much of this was actually down to me trying again to be a perfect patient, and always doing my homework, like I was at school trying to please the teacher all over again.

Whenever I was struggling or in the middle of a lapse, I was scared of reaching out for help because I wanted to recover perfectly. Again I never wanted to be seen as struggling. It is impossible to keep this up, the more perfect I tried to be the more I seemed to struggle.

Tackling The Perfectionist

There is nothing wrong with being a little bit of a perfectionist, however when it starts to interfere with your life and effect your overall wellbeing, then it needs to be recognised and those behaviours need to be challenged.

The first and most important thing I did was actually recognise I had this trait. I felt far from perfect, never good enough and yet I was a perfectionist. This took quite a while to get my head around, although I started to recognise what my therapist meant. Everything had to be done just right and my way. From my work to my home, perfectionism followed me everywhere. I also realised I was chasing perfection in my appearance; I was trying to look perfect, chase the impossible, try and be perfect.

One of the biggest things I struggled with regarding my perfectionistic trait was my house. I had to have things a certain way, I did not trust my husband to clean as he did not do it properly or my way, and it just was not good enough, so I would end up cleaning things again.

Everywhere had to be completely spotless if we had guests coming over, clean from top to bottom. I could not leave washing up on the side - it had to be washed, dried and put back away that evening. My husband used to tease me and say

"The queen will not be visiting tonight; you can leave it until the morning."

However, what happens if someone stops by first thing in the morning and sees the washing up and thinks we are some sort of lazy animals who cannot even look after our house?

I spoke openly about this to my therapist and we decided to do a little experiment, to try and challenge that perfectionistic trait. I had to leave one pan on the side overnight unwashed, just to prove to myself it did not need doing. That evening we had a simple pasta meal, I washed up everything except for one pan. I left it on the side and reminded myself it did not matter, the sun would still rise tomorrow if there was one pan left on the side. I continued my evening with my husband, we curled up together on the sofa and watched a film, he noticed my legs were twitching and asked me what the matter was. I exploded,

"I just know the pan is still there, what happens if it attracts insects and then we get an infestation?"

My husband looked at me and laughed. I was furious, how could he laugh at something so serious? I look back now and to be honest, I laugh too, but at the time trying to challenge that belief, and that everything had to be done perfectly was no laughing matter. It got to around 10pm and we were heading to bed, I shouted upstairs to my husband that I would be up in a minute and decided quickly to finish off the washing up. I could not leave it overnight dirty, but I could leave it to air dry.

The next morning my husband realised what I had done and questioned it. He reminded me of my perfectionistic trait and that if I wanted to recover, I needed to realise everything could not be perfect 100% of the time. I was a little embarrassed that I could not leave a simple pan on the side.

The following week, we tried again. I left the pan unwashed on the side and then distracted myself by watching a film with James. I headed up to bed knowing it was still there, knowing I had not finished my jobs. I tossed and turned all night, unable to even sleep as I felt like I had failed somehow. Then in the morning when I realised it was still there, I laughed. It really was not the end of the world. This idea that everything had to be perfect in the kitchen every night was just not a helpful behaviour.

I then started challenging other areas of my life where I realised I was being a perfectionist. Another big area was my baking. I could not give out imperfect cupcakes, I would re-ice them or remake them, even if they were being given away for free, they still had to be prefect. I started baking imperfect cupcakes; instead of weighing everything out precisely, I would add a few extra grams of sugar or flour, just so it was not completely perfect. They tasted no different, which surprised me and further challenged that trait, I had made an error on purpose and it did not matter.

I pipe roses on to my cakes in pink buttercream, just to finish them off, and if I piped one a little imperfectly. I challenged myself to leave it. It did not matter, this of course drove me insane, and made my anxiety bubble away - how could I give out something that was not completely perfect?

I wanted to continue challenging this trait, so I started taking my imperfect cakes into the clinic with me for the staff. I was always complimented and thanked for my gift, but I always hated it as I knew they were not my best work.

Truth is, nine out of ten of them would be perfect but I hated one of them not being so. However, over time and with practice, continuing to practice perfectly imperfect cupcakes seemed to do the trick. I continued to take my "misfits" as I called them, into work with me and make myself hand them out. Now when baking, if one or two are not quite perfect, I am able to think rationally about it and remind myself the other ten are. If they are a gift and not being paid for, it does not matter, they will appreciate the free cake and the gesture that went alongside.

My appearance and size were another thing I needed to challenge regarding my perfectionism. I was chasing after the impossible concept of having a perfect body. Pursuing the perfect body weight, I could see the number go down on the scale and I hit my target weight - my perfect weight - but automatically it would change again to another perfect weight, lower than what I was. In the eyes of ED that number would never be perfect. My measurements would never be perfect, I am not perfect. The only way I could stop trying to achieve perfection was recognising I am not perfect.

I worked hard and challenged my day-to-day perfectionism by practicing imperfect baking and not blitzing the house from top to bottom like some sort of cleaning genie armed with Zoflora. So now I had to start practising on my looks.

I needed to concentrate on accepting who I was. I started off by not always wearing make-up. If I was meeting friends, I would always make sure my make-up looked immaculate, if that meant taking it off and reapplying it, so be it.

I was going to a friend's house just for a drink and a film one evening, not going anywhere just a pyjama party. AKA an excuse for gin. I started to get ready and realised I had started to put make-up on. I questioned why? I was going for a drink; film and sleep over, why did I need to look perfect. I then thought *what happens if we take photos?*

I had to really think, so what, this is my face, does it really matter if I am not covered in foundation? Even if we do take photos and they go onto social media, the only people that will see them anyway are my friends, who have seen me at 4AM after drinking, I looked better at that minute than I did then. I also realised that in a few hours I would be taking the make-up off anyway.

This was the perfect opportunity to challenge that trait. I stopped in my tracks and decided, I did not need to look immaculate to visit one of my closest friends, and I was going as I was! I got to my friend's and was instantly calmed. Both of us had our hair in some sort of messy bun, neither of us had make-up on and she had gin ready for me. We took photos and yes, they were posted on social media, however no one commented on our lack of make-up or messy hair, they commented on our smiles and friendship. That is what really mattered that evening.

I then realised I did not need loads of make-up every day, I stopped wearing large amounts for work, and just wore it at weekends and special occasions. I was trying to make myself look better somehow, disguise the real me. Trying to be something I am not, trying to look perfect.

I made a list of all the things I did that was perfectionistic, and one by one I challenged them, like the example I used about not wearing make-up and leaving pots on the side. One by one I went through them all. Even now as I am well into recovery if I notice I am being extremely particular about something, I recognise it, and ask myself, am I trying to be a perfectionist, will this matter in a weeks' time, and work through my thoughts accordingly. There is no such thing as perfect. I will never be perfect no one is perfect, and I am okay with that.

Harm Avoidance

I have always been a very worried person, not just the day-to-day things that most people worry about, like being late for work or did I just say the right or wrong thing, but things that were completely out of my control. I was terrified of flying for example, I was convinced every bump or jolt on the plane would mean it was in trouble and something was wrong.

When my husband and I got married, we were lucky enough to honeymoon in Mexico. We booked the holiday and planned some incredible activities, it really would be a once in a lifetime holiday - snorkelling in the coral reefs, scuba diving with sharks, exploring and walking along the Caribbean coast, five-star all-inclusive hotel, and more importantly time away together to celebrate married life and celebrate each other. The flight, however, was over nine hours long. My heart plummeted when the travel agent told us this. Nine whole hours in a plane, I was being torn in two with worry, sick with anxiety. I desperately wanted to go, of course I did, something we would never be able to do again. Yet I was worried that if I let my true fear show and said I didn't want to go because I was scared of flying, my husband would be cross with me. He would be angry because he really wanted to go, and would just think I was being silly, I was convinced he would go anyway. I was also worried that if I did go the plane would crash or something would go wrong on the flight. I wanted to cry right there and then again in the travel agent.

Just before we booked, I plucked up the courage and spoke to James, who said I was more likely to be hit by a bus than to be in a plane accident (which by the way was not helpful, as now I am afraid of busses), but I did agree to go. I was desperate to do all of these amazing activities alongside my new husband.

The day before we were due to fly, I could feel the anxiety and worry starting to bubble up. I was so scared of the flight that I had started to be physically sick, my chest was tight and I was dizzy. We got to the airport and I headed straight to the bar and had a drink. As we boarded the plane I was visibly shaking, all these thoughts swirling through my head, but it was too late now, I had to go through with it and I wanted to go. Throughout the whole nine-hour flight, every jolt, slight bump or tiny bit of turbulence we hit, I was convinced that was the end. I ended up quite unwell during that flight. However, we had the most amazing time away, made the most wonderful memories, the worry and anxiety had been worth it, unnecessary, but worth it.

It was the day to day worrying that I struggled with the most though. One example of this was that I was constantly worried others were upset with me, or that I had said something wrong. I would also worry and obsess that if someone did not reply to my message, email or text, that it was because of something I had said. I must have done something wrong or said something to upset them. I would spend hours analysing messages I had sent making sure it could not be misinterpreted or taken wrong. I would annoy my friends by constantly asking if I had done something wrong to upset them. Quite often they would reply with,

"No stop asking me that, it's really annoying"

and then of course I would worry because my worrying had annoyed them. Oh, the irony!

I was also a massive pessimist. I always assumed the worst would happen, I would prepare for the worst-case scenario, which made me worry more and make me anxious a lot of the time. I firmly believed the glass was half empty and completely missed the point that the glass was refillable. It made me have a negative view on the world, always assuming the worst and holding back on opportunities, because I was convinced that I was going to fail. I have got better at remembering the glass is refillable, but often slip back to old habits.

I was in recovery, still in treatment and I explained to my psychologist that I had applied to do a TEDx talk, and actually got selected to go on to give the full talk, but I was going to pull out as I had made myself believe that I could not be a public speaker and I was regretting even applying in the first place.

I told him that I thought they only let me go through to laugh at me. I compared myself to the terrible acts we see on Britain's Got Talent, the terrible ones that get through just because they are so bad that they are entertaining. I was convinced this was me.

My psychologist reminded me that TEDx is quite a big organisation and does not really work like that. He suggested I have a chat with the organisers and see what was going on and to put my mind at rest. So, I decided to do just that. I contacted the curator for TEDx Lincoln and had a very honest chat with him, I was truthful about how I felt and explained my pessimistic views on why I had been put through. He was shocked I felt this way and reassured me that my idea and talk during audition was passionate and needed to be heard. He assured me I was not secretly being laughed at by everyone and he calmed me down. However, the negative voice could not leave it there, I then walked away convinced he was lying to me, convinced he was in on this massive plot to publicly humiliate me. I nearly pulled out of the event on so many occasions, convinced I did not belong there. My anxiety made me believe everyone was laughing behind my back and I convinced myself I would fail.

I was ready to completely throw away this amazing opportunity I had been given just because my negative way of thinking didn't want me to succeed. Since opening up and explaining my thoughts, I found the organisers to be very understanding and the constant reassurance helped.

However, even on the day I was about to speak, I was adamant I would mess it up and let everyone down. The pessimist inside me was bursting with poison, I was fortunate to have made the most amazing friends throughout the process, who could recognise when these thoughts were happening and they managed to calm me down. Turns out I aced the talk, but the pessimistic trait nearly stopped me from passing by this incredible opportunity. It convinced me people would always have an ulterior motive.

Tackling Harm Avoidance

We all worry, it's natural to worry and be anxious, however when the thoughts are incredibly intrusive and you find it difficult to concentrate on anything else, perhaps some alternative ways of thinking are needed.

After lots of talks with my therapist he suggested many ways I could try and manage my constant worrying. One of them was allocating myself a time to worry each day and think about all that was bothering me. I figured it was worth a try. I decided every evening before bed I would allow myself fifteen minutes to go over everything that was bothering me. If my mind wondered during the day and I found myself panicking, I would simply turn my mind to the present moment and say, *"I am not thinking about that right now, I will allocate time to this later, right now I am concentrating on this task."* It seemed impossible as when it got to the evening, I had so many different things that were bothering me I could not get through them all, and then with it being the evening I could not switch off, and it just wasn't working.

I then changed my worry time to when I was showering, as I was always calm in the shower. Something about being under warm water and the smell of my shower gels were always soothing. I then kept notes on my phone, so if I started to worry about something during the day, I could make a note of it and then tell myself that I had made a note and I would try and find a solution later.

I often found that before going in the shower, half the things on the list did not matter anymore and did not need solving, and the other half were out of my control anyway. I could not personally solve them, so worrying was not helpful. So, I used my allocated time to remind myself that I couldn't control every aspect of my life and I needed to accept this. I'd practice some mindfulness techniques to calm my anxiety, for example how did the bubbles feel on my skin, what was the temperature of the water like, what aromas could I smell? By turning my mind from worrying about things out of my control, to turning my mind to the present moment, my mind calmed.

One of the things I do worry about is my mum. As previously mentioned, she is disabled and has complex health needs. I remember when we were first told she may have to have a feeding tube fitted, I worried for her. She is a warrior, nothing phases her, as she has a 'what will be will be' attitude, she knew it could save her life so that was it. However, me being the opposite, the worrier not warrior, I fretted. How would she manage to feed herself with her hands with severe arthritis? How would she feel if we all eat around her and she cannot physically join in? What would happen if she continues to get infections in her lungs? The next infection could potentially kill her, could any infection kill her? I fretted about so many different things regarding this, but then she told me something which I admired, she told me *"I have no control over what happens, worrying about it is not going to change what will happen or the doctors' minds."*

I then remembered seeing a quote online, *'worrying does not take away tomorrow's troubles, it only takes away today's peace'.*

I realised that they were both right. There will be things I have no control over and it is pointless and wasted time worrying about them. This also applies to worrying over things that have already happened. I cannot change the past, but I can change how I think about them now. When I find myself worrying about something that has already happened, I repeat the following phrase:

There is nothing I can do about it now, it has happened, done with, worrying cannot change that.

I then continue to do whatever it was I was doing, reminding myself the past cannot be changed, but how I handle the situation and my feelings can be changed.

There are a few things we may worry about that can be solved. If I wake in the night worrying about something, I will add it to my list, instead of worrying all night. I still do this now and use my allocated time to worry. I remember waking up in the night worrying about something I had said to someone at work; they seemed a little off with me, had I upset them? I wrote it down and reminded myself to just ask my colleague if I had upset them, so that is what I did. I found that my colleague had no idea what I was talking about, I had not upset them at all. I felt somewhat proud, something that would have kept me up all night, worrying and fretting, going through every detail of the day to see if I had said anything that could have caused upset, was solvable by me writing it down, allowing myself a specific time to solve the problem and then actually following my plan. Problem solving and dealing with an issue instead of trying to ignore it and worrying over what could or could not be the case.

Forever The Pessimist

Knowing I was a pessimist took some readjustments in my thinking. I now pause, take a deep breath and think, "*but what could go right, am I missing something here?*"

An example of this is my career as a public speaker. When I was first approached by an agent, I automatically thought, "*I am not good enough, I will fail, this will not work out and it will just be a disaster*." Recognising all these destructive thoughts I allowed myself to pause and think, "*but what could go right?*" It was so hard to think positively so I took to pen and paper and wrote down what I would say to a friend in my situation.

A view of the situation from a different perspective.

I wrote down my negative responses, my automatic thoughts, and then wrote down what could go right. I then wrote down a compassionate response, so what would I say to a friend in this situation, and finally what is a more realistic way of looking at this, my example being my career;

- **Negative automatic response** – I will fail, it will be a waste of time, I am not good enough for this.
- **What could go right, what am I missing?** – It could work out and I love doing it. I could potentially have a bit of a career out of this. They approached me so must think I am okay at what I do otherwise they would not be investing in me.
- **What would I say to a friend?** – Go for it, if you do not try you will not know. If it does fail, never mind. At least you will not regret passing by on the opportunity.
- **More realistic approach** – It might not work. However, I am not losing anything by trying, and it might turn into something really positive. If I pass it by without giving it a go I could be turning down a really great opportunity.

I find myself taking on this approach every time I recognise I am being a pessimist, and after a lot of practice I am able to do it on the spot instead of writing it down and working through it. I also hear myself saying when I hear others being a pessimist; "*You are thinking what could go wrong, but what could go right?*" Then I am greeted with a confused look and a different response. A little example was a friend was thinking about going back to university, she was fretting she would fail and had talked herself out of it. I reminded her she was looking at the pessimist reasons and should look at what could go right instead. She was able to come up with a more realistic response, she turned to me and said, "*You are right. Yes, I might fail, it might not work and it could go a bit pear shaped but at least I tried and gave it a go. It could actually all go okay, and I could be a teacher at the end of it, my dream job.*"

Shyness

This is a strange one for me. After doing research and meeting others with an eating disorder, shyness seems to be a common trait. I know a few people that would severely struggle in groups of people and the thought of public speaking and talking in front of crowds could make them physically sick. I used to be quite shy as a child, my mum always said I would not say boo to a goose. At school I was always afraid of answering questions in class in case I got it wrong and was laughed at. I was not a 'popular' child so I kept myself to myself and only had a few very close friends who I could be my complete self around and trusted.

I was socially anxious and struggled to make new friends, although once I did make friends and fully trusted them, I was able to be me. Some of the closest friends I have now are ones I met at school.

But I started to change when I was at university. I had to teach a variety of different age groups and was put on the spot so many times. One day we could be teaching steel drums to prisoners, the next day we could be doing a samba workshop with a group of primary school children.

I learnt how to perform and adapt my language and behaviours depending on my audience or class. I had to adapt quickly and learn how to communicate with a variety of ages and groups of people. It was terrifying, but after being put in these situations constantly over the three years studying, I became used to it.

Now I am thankful that I am able to adapt and assess the crowd confidently and with ease. I also completed many recitals, individual and ensemble, and had to do many performances as part of my degree, so again I was somewhat used to being on a stage. I was also part of a choir, and again I was able to perform in large venues with my fellow singers and class friends across the country, so this was more practice at being on a stage.

But put me in a one-to-one situation with someone new, I panic. I close up, and my armour comes up.

I realised, to quote Jordan Raskopoulos' brilliant TEDX talk that I am indeed '*shy/loud*'. This sounds ridiculous, but for me is exhausting and makes so much sense. Put me on a stage in front of hundreds of people, I am anxious, but I am okay, I can wear my mask well and appear confident and together. I can talk when I am in a large group, as I can bounce off what other people are saying, making conversation easier. I can play the clown and make others laugh. I can also hide easier if needed to.

I was also a supply teacher for a while, so I have had training somewhat, on how to teach and be in larger groups of people. I feel safer when I am in a crowd but put me in a small group of two or three, I panic.

Who speaks first? What if they argue back at me? What if I interrupt by accident? I'd think, "*It's best to stay quiet Zoe, you do not want to upset anyone*". I also try and over analyse people's body language, spend so much time focusing on how others react and before I know it, I have lost track of the conversation. I feel insecure and vulnerable, especially on a one-to-one basis, I have difficulty trusting people so will struggle to communicate. I often feel anxious when I am meeting up with an old friend who I have not seen for a while. It takes me a while to calm the anxiety and remember, "*Oh it's okay I trust the person, I can be myself around them"*. Whereas in a large crowd of strangers, I can be whoever I choose to be.

I was delivering a workshop on body image and helping others to learn to love their bodies. I was teaching techniques I personally used during my own recovery and who better to deliver a workshop, than someone who has gone from hating every bone in their body, to learning to appreciate, thank and actually love their body.

At first, I was speaking to two people who were about to take part outside the room, they were asking questions on my history of eating disorders. I was nervous and stuttered, I was trying to remain focused but was panicking, was I triggering them? Were they judging me? The anxiety was rising, and I was starting to panic. I am well aware I was starting to come across as unprofessional, so I made an excuse to leave the conversation. However, the second I entered the room, full of people, I was able to take a deep breath and deliver the workshop with confidence and ease, teaching almost. Getting good conversations going, encouraging everyone to have a try at the tasks, and I was bouncing with energy and enthusiasm like I always am when delivering talks and workshops. After the session, the same two people approached me to say thank you for the workshop, they told me they loved it and that how they viewed themselves had completely changed. I had gone back to being shy and trying to analyse everything they were saying and pick up on their body language. One of them actually commented, *"How on earth are you so confident on a stage and able to talk to so many people? You seem so lovely and shy but on stage so energetic and self-aware."* Of course, the compliments made me shudder. I struggle to accept compliments. However, I started to think about it more and this was when I started to realise, I am indeed shy/loud.

Tackling Shyness

Being shy is not necessarily a terrible thing. However, if you find you are changing your personality to try and fit in with others, avoiding situations and letting people talk over you, then perhaps trying to become a little more confident would not hurt.

This is something I still struggle with and do not ever think I will overcome. It is part of who I truly am. However, what I have changed is my attitude towards social situations. Whereas before I would avoid certain events and scenarios where I may not know anyone, I now make myself go and once again feel the fear but do it anyway. I was terrified of what others might think of me, terrified of not being liked. I hid my true personality and pretended to be someone I wasn't. This would feed my anxiety.

I was attending James' work's annual dinner, every year it is an excuse to wear a ball gown, get glammed up for the evening and enjoy a meal, open bar and disco. I decided to conduct a bit of a social experiment. These people liked my husband, did it matter to me if they were not keen on me? At the end of the day, they are all accountants, had to wear suits and I was a bit of a hippy working in a nursery constantly covered in paint or glitter. You could not get more opposites.

I decided not to wear my mask, but be me, I did not need to be the perfect accountant's wife. When I arrived, I was introduced to another couple by James, he and Michael began talking numbers and figures, and I noticed Andrea looking a bit nervous. Instead of smiling and attempting to join into the conversation and act interested, I turned to his wife and said, "*I have no idea what these two are on about, can I get you another drink?*" She laughed and replied, "*My goodness yes!*"

I returned with two drinks and I started talking to her. Within an instant we clicked. She had two younger children, so we were able to talk about children's TV and nursery rhymes. We then discovered we were sat at the same table.

Determined to keep being myself and not put on an act, I let my guard down. Everyone else on our table were all lovely, and we were engaging in conversations well. After a few more drinks, Andrea and I were beginning to get a little worse for wear, however instead of being conscious about what others may think of me, we continued to have a giggle. I was not there to be impressive, I was there to have a good time. As the conversation turned to work again, our conversation heading towards childcare and I was proud of my job, then I found another lady on the table also worked in a nursery.

By being me, not trying to be anyone else, I was able to make some friends that evening, and I cannot help but wonder, if I had worn my mask, tried to impress instead of being myself, what would have happened? I recognised I always tried too hard to ensure people liked me, and I was not meeting the right people by putting on this act. I was meeting people I could not really connect with and therefore would never speak out against or voice my opinion around, only adding to my shyness. James then told me when he returned to work that his colleagues did in fact like me anyway, they thought I was refreshing and a good laugh. I had let my guard down, did the opposite of what I normally did, engaged with people I could connect with and ended up actually being quite confident on the evening.

Agreeableness & Passivity (not saying no)

As I look back, I have realised just how passive I really was. I had this intense fear of saying no to people. I could not say no, whether it was to working overtime, or simply giving someone a lift. I had to say yes, no matter how inconvenient it was, or if I had already made plans, I would always say yes.

Deep down it was a fear I clung to, a fear that if I said no, I would let that person down and they would dislike me, a fear of being rejected. I had a core belief that I would be letting people down if I could not help them and that idea hurt me. I was always the reliable friend, the friend someone turned to in a crisis and if they needed something, I was always there. Which is absolutely fine, however not when you are putting your own mental health at risk and burning yourself out which I did on so many occasions. There is a famous saying, '*you cannot pour from an empty jug*', and this is what I found myself doing, time after time. I could feel myself getting exhausted. I could tell my body was tired physically and mentally, but I could not stop, I could not rest. There was always something that needed doing, someone that needed a hand or a favour. I hated the thought that others may not like me.

For me being disliked could result in bullying or hurt somehow, so I tried my best to please others and was often taken advantage of. I would bend over backwards for people who I knew deep down would not do the same for me, and yet I could not stop. I was very much a people pleaser, with no regard for my own health and wellbeing.

Everything about me screamed passive, the way I spoke for example was hesitant. If I did not really agree with what was being said or a suggestion, I found myself saying things like, *"Well erm, I suppose you are right on this, ignore what I said, I do not know anything really."* I could never say what I really felt, never say my opinion in case it was wrong.

I would agree with everyone else in the room instead of expressing my own valid opinion.

Even when I am watching the Rugby for example, (yes I am a massive rugby fan) if I feel the referee made an unfair decision, or something happened in the game I knew was not right, a foul for example, I would not dare speak up. What if I was wrong? I'd wait to see what everyone else thought and then simply go along with what they said. I agreed with what they thought and said, even if deep down I had a different opinion.

I belittled my own views on so many occasions as well. If I did dare to go against everything I believed in and tried to speak out, I would find myself saying, "*I could be wrong but*," or, "*I mean I am not an expert really but*," instead of "*I think this*". I always started my sentences with a put down, without even realising. I look back at meetings I have had in the past and one example springs to mind.

I have monthly group meetings with my agency in regard to public speaking. Every month all the clients come together, and we discuss and practice skills and topics. One week we were discussing stage fright and mindfulness techniques, something which I do struggle with but now have under control. A few people know I can manage my stage fright quite well, and during the meeting asked my specific advice. I of course stumbled, "*Well, I am not really an expert and it might not work, it's silly really, but I use this technique.*" I explained the technique to everyone and then finished the example with, "*but it's silly really.*" Completely dismissing my own knowledge and disregarding a positive quality which I have.

Another way I spoke which I have picked up on, is approval seeking. Any suggestion I had I needed to make sure it was approved, an example being, with friends. I was with a friend in a shopping centre and I wanted to pop back to a shop to buy some shoes I had seen but put back, rookie mistake I know. Instead of saying, oh I need to pop back to that shop I found myself saying, *"if it's okay with you I could do with going back to the other shop quickly, if not it does not matter."* Which completely disregarded my needs. I would always put other people's wants first. I was incapable of making a decision in case it was the wrong one. I have a friend who is also quite passive. I remember we had agreed to go out for lunch in the early stages of my recovery. I had a few 'safe' places where I would feel comfortable eating at. I arrived at my friend's house and she asked me, *"where would you like to go for dinner"* I automatically said, *"oh I don't mind, you choose"* even though I did mind, and it was actually a big deal. She is also rather passive and replied with *"no you choose I don't mind either"* we spent at least twenty minutes ping pong-ing this before we were in fits of giggles realising how daft this was. I then admitted I have a few safe options and listed everywhere I felt safe. She then picked one of my safe options. A compromise.

However, if I was with someone that was not so understanding and passive, I could have ended up in a place I did not want to be, making myself anxious, uncomfortable and feeling sick with dread. This has happened on more than one occasion.

I really struggle with making decisions, I always let other people decide regardless of my thoughts, and I would find myself using phrases like I have listed above, then trying to express my views. Of course, I was never going to be taken seriously. Whether it was as simple as where to go for dinner or making group decisions at work. I followed what others wanted, trying to please everyone else and making sure everyone else was happy. I always assumed other people's needs and wants were more important than my own, I was unimportant, I did not matter.

Tackling Agreeableness & Passivity

I was a little clueless on just how much I did for other people and how little I did for myself. I had no time for self-care, no time to recharge my batteries as I was so busy making sure everyone else's wellbeing was okay. I was not important in my eyes, I had to say yes to everyone's request, I needed to say yes or I would be a let-down. I would become unreliable. I would become hated. These were my core beliefs that needed shattering, but how on earth could I learn to say no when I needed time to actually look after me.

The first thing I did was over two weeks, I made a list of everything I did to help other people, every request or thought no matter how big or small, I kept a note of. After writing it down I also colour coded it with red orange or green, which represented how I was feeling at the time. Red for really tired burnt out, no energy. Orange was feeling a little worn not quite right. Green was I feel great at the minute no problem. I then evaluated it after the two weeks and circled everything that was on red or orange and then looked into whether it was actually necessary that I did that request. There were things on there like could I bake a cake for the weekend, for someone I did not even know, for free? Could I pick up a parcel for someone on my way home, so they did not have to? Things that were highlighted red that I could have said no to and it would not have mattered at all. The cake I was not being paid for, it was just because they knew I could bake and wanted one for free, and the other without being rude, was that particular person being lazy.

I then decided that the next time I got a request, and I was feeling a red, I would say no and see what actually happened. Would they believe I was the worst person in the world, or would they understand I was burning out and simply in need of a break?

The next request I got was from a friend. I had just finished a ten-hour shift at work, the ED voice was extremely loud, I had yet to face tea and I felt physically and mentally exhausted. I got a text asking if I could meet her for a drink later, she had a bit of a bad day. I wanted to help her, but I was exhausted and knew I could not do this. Instead, I asked if we could chat on the phone and catch up properly another time. This was no issue for her, we had a chat on the phone and agreed to meet soon when I was feeling 'green'. I thought she would fall out with me, accuse me of being selfish, she needed to rant, and I was denying her that. Instead, we compromised and agreed a time where we could go out where we both would feel more up to it and it would actually be more enjoyable anyway.

Every time I got asked to do something from that moment on, I asked myself two simple questions:

What colour am I feeling?

Will this affect my own mental wellbeing if I agree to this request at this present time?

I exhausted myself too many times, constantly trying to please everyone. I needed to realise this was impossible to keep up if I wanted to be mentally well. I needed to learn to say no and look after my own mental wellbeing. I kept repeating this task, until saying no did not feel like the end of the world.

I am now able to evaluate whether something is important or whether someone is trying to take advantage of my good nature, I know it sounds a little ruthless, but it had to be done. Also, because I was feeling a little mentally better, and had a little more time, it made challenging that eating disorder voice easier too, as I had not exhausted myself already.

Confidence

I have always been scared of saying what I really think, my opinion did not matter, I did not matter. However, what I realised is, we are adults, capable of disagreeing with each other without us then loathing that person. One of the best examples is politics. I have very different political views to my parents. I have nick named my mum *Mrs Daily Mail*, however we can debate and have a different opinion but we never fall out over it, and we can agree to disagree.

Also, if I do voice my opinion in front of a group of people, and they do not agree and do turn horrible, do I want to be in their company? Do I want to try and befriend and impress them? Or would it be better to spend my time finding a group of people that did share similar views and opinions to me.

I wanted to try and become a little more confident, start standing up for myself a little and actually have a voice. However, going from not saying boo to a goose to voicing my opinions in a crowded room took a lot of work. I started small, with people I trusted. If we were having a debate about something at home or with friends and something was said I was not sure on, instead of fretting I would be hated for voicing my opinion, I started to be brave and speak up.

I was in safe company, those who loved me, so even if I did offend someone, it would not matter as they would still love me. I practiced this all the time and started to become more confident in doing so.

Once again feeling the fear and doing it anyway, putting myself out there to overcome it. Then once I was doing this more confidently, I upped it a notch. When I was with newer people, I would try and voice my opinion too, remembering that it did not matter if they disagreed, we were adults and capable of a debate. It did not always end in a massive argument like I thought it would.

Once I had proof that people would not become nasty about my opinions and it would not escalate, I felt safer to voice my opinion more, and if it did ever turn heated, I could always remove myself from the situation. It was okay to do so. I knew that it was safe to have an opinion and had learnt how to have debates without fretting it would turn heated.

Making decisions was also something that I just needed to overcome with practice. I recognised I was rubbish at this and confided in someone I trusted, a good friend. I told her about my inability to make decisions and would she object if next time we go out, I decide or suggest where we go. She of course agreed. She arrived on my door step a few days later and asked where we were going, I froze, oh no, I forgot about that, automatically I said, "*Where do you want to go?*" She laughed and said, "*no you choose*".

I could not, we compromised I made her choose 3 places she fancied visiting and I made the final decision. That way I still managed to make a decision, but I knew they were all options she wanted too. We tried this a few times, and I also practiced with my husband.

Once I became more confident in doing this, I then decided it was time to push myself. Next time my husband and I were stuck for things to do, I made two suggestions, he agreed to them both then I made the final decision. My heart was racing, what if it was wrong, what if he didn't want to do either? Then I remembered, he is a fully grown man, if he did not want to do something, he would tell me. I knew this, I started to relax as we agreed what to do based on my decision.

I then found I was more confident in making other decisions in my life, such as work decisions. I practiced small, gathered my confidence in a safe space, watching my language trying not to put myself down but instead sound confident. Then started to push my boundaries making myself feel uncomfortable to overcome my fear of making decisions.

Competitiveness

I have always been very competitive, not just with others, but with myself. My best running time for example, could be better next time, I could do better next run, I needed to beat it, I needed to beat me. It was the same with grades and marks in school, constantly obsessing with how I could do better next time, how I could beat my mark. I constantly compared myself to others, people would not know, but I was in competition with everyone and anyone.

If I saw someone in the gym lifting weights, I would try and match what they were doing, or try and lift more. If I saw someone had posted their run on social media, I would automatically take note and try and beat it. I could not seem to help it, I seemed to have this competitive streak, I needed to win to prove myself, prove I was not a waste of space that I had always thought I was, prove that I was worthy.

My husband and I were squash players, on a Sunday morning we would often be on the squash courts having a friendly game, a bit of fun. It was never fun for me, I always analysed every move I made, every shot I went for, overthinking every technique, trying to better my game. I hated losing, I felt like I was a loser in life, and every time I lost a game it would feed into this core belief I had that I was not good enough. If I lost a game, I could not just let it go, I would replay the game in my head, over and over again, trying to figure out exactly where I went wrong, what I did wrong, what could I have done differently. I would torture myself and be extremely unforgiving for my performance. I often won, I was very quick on the court and was quite strong, so therefore I could return with a powerful shot. But again, even when I won, I would still analyse the game; where did I lose a few points, how could I have made my lead larger, what could I have done to get even more points.

Unfortunately, this played right into my eating disorder's hands. I would compete with myself every day, eating less and less. Competing with myself to exercise more and pushing myself to extreme physical limits, determined to do better than yesterday, determined to beat yesterday's me, determined to be better than what I was yesterday. It was the same with the weight and the scales. I had to move that number down, every week a new goal, a new challenge, a new way I could compete with myself. A new way to torture myself.

Tackling Competitiveness

I am competitive, I always have and always will be. There is nothing wrong with being competitive, but what I needed to overcome was being competitive with myself and others when it comes to exercise.

I have mentioned when I was at the gym I would become competitive with others around me, challenging myself to do more reps and lift heavier weights. I realised this was fuelling that eating disorder voice, so I started listening to music more and going to the gym during quieter times.

If I found myself being competitive, I forced myself to stop whatever it was I was doing, and ask myself *"is this helpful? I am me. I am training my body not theirs. We have different goals, different aims, this exercise is about what my body can do"*. I had to remind myself constantly everyone is different, and what someone else is doing may not be suitable for me, I could end up with serious injury or straining my muscles. I would then turn my mind back to my music and focus on something in front of me instead of the people around me.

I was competitive with myself, I seemed to forget that some days I may be able to run more, I may be able to do a little more. There were extenuating circumstances, have I had a long day at work? Had I already exercised that day? Many things can contribute to performance, and yet I still fought with myself. I realised this was down to my exercise addiction, it was due to my eating disorder. So to overcome my competitiveness with myself regarding exercise, I needed to overcome my addiction first.

I have written about this later in the book, so please do look at this in great detail if you are struggling with exercise addiction. I found once I had dealt with that addiction, I was no longer severely competitive with myself as the need to strive had diminished.

Low Self Esteem

You may have noticed a very common theme amongst all of these personality traits was the way that I spoke to myself. Everything I did I could criticise, and nothing was ever good enough. I was terrified of failing and felt like I was a waste of space. I was so scared of being disliked and thought everyone I came across secretly hated me. All these traits and the way I thought about myself all tied in with the fact that I had extremely low self-esteem. Everything about myself I seemed to hate, even if I could name a few good qualities, I would find a way to sabotage them, to turn it around and turn that positive into a negative. For example, I do a lot for charity, in particular BEAT. However, no matter how much money I raised, how much I did, I always felt it was not enough. I could have done more or would simply say, well anyone could do it really, it is no big deal. I would never be able to take praise given to me and I was completely unable to accept any type of compliment, I did not deserve compliments.

One example does spring to mind when I think about how I have completely dismissed compliments. I decided to do a skydive to raise money for BEAT. They did so much for me in my recovery I wanted to give something back. I am terrified of both flying and heights, so this for me was a very big challenge. Jumping out of something that should not be in the air at 10,000ft seems like a big enough challenge, and if I could face that I could face anything that ED threw at me.

I decided I wanted to try and raise as much money as possible. I went to car boots and sold the clothes that reminded me of being ill, I ran wine or water games at local street markets and fairs, and did a lot of cake sales and competitions around the community. I worked tirelessly for months, fundraising and also raising awareness as I raised funds.

I met and signposted many people on my fundraising journey and was able to help many people in need. I managed to raise a total of £2,207.75 for the charity. Looking back, I am now of course over the moon with this, but at the time, I was disappointed.

Anyone else would have been thrilled with this amount, and I got a phone call from the charity thanking me for my hard work and donation. It was a huge amount one person alone has raised, and all I kept thinking was, I could have done more. If I had done another street fayre, I could have raised another hundred or two, if I had only done another cake sale somewhere, I could have done better. Completely dismissing the fact that I had raised a lot of money, disdaining the fact I did this on my own and the money was going to help so many people. They were over the moon with the donation, so why wasn't I?

Everything about me screamed that I had low self-esteem, from my extreme passiveness, assuming everyone else was right and being too afraid to speak up as I was afraid of what they would say, to always putting everyone else's needs first and dismissing my own needs. I was terrified of being rejected so would never add my own thoughts to conversations and the thought of making decisions sent shivers down my spine. All of the things I have talked about in this chapter are all some typical examples of having low self-esteem. The fact I could never take compliments only added to this, as I could never raise my self-esteem, and would only pull myself down more by twisting the compliments. I had a very distorted view of myself and could only see negatives and assumed everyone else could only see my negatives too.

For me, I believed that a way to improve my self-esteem and become more liked would be for me to change. I needed to change my appearance, I needed to be better, and for me this meant thinner. If I could shrink my body maybe I would fit in more? Low self-esteem did contribute to my eating disorder, I also became depressed due to having low self-esteem, and again could not deal with this emotion so found a different way of coping, yet another way that low self-esteem contributed to this illness.

Tackling Low Self Esteem

Improving low self-esteem is a whole book on its own. It takes time, a lot of therapy and also a lot of hard work. Challenging those negative automatic thoughts, as we have already discussed, will of course help with your self-esteem. I was given a top ten from my community support worker, which I will share with you. These tips are a starting point and a few things you can start doing immediately to help improve your self-esteem.

- Ensure you are providing your body and mind with the basic necessities of healthy living. Get enough rest, fuel your body and enjoy movement because you *want* to not because you *have* to.
- Spend more time with those who encourage you, less time with those who discourage you.
- Make a strong commitment and conscious effort to succeed in building your self-esteem.
- We all make mistakes, next time you have made a

mistake, be forgiving. What would you say to a friend?

- Celebrate your achievements, no matter how small or big. Recognise the good choices you make and congratulate yourself. Try not to brush it off.

- Watch the way you speak, try and avoid negative self-talk, speak clearly and slowly being aware of your body language, and the message it conveys, to yourself and also to others.

- Do things you enjoy and know you're worth it. Make the time to do things that make you feel relaxed, calm and happy. Whether it is a little reading or watching a film, prioritise these activities especially when you are feeling low. Self-care is a necessity especially during recovery.

- Redefine 'selfish'. Learn to love yourself and take care of YOU. Make sure you are meeting your own needs. You cannot pour from an empty cup.

- Take responsibility for your own life and wellbeing. This is something only you can control. Stop taking responsibility for the lives of others. It is great to help people, but they are ultimately responsible for their own situations, actions and behaviours. Just as you are responsible for yours.

- As you make new choices, set out goals and strategies for improving your thinking styles, the way you act and live. Treat yourself with deliberate acts of loving kindness. Refuse to dwell on negatives and seek out positives in all situations.

This list became somewhat of a bible for me, I followed them religiously and ensured I was doing all of these things. However I also added to it, one of the things I did was learn how to accept compliments. For example, if I was delivering a lesson and being evaluated, instead of focusing on the six or seven good elements, I would focus on the one improvement, dismissing the compliments focusing only on the negative. This of course was only adding to my low self-esteem. What I should have done in that situation was think - oh I did well, I cannot deliver a completely perfect lesson, there is always room for improvement and personal growth, I will work on what was suggested, however I am pleased with all the things that were said.

If someone complimented me face to face, I would automatically cringe, and then diminish what they were saying or ignore it completely. "oh, it was nothing" or "it did not really matter." Again not absorbing that I have any good qualities. Whereas the slightest criticism I would take to heart and dwell on. When receiving compliments now I simply say, thank you, and remind myself it is an opinion, everyone is allowed an opinion. And if I am receiving feedback or a criticism, I take it as a positive as it is something that will help me grow and benefit me in the long run and that's not a bad thing.

I also needed to accept I have got some good qualities. This was especially difficult for me, I truly believed I was a waste of space and offered nothing, I was worthless. Constantly thinking this way was another contributing factor to having low self-esteem. During day programme we had to list our good qualities. I sat there panicking, I had no idea who I was; I had no good qualities surely. When it came to sharing them everyone in the room realised, we all felt the same way, we all shared low self-esteem and struggled to see good qualities. We then wrote down what we thought of the other people in the room, and listed each other's good qualities which we found easier, and learning to accept the compliments I was being given I started to see these good qualities. I was determined to overcome this, so I also asked my friends to list my good qualities. When they replied instead of instantly dismissing them, I wrote them all down, on a flash card, and kept it handy. Then when I heard myself saying things like "I am worthless" I was able to look at the flashcard and think, well actually they think this, that is their opinion of me.

I also needed to accept that I did do good things. However again in those times of high stress I could not see the goodness within, so it was suggested to me to keep a positive-me journal. I wrote down all these things I did to help others and also wrote all the good things I had done during the day. So once again during those times when I was tearing myself to shreds, I was able to look back at that positive-me journal and remember, actually I am a good person, look at these things I have done. I wrote down everything no matter how small it was, every success needed to be celebrated, whether it was going to work to earn money to pay for the mortgage or doing a fundraiser for charity. Everything needed logging and celebrating, I had worth.

Key points to take away

- No matter what personality trait your eating disorder has latched onto, you can detach it.
- It's ok to step out of your comfort zone and be yourself.
- If your friends do not like you for you, they are not friends. You deserve to be loved wholeheartedly for being your authentic self.
- It will feel so uncomfortable to begin with, but keep practising and trying, over time challenging these traits will become easier.
- Saying no does not make you a bad person. You need boundaries to look after yourself. No reasonable person would be cross with you if you could not do something for them if it was a risk to your own well-being.
- These personality traits are not necessarily a bad thing, however if they are affecting your life, it's worth spending some time on them.
- Take the time to analyse if these thinking styles are serving you a purpose, or fuelling ED?
- When focusing on your self-esteem, ask yourself who you are spending time with. Are you spending time with people who make you feel good about yourself? Are they cheering you on? Or are they those who drain you and pull you down? Spend your energy with those who love you for you.
- Perfection simply does not exist. If everything was perfect, there would be no room for growth and improvement.
- The world would be boring if we were all perfect and the same.

Chapter 9
Restriction

"It is just a diet", I thought to myself. *"How much harm could it do?"* I remember this thought well. I was a 14-year-old girl and the pressure of fitting in at secondary school was real! I was surrounded by others constantly trying to change their appearance by engaging in different diets, different exercise regimes, beauty techniques I could never master. Lunch times were particularly terrifying as I could not help but compare what I was eating to others around me.

My mind kept resorting back to, *"should I be eating this?"* I had no idea just how obsessed I had become. How much of my thoughts and feelings were to do with food and more importantly just how much of my life it would unfortunately take up.

So, I decided to start a diet. I started to cut down what I was eating during the day and eating a normal amount in front of my parents, and I continued to do so throughout all of school. When I was alone, I would restrict, but to avoid being "found out" when I was with others, I would appear "normal". I hated conflict and found the idea of being confronted absolutely terrifying. I lost weight, and quickly other aspects of my mental health started to deteriorate, I had become addicted. I went to my GP as I knew I was struggling and was told I was a teenage girl, hormones were making my moods up and down and I would grow out of it.

So, I had validation that this was normal.

This began the fourteen-year diet yo-yoing hell I became trapped in.

Calorie Counting

The thing with restriction (for me anyway) was it became very addictive. I allowed myself to eat so many calories a day, then after a few weeks I realised I could consume less. Then after another few weeks, the number of calories I allowed myself to eat got lower and lower. Until it was next to nothing. For me this was something I was good at. I was in competition with myself and I was winning.

I kept setting myself new challenges and when I achieved it, I felt a little more positive about myself, but then something inside told me, it was not good enough, I was not good enough, I need to do better.

At this point I was still eating three meals a day, but I had become very strict with myself as to which foods I could and could not eat. I became hooked on looking at the calories in everything so I could work out exactly what I was consuming. I had to weigh out everything and enter it onto my fitness tracker, so I knew exactly what I was putting into my body.

This may not sound like such a horrible thing, portion control, right? WRONG! More like unhealthy obsession. I remember having an argument with my husband one evening as I was making a tuna salad for my tea, while he was cooking up spicy chicken pasta. It took me over an hour to make this salad, as I had to weigh everything out individually - lettuce, cucumber, tomatoes, pepper, how many calories is that so far? Maybe if I added less pepper it would make a difference?

Ok I can't have that much tuna, too many calories, let's try halving it - trying to consume as few calories as possible. Not only was it exhausting but it became incredibly problematic for my day-to-day routine. Evening meals took ages to prepare and it took me longer to get ready in the mornings due to having to weigh out my low fat, low sugar, low nutritional value, tasteless yogurt and my handful of blueberries.

Preparing lunch for work took too long, and I could not face eating sandwiches as 'carbs are the enemy', so I started to resort to slim-a-soups (basically like cup-a-soups but nothing actually in them, it's like drinking hot water with essence of noodles). The problem was, I did not enjoy my lunches anymore, no surprise really.

My fitness tracker, which allowed me to access and figure out exactly how many calories were in everything - and I mean everything - completely enabled my disorder and allowed me to have a database on my fingertips. For those few foods that were not on the database, I quickly figured out I could use google to find the missing numbers which I desperately needed.

I knew exactly what I was putting into my body every time I ate. It became very addictive, very quickly and I refused to eat anything I could not track, as I could not be sure exactly how many calories were in it. This became problematic on the few occasions I had to eat out. Luckily for my ED, a lot of restaurants now have the calories for each meal listed, so I could see which had the least and go for that. However if we went anywhere new or somewhere where the calories were not displayed, I would be constantly trying to figure out what it could be, or Googling similar recipes, trying desperately to work it out.

I couldn't just go out, I had to plan and look at the menu online first, so I knew the calorie content and knew what my safe options would be. One of the first realisations my husband had that I had an issue, was when we were travelling back from Cornwall. It was late and he had not had tea yet, we pulled into a service station to rest and I had such a meltdown. My husband suggested we grab some fast food, as we had been travelling for about four hours and still had two more to go. I tried to google this particular chain of restaurants to find what I could possibly have on the menu, but I could not find anything that would allow me to stay under my ever-decreasing calorie limit for the day.

I was in public with tears streaming down my face as I just could not face anything on the menu, yet my stomach ached as we had such a busy time away. I felt like everyone was judging me. I kept glancing around and became more and more panicked fearing what everyone must have thought of me. I assumed they thought, "*Oh look at the fat woman crying over food, look how hideous she looks, she should not be eating at all.*" I felt trapped, my breath was getting quicker and quicker and I thought my heart was going to leap out of my chest. I did not know what was going on, just that I knew I could not possibly eat, and I had to get out. I turned and walked briskly to the door. After a few minutes my husband came to find me, I was pacing outside getting some fresh air, counting my steps in a way to burn a few extra calories, as punishment of even thinking about going over my limit.

What was I thinking? How dare I think it was okay to grab something 'unhealthy' for tea. My husband suggested we just grab a sandwich or something small from the shop instead. He wrestled with ED, pleading with me, trying to get me to have something. But I couldn't I was too distressed, I felt like I had let him down, I felt worthless and I did not deserve to eat.

This, ironically made the ED voice stronger, making me want to restrict more. I had entered a vicious circle of calorie control and self-hatred and I was drowning. Fast.

As this illness progressed, I would find myself working out the calories, not only in my food, but everyone else's. Constantly comparing and doing maths, adding up roughly how many calories each person is consuming, and trying to work out, if I had their lunch, what would I have to do to burn it off? It was like practice to me, practicing trying to estimate, checking to see if the database in my head was accurate. I would also do this at work when giving the children their food. I would again try and guess how many calories would be in each portion, wondering how the children used their energy, wondering if I could learn something from them. It never stopped, the obsession working out calories was exhausting, I could not stop! I became an expert on knowing exactly how many calories were in everything, and I mean, everything. From a small Sunday roast to a handful of grapes, my ED knew, and I knew exactly how to burn off what I had eaten and remain in my calorie daily defect. I wanted to think of something else, anything else other than numbers, but I could not switch it off, I could not stop, it had become who I was.

Skipping Meals

I started to become very disinterested in my meals. I hated my tasteless lunches and did not dare to have anything with any calorie content, therefore anything that tasted any good. So, I figured if I skipped them it would not be the end of the world. I started skipping lunch, however I found it quite difficult at work to sit in the staff room for an hour, surrounded by the smells of other people's lunches.

So, I kept myself busy, distracted. That way, I had no time for lunch, no time to think about those pangs in my stomach and the fact that it hurt. I got a weird high from knowing I could go from breakfast till tea without eating. So again that competitive streak appeared. I felt fine, surely if I missed that little bit of breakfast I was allowing myself to eat it would be okay? Would it really matter I missed those few berries and that tasteless yogurt?

I managed to cut out breakfast and lunch and just eat at teatime. My husband hadn't noticed what I was doing, and I appeared well to those around me, as I still appeared to be functioning. Or so I thought.

I continued on one meal a day for ages, and everyone had started commenting on my fabulous weight loss. "*Wow you look great." "Tell me your dieting tips."* I would say that I ate well and exercised. I did not dare say, *"well actually I am only having one meal a day and spending how many hours at the gym."*

I was enjoying the compliments. I enjoyed being referred to as the fit one. I was so use to people shaming my body, this was a strange welcoming acceptance that I had never had. However deep down, it still was not enough, I was not enough, I could do more. This is where I fell, my cover blown.

I started to restrict even more in the evenings. I had been okay with eating an evening meal with my husband, but we argued constantly, as it would have to be a healthy meal. I would only eat stir-fries and fish with vegetables. For my carnivore obsessed other half it was boring.

I felt guilty, so I started occasionally skipping tea. Eating nothing at all during the day. I remember the first time I did this. I felt an uneasy sense of pride, I was proud that I went all day without consuming any calories.

My fitness tracker would show how much of a deficit I was in and it made me happy. I was in control of my weight; I was in control of those numbers. Little did I realise it was the number obsession that actually had control over me.

The next day I went back to my one healthy meal a day, but I had proven to myself I did not really need that one meal. I felt okay without it, so when I ate that evening meal I was plagued with guilt and shame.

I very quickly started to spiral even deeper into my disorder, every time I tried to eat something, no matter how many calories or no matter how little the portion, each time I ate became a battle in my own mind. I called myself names, like fat, worthless and a failure, told myself I was failing the diet, convinced that the compliments I'd been getting would stop. That everyone will see me for the failure I was. I needed to push harder!

I was consumed by negative voices and my house became a battle zone. Every night my husband would plead with me to have something, I would lie and say I had eaten at work, I was too tired, I was going out with friends.

The lies became too much for him and he actually messaged a colleague of mine, to find out if this was true. I felt hurt, he went behind my back and called out my ED.

He became very concerned as he could see my health quickly deteriorating. I was still adamant I did not have a problem, I was fine just on a strict diet. My husband became a bit more tactful at this point, he would purposely try and cook evening meals that he knew I would love, to try and coax me to eat. The house would fill with the smells of spices every night. I adore spicy food, always have always will, we joke all the time that my taste buds must have been burned off as nothing is too spicy.

He would constantly try and plead with the rational side of me. At times I would cave and enjoy what was cooked however, the days that followed that were torture.

How dare I eat a meal! I would have to double my exercise the day after to compensate, or purge somehow. My husband kept doing this and I got more and more frustrated with him. What was he doing? Ruining my diet. I was weak for giving into temptation, the only way around this was if he cooked and ate while I was not at home.

I figured out if I spent a bit longer at the gym, he would have had his tea and cleared up before I got home. So that is what I started doing. However, we would argue so much when I got home, as I could smell the food, it smelled so good and it made me think about wanting to eat. That was not an option. I made James open a window and light candles after he had finished cooking, so all traces and scents of food were gone by the time I arrived back from the gym. Helping my ED to run riot, I had no idea just how much damage I was doing by not fuelling my body.

Good & Bad Food

At a very early age it is drilled into us what foods are "good" and what foods are "bad" we are constantly told what we should and should not be eating. In schools we teach our children to categorise food and it is so easy to label certain food groups as 'bad' as they are deemed 'unhealthy'. Everywhere I turned I was drawn into the diet culture we live in more and more, surrounded by people saying, "*Oh that is bad for you, you should not eat that.*"

My ED clung to this, every time I heard someone say a particular food was "bad" it became a new fear. When the truth is all food has nutritional value, and yes while we should be eating a variety of foods, it never seems to be taught to us that moderation is key. Through every diet I ever engaged in, it became apparent that I should not be eating carbs and any sort of sweets, chocolate, cake, sugary products of any type, basically anything damn good!

These were very much deemed my 'unsafe' foods. However, I also started fearing other food items, such as red meat, the only 'safe' or "good" foods I allowed myself to eat were, fish, chicken, fruit and vegetables.

However, ED has a way of making even the safe foods seem scary. For example, certain fruits became terrifying because of the sugar content in them. I became scared of eating bananas, they were huge and had loads more calories (thank you constant database) than any other fruit. I remember passing out at work one day and my manager at the time gave me a banana and said:

"*It's a banana, just eat it, what is wrong with a banana? I do not get it?*"

My ED voice was screaming back at me, I wanted to shout, "*do you know how many calories are in a banana? It is massive, too much, I do not need it! I am fine*" (clearly) but instead I remained silent. I sat on the floor with a tear trickling down my cheek, too embarrassed to voice what my

ED was telling me, as even I had realised just how ridiculous this seemed. Those words, "*I don't get it*" swept over me, because truth be told, I did not understand it either. Too afraid to eat a banana.

Each time I did a new diet, I became fearful of another food group and would do anything to avoid eating it, until all pleasure in eating was diminished.

I became such a fussy eater, which drove my husband mad, as we were having the same things for tea week in week out. Fresh fish with veg one night, then stir fry the next, then chicken and veg and maybe another sir fry. Very bland, dry food, no sauces allowed as they added, in my eyes, unnecessary calories.

The arguments continued with my husband as we did the food shop together on a Sunday, our weekly trip to Tesco had become another battle zone. I was obsessed with trailing through each type of the same product, to see which brand had fewer calories. It would take us ages to do a simple shop, as I was so busy calorie checking and going through the fat and sugar content. I refused to buy anything that was not low fat and low sugar, therefore low nutritional value and low taste.

These products should come with a warning - may leave you feeling unsatisfied and may cause low mood. I even resorted to buying skimmed milk, as I truly believed if I bought and consumed normal milk it would instantly make me the size of the house. I ignored the fact that all the goodness and nutrients that makes milk beneficial gets taken out too, logic went out the window as ED took over.

As well as only buying low fat food, the fluid I was consuming changed. I became fearful of anything other than water or tea with the smallest amount of skimmed milk in or black. I refused to drink squash or any sort of soft drink with calorific value. Now and then I might have had a Pepsi Max or Diet Coke, but I limited myself to one as I found it helped cure my sweet tooth from time to time and made me feel full when my stomach was growling at me.

I consumed alcohol, but it added toward my calorie count for the day and I made sure I entered it onto my fitness tracker. Very dangerously if I knew I was consuming alcohol I would not allow myself to eat as I was too frightened of doing both. I could not possibly do both! I could not possibly live my life.

Time To Eat

Before I started skipping meals, I developed very rigid times I would allow myself to eat - very strict. If I missed that time slot, that was it. The chance for that meal gone. It started with breakfast, I refused to eat after 9am as lunch was mid-day, and I truly believed it would not give me enough time to burn off my breakfast before eating my lunch. Therefore, I would instantly gain loads of weight.

If, at the weekends I woke after this, tough. No breakfast. Lunch was difficult anyway, and if we were out and I missed my slot, again that was it. However, I became crafty and quite deceitful.

When someone mentioned lunch time I would simply reply with "*oh not quite yet, in a bit maybe*" and keep them busy until it was 'too late' as tea was soon. So, I could avoid that meal. If I was at work, I would find tasks to do during my lunch time so I simply did not have time to eat, and would make myself too busy to possibly sit and have lunch.

Again, with the evening meal, I would not allow myself to eat past 7.30pm as I truly believed if I did not exercise after the meal, I could not burn off what I had eaten before going to bed. Therefore if it got past 7pm, there was no time to cook and have tea before my time limit was over.

This was very easy to skip as by the time I had finished work and been to the gym, I rarely got home before eight pm, which was without any staff meetings or extra tasks I had to do. This therefore enabled me to miss my time slot, therefore allowing me to believe I could not eat.

During the weekends and if I was not at work, again I would try and procrastinate and delay the meal until it was 'too late'. Those around me never questioned my motives throughout the day, if I missed lunch it was no big deal as I was having tea, but they had no idea I also had every intention of skipping tea as well. Colleagues never questioned where I was on my lunch breaks, as a lot of people did not use the staff room and getting a bit of work done on my break was commendable. I had become completely unconnected from my hunger signals and constantly ignored them. Snacks were not an option, as it was always so many hours till my next possible meal so, I could not possibly have anything, even if I did feel hungry. I would convince myself I did not need it, I did not need the fuel, I could wait.

Social Interactions

Sunday, yes! My favourite time of the week. The time when the family came together, we'd cook a roast dinner, enjoy time with my beautiful nieces and have a bit of a giggle. Well, that is what use to happen before ED completely consumed me. I used to restrict all day to 'save my calories' for my roast dinner.

I allowed myself to have this one 'treat' a week, however, very quickly restricting all day was not enough. I then started to get very possessive whilst serving out the portions and made sure everything was cooked in the one kcal spray instead of oil. The mash potatoes could not be creamed, why would you need the extra calories? I would restrict as much as I could without being noticed.

This worked for a while but again it soon was not enough for ED. I started to have the same amount as my, at the time, three-year-old niece. I would make excuses like, oh we had lunch out, I am not feeling great today, and I am just not hungry. I got away with this for a while but then as my weight dropped suspicion started. I was terrified of the conflict with my family, so we would make excuses not to go for our Sunday roast anymore. This for my ED was brilliant, I had more time to exercise.

However, a piece of my heart broke I was seeing my beautiful nieces less. I was unable to play with them as well as I didn't have the energy. I had gone from being fun Aunty Zoe, to a constantly worn out, boring shell.

The genuine fear and anxiety I faced in social situations, would have me keeled over in pain. The joys of anxiety can take many forms, however for me, it caused palpitations and dizziness. If food was mentioned, it felt like my heart was going to leap out of my chest, my breathing got quicker, and I became very flustered. If I were to eat in an environment I had not researched beforehand, the panic would set in even more. I was not in the present moment, my mind was elsewhere. I completely ignored the conversations that were taking place around me, completely disengaged from everything else that was going on. James used to tell me off for being rude and remind me constantly it was more about the conversation then the food, however, I just could not seem to switch off my calorie counting brain. I could not focus on any conversation.

Even after working out my meal, whilst forcing myself to eat it so no one would suspect my issues, I would constantly be thinking what exercise I needed to do after eating. How could I burn off what I was consuming? How many laxatives should I take or was it safe to purge? Going out for a meal became another fear, another thing ED took away from me, another pleasure gone.

It was not just going out for meals that became so problematic. I adore my friends, some are more like family. I started to distance myself from them as I became fearful of being in their company if food was present. Meaning I could only see my friends certain times of the day, between meal times.

Going for days out became a big no, as again it meant I would have to eat in front of them and it seemed an unnecessary stress to me. On so many occasions we would be with friends for a few hours and someone would invite us to stop for tea and play a few games. James would always be up for it and I would have to think of an excuse fast, as to why we could not do that.

Not only was I depriving myself of spending times with those I absolutely adored, but little did I realise at the time, I was also denying my husband time with our friends, so I could continue my path of self-destruction.

Physical/Mental Elements Of Restriction

Even though I looked physically OK, my brain had started to do funny things. Deprived of the nutrients it needed. I was not sleeping properly as I was constantly thinking about food. I became obsessed with recipes and would waste countless hours trawling Pinterest and Google for low calorie, low fat recipe ideas. I never made any of them, but would still look and save them. Hording them.

I had constant brain fog, unable to concentrate for long periods of time, unable to take in information as well and I struggled to keep up to date with the paperwork side of my job. It took me longer to think and make decisions, as my brain always felt two steps behind me.

I became severely depressed, as my mood was constantly low as a result from the lack of nutrients. I would continuously pull myself down, insult myself and I lost who I was. I lost my bright, bubbly personality as ED consumed me.

I got stuck in a cycle as I struggled to do day to day things. I therefore felt completely worthless and a waste of space, I wanted to improve myself so would restrict further, and this would continue over and over again. Stuck in a loop, believing if I restricted, I was being good. I was successful at something, successful with my diet.

I could not see that my body was struggling, as all I cared about what becoming a smaller version of myself. The smaller the better right? The physical side effects of restriction can happen after missing one meal. My biggest giveaway was my hands, they become like blocks of ice, cold and clammy.

As my body struggled more, the coldness would sweep over me, it was impossible to regulate my temperature. I would get very cold very quickly. I remember, myself, James and a few friends walking around the Christmas market one year. I was in such a rush to get round and get home as I felt so cold, it completely took the joy out of it. The spirit of the Christmas market and beauty of the atmosphere lost. All because I was restricting, not allowing my body to have the fuel it needed to keep warm.

I also got very tired very quickly, constantly feeling exhausted and weak. I hated this feeling as my job was very active and involved me being on my feet for over ten hours of the day. I always put 110% into my job, so the fact that I was struggling to keep up and constantly feeling like I was about to pass out, fed that negative voice even more. I found my ridiculous exercise regime a challenge, which again fed the ED voice. If I could not exercise, I could not eat, if I could not eat, I did not have the energy to exercise. Again, another vicious cycle I seemed to get stuck in.

I started having heart problems, my body was eating itself to stay alive, even though I was a healthy weight I was at risk of death. My heart simply could not keep up with this illness.

A symptom that I feel is not talked about enough, is Amenorrhea. I never had normal periods, because I was always restricting or binging or purging, or on some crazy diet. My whole life. So never realised how much of an issue it was until it came to thinking about having children.

I sat with my GP and we went through reasons why I did not have periods, I had no idea it was due to ED. Once I learned what had happened, that ED could have damaged my chance to have children, that was a wake-up call.

I wanted to start a family one day and did not realise that restriction was the reason I had lost my periods.

My hair has always been something I liked, long and thick, and I was fortunate enough to have lovely long nails as well, however, again as the restriction became more prominent, I lost these. My hair thinned and fell out in clumps, my nails became brittle and broke easily. I used to enjoy painting my nails, however as ED took over, another pleasure I once found peace in had been taken from me. A piece of me lost, my femininity ruined. Another reason to hate myself, therefore another reason to restrict.

Key points to take away

- Regardless of body size, restriction can have serious mental and physical complications on your body.
- Even if bloods and tests come back OK. This does not mean you are fine. You never know when things could change all of a sudden.
- Restriction effects your cognitive ability more than you may realise.
- The mental elements of restriction can be just as dangerous as the physical.
- Restriction robs you of so many happy memories. Time spent avoiding meals out and socialising with friends is time wasted.
- Not fuelling your body stops you from having the energy to live your life to the fullest.
- Loosing your period due to restriction is not a good thing, it can lead to being completely infertile.
- Your body will eat itself to stay alive, this means your muscle too. Including the muscles around your heart and brain.
- If you are eating meals just because they are low calories, you need to re-evaluate your eating habits. Food should be enjoyed.
- No one should be scared of fruit.
- Try not to get frustrated if people do not understand, from an outsider's perspective it may be hard to understand your behaviours.

Chapter 10
Working Towards Recovery From Restriction

Once I was educated about all of the terrible side effects restriction has physically and mentally, I was willing to try recovery.

Throughout this section I will talk about a few techniques I learnt, although trying to remember and practice these techniques when in high levels of anxiety was nearly impossible.

To make it easier, (and this is something that you can do) I made myself flash cards. Little cards with bitesize information on them, reminding me how to do each technique. I also had flash cards with little quotes on, recovery quotes I had found, and also a few cards reminding me of my long-term goals and why it was important to recover.

I took these cards everywhere and had them handy at mealtimes; I was able to use my flash cards to help settle my anxiety. In public places I used them too, when I was in a café, if I could feel my anxiety bubbling away, before I abandoned the situation, I would pull out my flash cards and work through the techniques, working constantly towards recovery. I also had a few deep breathing exercises on some cards, for when I was struggling to calm my anxiety, and I could not challenge the thoughts as my mind was still racing, quick and easy mindfulness techniques in bitesize chunks.

The cards were not special and very easy to make, all I used was coloured paper, coloured pens and a laminator. I would add more cards as I learnt more techniques and if I saw an inspirational quote I liked again, it would become a flash card.

Upping My Intake

I was a normal weight… so why did I need to eat more? I was just going to end up obese. Believe me, my mind went through all of these, but once I accepted that okay, I may indeed gain weight, that it was okay to gain weight, my body needed to heal. I indeed started to heal.

However, I couldn't simply go from barely eating to eating three meals a day and snacks, I had to work very closely with my dietician as I talked about earlier.

We outlined a meal plan, that was to begin with, still restricting but was an increase. Then week by week we upped the meal plan until I was on three meals a day and snacks.

This was far from easy but with the help from everyone and the techniques I was taught to manage my distress, it was indeed possible. I was taught about the importance of all food groups and I had to make sure I had lots of calcium to help mend my muscles. I learnt how important fats are in a diet and also learnt the dangers of diet products. I was given all the information by the dietician, but it was up to me to work towards my goals.

I was able to learn about my metabolism and I realised that missing meals was actually detrimental; I learnt the importance of regular eating and was given so much evidence from the dietician around this. My disordered brain tried to argue with the facts, but the more I read about it and the more I read up about the effects of starvation, the more I began to realise that actually, the dietician was right, and not trying to trick me into gaining weight, but was indeed trying to help me. I printed out information from the dietician on what my body needed, and pinned it onto the cupboard doors, along with some other techniques I had learnt.

Calorie Counting

This is so difficult, calories are displayed everywhere, and if it is not calories it is the traffic light system used to fuel your eating disorder thoughts even more. I was obsessed with working out the calories in everything; I needed to know exactly what I was eating. For me the only way I could get over this was to get rid of the food scales.

I am a baker so, I did still need them and couldn't get rid of them completely, but I made my husband hide them, and only get them out for me when I wanted to bake. I realised, working out the calorie content was a massive contributing factor to my ED, so it definitely needed to stop.

I started off with breakfast, not weighing out my cereal and trying to determine a normal portion without measuring it out, of course this was hard. I questioned everything I was doing. "*Is this too much? Am I over eating?*" I was so confused but knew I had to face this fear. When I went shopping, I tried to stand back and pick something that looked nice and not look at the calorie content. Picking items of food that I didn't know the calorie content of. Thanks to my brain I had memorised every food I ate and knew the calorie content in those things.

I had to challenge my thoughts, remind myself that yes, it had X amount of calories in, but I needed to fuel my body; I needed calories to help my body work properly. I had to constantly refer to the information given to me by the dietician to fight the voice and remind myself why getting enough calories was important.

When I was out, or when I was in cafes, I needed to refer back to why it was important I chose something I liked instead of automatically choosing the option with less calories. I had to do this to recover. In restaurants I always went for the lighter calorie options, but now I just had to bite the bullet and not even look at those options, look at the whole menu not just the 'safe' section. This was one of the hardest things I had to overcome. I had become so used to doing it and I automatically started to add things up as I was eating, when I recognised I was doing this I paused, I stopped myself and repeated this sentence.

Is this helpful? Is working out calories helping me recover?

I then took a few deep breaths and carried on. I had to repeat this many times, and sometimes it would take me ages to prepare something as I kept having to stop to reset my mind, reminding myself of the dietician information, reminding myself to breath.

SMART Goals

Challenging these thoughts was far from easy. The first thing I did, was I set my self a long-term goal - what did I want? Why was recovery important to me? For me I wanted to start a family, I was unable to do so whilst engaging with ED, this was my reason to recover. My ultimate goal.

I also set myself short term goals, every week I had a new aim. In the early stages of recovery these goals included, only weighing myself twice a day, eating more than one meal a day and exercising only twice a day.

Then as my recovery progressed the goals were reset. I challenged myself to not weigh myself at all, eat everything off my meal plan and only exercise once a day and plan it in advance. These goals kept me focused and gave me something to work towards every week. Sometimes I had to repeat a goal, and that was okay. If I was having problems with a particular goal, I would discuss it with my team and work out ways to tackle these goals.

I used a SMART goal approach meaning;

S – Specific – Who what where when.

M – Measurable – Is there a way to track your progress?

A – attainable – Make sure your goal is ambitious but not outrageous.

R - Relevant – Ensure your goal is relevant to you.

T - Time based – Set a time limit and go for it.

An example of a SMART goal for myself was:

S – Specific – To stop self-weighing altogether.

M – Measurable – Thought diary, log your thoughts and make sure you are cutting down throughout the week.

A – Attainable – Cut down on scale use, it is possible but will be difficult.

R - Relevant – This is important; the obsession over this number is fuelling my disorder.

T - Time based – By the end of the week.

I also listed the barriers for the goals, things that might halt me from achieving this goal and again worked through them by challenging the thoughts and talking to my team, to find ways to work around the barriers.

Radical Acceptance

I used many techniques to help me during mealtimes, as my anxiety was hard to manage. One technique I found incredibly useful was a technique called radical acceptance.

For my stubborn personality trait this worked very well for me. The way I interpreted Radical Acceptance was very simple, I needed to accept the present moment, not fight it or get angry with it, but accept that the present moment was due to a chain of events, and then either jump off the distress hill or ride the wave. An example of this is:

- I am feeling anxious and scared about eating this meal, this is because of ED. I can either not eat this meal and continue to feel anxious and never recover. Or I can accept the fact that I am anxious, accept it's because of ED and then try and ride the anxiety wave. It will pass.

I saw radical acceptance as giving myself two options and one choice, choose recovery or choose ED. It also helped me to acknowledge what was going on in my body, I said out loud where my anxiety was affecting me.

For example, I feel hot; I am noticing my heart is getting faster. This was also a way for me to observe and acknowledge that it was the anxiety making my body react this way, and again this was because of ED. Radically accepting I felt the physical changes in my body, and that was ok.

Distress Hill

I mentioned the Distress Hill previously. I found my anxiety and distress around eating were like a hill, once it peaked, the anxiety started to ease. However, if I abandoned the meal and did not allow my anxiety to come back down, I would never be able to learn how to manage that anxiety.

I used the distress hill alongside radical acceptance, accepting why I felt this way and fighting my way through the meal. When I could feel my anxiety peaking, sometimes I needed a few moments away from the situation to take a few deep breaths, allowing that anxiety to come back down.

Quite often, I found that these hills were more like waves, they kept coming back, waves designed to knock me down, again, during these waves I had to learn to surf, I had to remind myself about all the information the dietician had given me, all the information why food was important and also remind myself constantly why I wanted to recover.

Talking my way through each mouthful, and focusing hard on that long term goal, whilst accepting the only reason I felt so anxious, so distressed was because of ED.

Good & Bad Food

All food has nutritional value, but, thanks to the diet culture world in which we live in, many foods have now been labelled good and bad foods, which for me is now a pet hate.

What has the food done to make it bad, has it robbed a bank? Has it committed bigamy? No. It is a food, unless it's off, it cannot be bad.

I really struggled with fear foods during my recovery. I had labelled so many foods as 'bad' and would not eat them, and I was scared to eat them. It was surprising the amount of fear foods I had, even toast had become a fear.

In my recovery I made a list of all the foods that I had labelled bad, and therefore would not eat. One by one I tried to challenge these fears, through the help of my community support appointments and help of family and friends. I started small, some fruits I had weirdly became scared of, I slowly started to introduce. I aimed to have a banana for a snack one day. Why this piece of fruit was a fear food still baffles me, but I wanted to recover, I kept asking myself, *"Is this banana going to realistically make me gain weight? No, why am I anxious?"* I had to remind myself, it was ED that was making me anxious, and I used a phrase that I really want everyone to take away with them:

My anxiety cannot hurt me, it is a feeling, and it will pass. My eating disorder can and will hurt me.

I kept reminding myself why I wanted to recover and use the techniques outlined previously to face my fear foods. This worked well for some food groups, but for full fear meals I needed a better plan. I used a stepladder approach, each week work towards a specific meal that terrified me. Let me give you an example. I wanted to be able to enjoy a takeaway pizza with friends, without using compensatory behaviours.

Step 1, Homemade pizza, from scratch, 3 toppings.
Step 2, Frozen pizza at home.
Step 3, 'Fake away' pizza at home.
Step 4, 'Fake away' pizza with friends.
Step 5, Takeaway pizza!

Each step was one up from the previous and each very challenging. Our 'fake away' pizzas were from a pizza counter at ASDA, I could control exactly what toppings I wanted, but did not make the sauce or dough from scratch like we would at home. I used this step ladder approach so many times and wrote down my barriers and thoughts along the way, logging all my thoughts and feelings, so I could challenge them with a more logical approach. An example taken from my thought diary;

Tonight I managed a 'fake away' with friends, I enjoyed the pizza and we all were having a giggle watching the Avengers in the background. I found myself having to bring myself back to the present moment so many time. I wanted to Google the calorie content but knew deep down this would not be helpful. When I got home, I went straight for the laxatives but stopped. I had fun tonight, with my friends, would they be taking laxatives right now or asleep resting? Are these laxatives helpful in my recovery?

The next day, I wanted to exercise but kept reminding myself I needed to recover. Yes, the anxiety was hurting me physically, making me feel sick, but it would pass. I wanted to restrict to compensate, but again, I had to fight these behaviours. I was at war with my mind, constantly battling away at the thoughts. I then turned to self-care. I needed to slow down my thoughts, so I went outside for some fresh air and read a few chapters of my book; my anxiety settled but remained with me. It was not a 'quick fix'.

One by one, I challenged all of my fear foods, it was not easy and many times I did fail or use compensatory behaviours. If this was the case, I amended my step ladder approach, added more steps if necessary and tried again.

There is no shame in having to repeat steps, it does not matter how long it takes to reach your goal. As long as you do indeed keep trying. When you achieve it, manage that fear, and smash your goal, it feels so empowering, and really does spur you on to do another.

One note though, when you do face a fear, complete a challenging meal, do not put it on the back burner and forget about it. Do it again in a week or two, otherwise before you know it, it will become another fear again.

Timed Eating

As I said in the last chapter, I had set times to eat, which allowed me to skip a meal if I missed the time slot. The first thing I did was make a list of all of the rules around times, then I made myself challenge these rules. I made myself purposely delay getting breakfast until later on. I started off leaving it only five minutes late, then a little longer, using radical acceptance. I then had to challenge the thought of it being too late for breakfast now so I should just skip it.

One of my other rules was eating my main meal at lunch time, surely if I was eating a big meal at lunchtime I did not need breakfast and then I would be too full for tea? I talked this through with my community support worker and we decided that he would challenge this. We decided to go out for lunch one day. I made myself stick to my meal plan in the morning, reminding myself that this was now and not looking at what I would eat later, but just taking each meal a step at a time. When we got to the restaurant, I had managed breakfast but was very anxious. We talked through my feelings, and discussed why it really did not matter what time I ate my main meals, people working night shifts for example may have their main meal at the middle of the night and breakfast at 7pm, it makes no difference. I managed my meal and then when it came to tea had to challenge the belief that I had already eaten and was full, I did not need tea.

Again, remembering to try and take one meal a step at a time, focusing on the present moment and not thinking about what I had already eaten or done, using radical acceptance to accept why I was feeling so anxious and riding the distress wave, I was able to enjoy my last meal of the day.

Every time my ED told me "*no*" or I heard myself saying "*I cannot do that*" I added it to a list and made myself do it, made myself challenge that belief.

Social Interactions

I used the step ladder approach for this too, I wanted to be able to go out for meals, visit coffee shops with friends and get my social life back. My first step was to visit a small quiet café with someone I trusted who knew about my disorder so would not push me, but would set a good example.

Before we went, I asked them to talk about anything, to keep me distracted and that I needed to have a milky drink with a snack, as it was on my meal plan. I took one of my closest friends, Gemma, to a very small, quaint café in my village called Tilly's Tea Room. There was only us and one other couple in there. If I panicked or could not eat what I had planned, it was okay, it was not busy, and I did not feel rushed.

We engaged in a conversation around work, as we worked together but I was currently off work to focus on my recovery. She was filling me in on everything what was happening, and general work gossip. We then talked lots about her son, it was November so getting close to Christmas, we were able to discuss all of her plans for her gorgeous little boy and I was able to engage well in the conversation. Whilst still battling with the ED voice at times I did zone out, I also used flash cards with my techniques written on them to remind me what I should be doing. It was very difficult and my anxiety was high but eventually it did pass, the wave broke and I was able to carry on with my day. Once I had done this task, I then set myself another goal; repeat this in a busier café.

This time we chose a Costa in town. I decided to have a snack and milky drink again and this time I was with my community support worker. The place was busy and there was so much choice it was overwhelming, I could see the calorie content on everything and I wanted to run.

I could not do this. Recognising I wanted to flee, my support worker talked me through the techniques I had mastered, helping me to calm down and choose something. *Would this snack really make a massive difference to my overall weight? Look around at all these people in here, are they panicking about eating a snack and having a coffee, or enjoying their company and enjoying the experience?*

I re-did this task a few times until my anxiety had settled and it no longer completely scared me.

Once I was comfortable with this, I needed a new task. This time it was to enjoy a meal out. I chose a café for lunch again with a close friend, a small independent café, not very busy with a relaxed atmosphere, a safe option. Once I did this a few times I rode the anxiety wave. Once I felt comfortable with this, the time had come to face the big fear, a meal out with friends.

It was Black Friday, a group of us go to Meadowhall every year to enjoy the chaos of the sales - manic I know. We decided to meet for dinner, I had already looked at the menu and chose something that was a challenge but not too challenging, the fact I was out for a meal was my main task.

When we arrived at the restaurant, the place was absolutely packed, full of people, everyone surely judging me. I was able to engage in a conversation with my friends whilst we waited for our meals. We were discussing what we had bought, what deals we had found and what we still needed to get. The conversation was lively and I soon realised no one was actually judging me for what I was eating, everyone was simply enjoying their own meal, enjoying the lively atmosphere and most importantly enjoying each other's company.

I had a bit of an epiphany. Nothing mattered - the calorie content, others in the restaurant and what I was eating. None of this was important, what was important was the present moment, seeing my friends smile, laughing and having a very good time in each other's company. This was what was important, this was what mattered, this could be my life if I was eating disorder free and this was what I wanted.

I then continued to do this, continued to go out for meals and ordered more unsafe foods by using the step ladder approach, challenging the thoughts, using radical acceptance and the distress hill, remembering my long term goals and how amazing life could be without ED. Every time I succeeded, every time I managed a goal, it simply spurred me on and gave me more confidence, more ammunition to fight that ED voice.

Physical/Mental Elements Of Restriction

Take it from someone who is in stable recovery, being warm rocks. I am able to enjoy the winter without constantly thinking about how cold I am. I knew I was in a stable recovery when it was the Christmas Market. The year before as I said, I couldn't enjoy it as I was too cold. The following year, I was able to enjoy the market so much more, enjoy roasted chestnuts and a Baileys hot chocolate. I was able to be more present in the moment and actually enjoy what was going on around me instead of focusing on food and my body temperature, the beauty of the market, the lights, the atmosphere, the music. I was able to enjoy it all, embrace the beauty. ED was there, being a little vocal, but none of it mattered. I found I had energy to enjoy the market as well, now I was fuelling my body I did not get tired and want to leave halfway around, I was full of life and loved it so much, we actually walked around again! This is just one example, just one day where I noticed a remarkable difference. Imagine every other day, every day having energy, feeling warm and well, focused and able to think so much more clearly.

The better I felt, the more I wanted to keep going. I logged the good days, wrote down how I felt after following my meal plans and after the anxiety had passed and when I was struggling I was able to read these back and remind myself why I was fighting, why it was important and most importantly, that it was possible.

Recovering From Compensatory Behaviours

When I had managed to complete a meal, or a challenge, I then had the difficult task of not trying to "get rid" of whatever it was I had eaten. My body ached from over exercise, my stomach was ruined from the laxative abuse and my heart struggled to keep up with my demands. I needed to slow down, but I kept telling myself again and again, that exercise was important. True, exercise can be enjoyed and keep you strong but there is a difference between punishing your body and celebrating what your body can do. My whole view of exercise was distorted. It was not about stretching my muscles and working out to keep them strong, I was punishing my body because it did not look like what I wanted it to, punishing myself for eating, punishing myself for not looking perfect. I needed to remember that exercise was not about mistreatment, it should be enjoyable and fun, a celebration of what my amazing body could do, and a way of praising my body. All of my compensating behaviours needed to stop; I had to change my views on exercise if I wanted to live my life free from this misery I was trapped in.

Over Exercise

This was my addiction, my go to. Every time I had eaten something I had to "burn it off" but my body needed the energy, it needed the fuel. I decided with my team that I needed to cut down on the exercise that I was doing. However, I still wanted to exercise, it helped calm me down and was a coping strategy, but also an unhelpful one at the same time. The first thing I did, was for one week to write down everything, all of the exercise I had participated in, whether it was planned or spontaneous. After the week had finished, I reviewed it with my psychologist, the amount of time I had spent exercising was quite frankly, ridiculous. We discussed what I could have done in that time, I could have achieved so much, academically and on my own dreams. I could have actually achieved something useful instead of chasing after the perfect body.

We agreed a set timetable, I was still able to exercise every day at that point, but only once a day, and it was planned, so any compensatory behaviours meant I had to learn to ride the anxiety wave. I then slowly cut down my exercise to a more realistic timetable. Three days a week and this included one run.

I really struggled with running. Every route I took, I knew how many calories I could roughly burn. I stopped taking my watch and just had my phone for music. I did not look at the time and tried to run until I started to feel tired then head back. But I found myself still checking the time, Googling the route I had taken on my return and trying to work out the calories. The only way I could stop this addiction was to go cold turkey. Running was too triggering for me, as much as I adored it and wanted to find a way around it, I knew it was just not possible at that point, so stopped running all together. Maybe once I am ED free it is something I will be able to participate in again, and actually see it as enjoyable instead of a punishment.

Sticking to this timetable was far from easy, and of course I wobbled more times than I would like to admit. It took time, like any addiction, it does not disappear overnight, it took months of fighting, determination and will power. After a meal I'd be reaching for my running shoes to compensate, I needed a few techniques to help me stop in my tracks. To ask myself "*is this planned exercise or compensatory behaviours?*" The first thing I did was of course, make a little flash card that read:

STOP, is this planned or compensatory? Is this behaviour going to help you recover? Remember your long-term goal and your reasons for recovery, use your resource jar (will come onto that).

The fact I had to take the card out of my shoes and put it down somewhere automatically made me think, was I compensating? Was this helpful? I was able to question and challenge what I was doing. If I recognised it was compensating I knew I needed to distract my mind until the anxiety had eased.

Eventually, this got easier, so I challenged my exercise addiction further. I started to miss workouts on purpose and diverted from the timetable. I waited to see what would happen when I did none at all. I kept changing my routines and days I would exercise, until I felt comfortable with not working out at all. I forced myself to have time away from it completely, to learn how to deal with the anxiety. I now do have a healthy relationship with exercise. I work out in a way that is fun, if I skip a workout, it does not matter. What matters is my mental wellbeing, how I use exercise for pleasure instead of punishment and in a way that feels good as opposed to torture.

Distraction Jar

As well as my flash card I created a resource jar to help when I needed to distract myself from engaging in compensatory behaviours, whether this was the urge to take laxatives, purge or exercise. This jar is simply a jam jar filled with lollypop sticks. Each stick has something written on it that I love doing. When the urges hit me, I panicked and couldn't think of anything to do to help myself; in those situations, I could pull out a stick and do whatever was written on it.

Here are a few examples of my favourite personal distractions;

- Play the flute
- Read a chapter from a book
- Do a puzzle from your puzzle book
- Learn a new song on the ukulele
- Listen to music
- Take a bath
- Play a game with James
- Cup of tea time

I encourage others to make their own and fill it with their own personal distraction techniques and when they feel or recognise they are about to use a compensatory behaviour. Pause and pull out a stick. I often did a few sticks one after the other until that anxiety wave had passed. The anxiety does pass, it's just delaying the behaviours until they do. No matter how long that may take.

Distraction Box

As well as my distraction jar, I also made myself a distraction box. Inside this box were items to distract myself when my thoughts were running wild, whether it was the need to compensate or general thoughts regarding ED. I had stress balls I could throw around to release some of the tension, I had a notepad to journal my thoughts, I had a colouring book and some crayons which distracted my mind. I also had a candle I loved the smell of, some hand cream and room spray I could use, engaging my other senses. My favourite book was in there, with post it notes marking my much-loved sections. I also kept a mindfulness book full of guided exercises, and a few photographs of my beautiful nieces, reminding me of my own long-term goal. My friends were amazing whilst in recovery, one of them had written me a variety of cards, saying open me when you need some encouragement, open me when you feel unloved and many more. I loved reading her words of encouragement and it helped push me through those difficult times. Part of my eating disorder made me feel worthless and unlovable so having my friends' voices nearby really helped. I also had a flash card in there (yes more flash cards) of what my friends had said about me, how they would describe me, as a reminder that they loved me, regardless of my size, regardless of my illness, they still loved me. I also had somewhat unpleasant reminders about where my eating disorder takes me. I had my hospital bracelets and get well soon cards in there, reminding me that is where ED leads.

I encourage everyone I meet to make their own distraction box and fill it with things that will distract them in those moments, similar to the jar, but again personalise it. All you need is a shoe box and then wrap it in some wrapping paper, fill it with photographs, flash cards, scented items, anything you can use to help you ride that anxiety wave. I leave it on the dining table so if needed straight away after my meal I can grab it and work through the next wave, work through the feeling that I have to exercise and burn off what I had just eaten. I found the jar and the distraction box really helpful as I did not have to think of things to do in these moments, I had already planned for it. I found this took away a lot of the stress and made challenging this illness more manageable.

How It Really Looked

These techniques worked, but not every time. Of course there were times when I did jump off the distress hill and times where our house became a battlefield. I knew what I should be doing and why, I knew the importance of recovery, but sometimes it was just not possible. I would shout and scream at myself, angry at myself for failing, angry at myself for letting the disorder win, angry for being weak. I used to get so frustrated with myself. I did resort to self-harm on more than one occasion, desperate to take my frustration out somehow.

I remember trying to eat my evening meal, it was pasta, a nice simple meal. I had my flashcards out and was working my way through the meal, the anxiety kept building and building, I needed a few moments to calm, so I took my mindfulness cards outside and did some breathing techniques. I calmed down my breathing and slowed my thoughts down. I re-entered the room, sat back at the table and straight away, it felt like I was going to boil again. I repeated the techniques, repeated the radical acceptance script and calmed but I was just getting angrier. I threw my knife and fork across the room in utter frustration, screaming at the top of my voice, letting all the anger out.

Once I had vented my frustration, I tried again, but it was just too much, again all the techniques just did not seem to work, nothing worked, it was hopeless. I was shouting at James, he was trying to encourage me to have a few moments, but I was done. I was tired, and my anxiety made my body ache. I ended up picking up my plate and throwing my meal in the bin, outraged that ED had led me to do this, I burst into tears. Angry for giving up, angry for wasting food and angry at myself. I could never recover, what was the point, I was just going to fail. I cried and cried until I did not have any tears left, I went upstairs and fell asleep, exhausted from the fight, exhausted from the emotional pain.

I woke up the next morning, refreshed and determined. I reset. Right, yesterday did not go as planned, that was ok. Recovery is not linear, hiccups happen, today was a new day, what happened yesterday no longer mattered. I couldn't change what happened, but I could change what I did today. A new day.

I learnt not to dwell on the day before, take each day as it came and start each day fresh. If I had dwelled on what had happened, it would have made it impossible to eat breakfast, then because I had restricted breakfast, lunch and snacks would have been difficult too, and so on, until I would of course completely spiral. Each morning I reminded myself it was a new day, a new chance, a new start. I was stronger than my eating disorder, I needed to fuel my body and my mind.

Key points to take away

- Slow down, remember that yes, exercise is important to stay healthy, but when it becomes excessive it is dangerous. The healthiest thing to do is sit with those emotions and allow yourself time to rest.
- Distraction and delaying the behaviours is key. Keep yourself busy after a challenge, engage in something you enjoy and create a whole toolkit of different activities to avoid it being repetitive.
- True, exercise can be enjoyed and keep you strong but there is a difference between punishing your body and celebrating what your body can do. My whole view of exercise was distorted, it was not about stretching my muscles and working them to keep them strong, it was mistreatment. I was punishing my body because it did not look like what I wanted it to be, abusing myself for eating, torturing myself for not looking perfect. I needed to remember that exercise was not about punishment, it should be enjoyable and fun, a celebration of what my amazing body could do. All of my compensating behaviours needed to stop; I needed to change my view on exercise if I wanted to live my life free from this misery I was trapped in.
- Understand that there will be set-backs, you will feel you've failed and you will slip back, it's ok. Just give yourself permission to heal.
- There is no magic pill to solve negative body image, diet pills can be extremely dangerous and addictive. These companies are making money from your insecurities, please stay away from them, they can be deadly.
- Laxative abuse and purging can have severe long-term damage on the body. My bowels no longer work properly, not pleasant at all, take it from me, they do nothing but dehydrate you.

- Every fear faced is a step closer to recovery.
- What may seem like small steps to some may feel like mountains to others. That is ok, take your time and set realistic goals and targets suited to your own recovery and pace.
- Setting unrealistic goals will set you up to fail and dishearten your journey, set goals that are achievable but also still challenging.
- Engage in the opposite action as often as you can. If your eating disorder is screaming something is wrong, chances are it is the right thing to be doing. Go against that voice and keep rebelling. This way you will become stronger.
- Not all of these techniques I used will work for you, try them all and see what works best. Remember, recovery is an individual process and no two journeys will look the same.

Chapter 11
Body Image

My husband was getting restless, we were supposed to leave the house over half an hour ago, however I had just gotten changed for the eighth time. Nothing looked good, I looked awful and nothing fitted.

I can't go out looking like that, I look dreadful. My mind was racing, I was under pressure to get dressed. The more pressure I was under the worse it got, the more panicked I became and therefore the more anxious I felt, which played into my eating disorder's hands.

I had gotten stuck in a cycle of self-hatred and anxiety. I tried to wear jeans with a baggy top, but it hung off me and had no shape. I then tried tights and a floaty dress, but my legs looked too big in the tights. I then tried leggings and a slightly smarter dress but then felt I looked too formal. I just did not know what to wear. It was not the clothes that was the issue, in my disordered mind it was my body, my body was the issue, the big fat ugly issue that needed fixing.

This happened daily, every time I got dressed and looked at what I was wearing, a sense of panic swept over me, and the negative voice started. "*Everyone will laugh at you Zoe, you look fat, you look awful, and you cannot leave the house looking like that.*" I could be visiting family or just popping to the local shop for some supplies, no matter what the occasion, I had this overwhelming issue with whatever I was wearing. The funny thing is, when I found something that was maybe half acceptable, maybe I did not look that atrocious in, the next time I would wear it, I would think it looked awful. No matter how many compliments received, again it would not satisfy that negative voice, nothing could please that disordered voice.

Here's an example of what it was like to be inside my head at one of my worst moments:

- Right, it is 6pm I have an hour to get ready before I am meeting the girls for cocktails.
- I am showered, I'll curl my hair.
- Oh, my goodness that looks awful, what have I done? My hair looks stupid like this. Everyone will laugh, I have to brush it out, it looks silly. Five minutes trying to brush it out it looked worse, I am going to have to re wash it.
- OK now I only have half an hour to get ready, I will blow-dry my hair and I will just have to leave it, no matter what I do it looks awful anyway so what is the point in trying.
- Right next step make-up.
- Make-up started but halfway through, is this too much? I look like a clown. I need to take it off and start again.
- Right, hair sorted - it looks messy but I cannot tame it. Make-up a little bit on, not too much, maybe not enough, I just don't know. Next step, find something to wear.
- Oh no. The familiar sense of panic as I open up my wardrobe and pull out a few outfits, one by one I try them on and send a photo to our group chat, I am now running slightly late, which I hate!
- First little black dress, quite fitted and my old faithful. But tonight all I can see is chunky legs. I needed something to cover up my legs, skirt, top and thick tights. Let's try that, but again nope, my legs are still out, they needed covering.
- Let's try jeans and a sparkly top, oh my goodness this is the worst one yet, the top looks baggy and unflattering and what was I thinking trying to wear jeans? Every part of my body looks awful in jeans.
- Continuing to seek my friend's approval and ignoring the compliments I'm getting back. They were lying, just being nice, they know I am running late and just saying it looks good to try and hurry me up.
- Nothing in my wardrobe looks nice on me. I can't go out

and embarrass my friends, they all looked gorgeous, they do not want to be seen with me, an ugly wreck.

- Stay at home Zoe.
- They will thank you, they do not really want you to go, they all think you look awful too. There is no point in trying to look good, you will never look good.
- The voice has won. I am defeated. I can't go out. I am too ashamed of my body, too ashamed of my appearance, too ashamed of me.
- I tell my friends all of a sudden I had developed a really bad headache and felt dizzy.
- After a few well wishes from them and a few tears from me I decide I need to sort out this mess of a body, and engage in my normal punishment.
- Running shoes on, jogging trousers and my sports top, out the door, fitness tracker watch set, go for a run.
- When I get back a few pictures have started to be uploaded.
- My friends look like they are having a great time, and part of my heart starts to ache. I wish I was there too, longing to be with my best girls, laughing and joking. But then out pops the negative voice, *don't be stupid Zoe, they are having a much better time because you are not there. They all look beautiful, your fat face would have ruined all these Insta-perfect photos.*

Sadly, this is not the only time something like this happened, this was a regular occurrence, where I had to cancel plans because of the shame I felt about my body. I had to, I did not want to embarrass those around me, in my eyes, my body was an embarrassment. I was an embarrassment.

Comparing

Wherever I was, I could not help but compare my body to those around me, whether it was complete strangers whilst walking down the street or my closest friends. I was constantly thinking, *"why can't I look like that, her legs look lovely why are mine just fat stumps, I wonder what exercise she does to get them to look like that. What is wrong with me?"* The worse place for this was of course at the gym. Everywhere I looked I was surrounded by different body types, and I would always fixate on the ultra-fit toned woman who I aspired to look like. I would take a mental note of what exercises they were doing and try and copy them the next day. I would look at what weights they were lifting, and how many reps and circuits they would participate in, and again try and match it in the hope I could somehow steal their body type.

It was a friend's wedding preparation, I was well into recovery, and doing well with my treatment, engaging and participating in therapy. I was so honoured to have been asked to be a bridesmaid for one of my oldest friends, however straight away was plagued with anxiety. I was going to look awful and ruin her wedding photos, I would be referred to as the 'fat' bridesmaid all day, everyone would laugh at me.

When I met with the beautiful bride to be and other bridesmaids to go shopping for our bridesmaids' outfit, I felt completely out of my depth and started to engage in this toxic comparing behaviour. Everything we tried on I thought I looked awful in and I felt everyone else looked so much better, and again my core belief of *"I was not good enough"* filled my heart with sorrow.

We found an outfit and when trying it on I tried my hardest to work on some techniques I had learnt in therapy, so I tried not to focus on my problem areas and focus on the fabric on my skin, the colour, was it comfy? It was, so I took a deep breath feeling somewhat OK, and stepped out of the changing room to join the others.

ED voice was raging, how dare I try and ignore it! What could it say or do to really get to me? Then upon seeing the others, the voice knew, it knew exactly what to say. *Zoe you are not good enough, you are letting everyone down, look at the others…* and one by one I found myself comparing my body to each of the other bridesmaids. They all looked absolutely stunning, one was tall and everything she wore looked elegant, she had the most amazing curves and could rock any outfit. One of the others had a beautiful petite figure and a personality that would make anyone giggle. Finally, the third bridesmaid again, had the most amazing curves and looked so feminine in the chosen outfit. Then I looked at myself in the mirror and felt sick.

All the techniques I had learnt in therapy seemed to have disappeared out of my head and the ED voice was very much winning. Could I try and think of one positive thing about the way I looked in this outfit? I'd been able to a minute ago. *Think Zoe think, just one thing.* Nope, all my disordered brain could fixate on was how amazing everyone else looked, and how much I did not fit in. I wondered if my friend thought the same and regretted asking me to be bridesmaid, my mind was racing. However, one of the other bridesmaids knew about my disorder, and knew I was working hard to battle it. After we got changed into our clothes again, she asked if I was OK, I nodded, fighting the urge to explode and say how I actually thought I looked awful and was letting everyone down. She must have read my mind; she turned to me and started to tell me that the colour really suited me, and I looked amazing in the outfit.

She then opened up a little about her own insecurities, and told me she felt self-conscious. She felt like everyone else looked amazing and how she needed reassurance. Straight away I jumped to defend her, how could she think like that? She looked stunning! However, it made me realise, we cannot help but compare our bodies to others. Disordered mind or not, everyone struggles at times with body image issues and finds themselves comparing their bodies to others.

I did not know how I had never tuned into this before, but now I was aware of it and I heard it everywhere. Work colleagues saying how fat they were, this was always the worst for me, I could not help but think, *Well if they think they look fat and they are actually slim and have an incredible figure, how fat am I? I must be huge!* After that event, I found myself really tuning into other people's insecurities, and my disordered mind found more ammunition to tear into my self-confidence. If I heard someone say their hair was a mess, I would automatically compare, *well if they think theirs is a mess and it looks that lovely, mine must really be a mess.* If someone said, they felt like their legs were big, my mind would again, compliment them and then compare, *well they have lovely shaped legs, if they are what fat legs look like mine must be like tree trunks.*

Before I knew it all the hard work on body image had been undone, my eating disorder had found a new way to torture me, to haunt me and to continue to make my life miserable.

Ending Comparing

Today you are you.
That is truer then true.
There is no one alive.
Who is youer than you – Dr Seuss

This quote got me thinking. I spent so much time comparing my body to others, I lost sense of who I really was and lost the unique style I once had. I was so obsessed with looking like someone else, anyone else, I also lost aspects of my personality by doing so. No one is better at being me then me, the same applies for everyone, we are meant to all be different and have different styles and shapes, I had to re-learn who I really was.

I started off by simply noticing when I was looking at others and pulling myself down. I would stop myself, and ask "*is this behaviour helpful?*" Instead of wishing I had her hair, arms or whatever it was, I would simply allow myself to notice them, pay them a compliment in my head and then move on, recognising that I liked that about them but not wishing to change myself. It was such a hard task to do but with practice it became easier. At first I did it on auto pilot, automatically criticising myself, and again I had to recognise the thought and think to myself, "*you are you not them, you cannot look like them*", and then move on. After time and a lot, I mean a *lot* of practice, I did not need to talk myself through it anymore, it became more natural. I was able to recognise others and things I liked about them without the need to then pull myself down for not being like that.

One thing I had to do was detox, no I do not mean with laxatives (aka diet shakes). I mean detox your social media. Unfollow pages that make you compare yourself, I unfollowed all the diet and exercise pages on Instagram.

I am enough, just the way I am, and it is true, these pages make you feel, made me feel, not enough. What would happen to these industries if we all realised we are enough? They make money from our insecurities, making us feel not enough.

However, I was scrolling through social media one morning, it was shortly before summer. The amount of weight loss adverts, people engaging in bikini body diets, pages from companies trying to play off my insecurities and invite me to different exercise programmes was astonishing. I was scrolling through and could not stop comparing my body to the people trying to sell these workouts and weight loss programs. I was clicking from one link to the next, once again my mind was racing as the ED voice loved it.

All the work I had done on overcoming my body image issues meant nothing. I then paused as I realised what I was doing, and recognised the thoughts were getting louder. I then went back onto my social media and started to unfollow all of the pages and people trying to sell these products. Deleting exercise programmes I had followed and personal trainers with the wash board abs promoting cucumber smoothies. I just deleted them all and then went on a massive following spree, flooding my news feeds with body positive accounts, finding new people to follow and also following others that had been through and recovered themselves, from eating disorders.

My massive deleting spree did cause fall outs, lead to a few arguments and result in a few people to becoming a little upset. One example being a pretty heated argument with my friend. She had tried to get me to like her new business page, but she was now selling weight loss tablets. I refused. This is something, that for me, was extremely dangerous. I was addicted to them and the content on her page was extremely triggering to me, but also, I did not agree with what she was trying to sell. Yes, it caused an argument, but I explained I am against everything they stand for and could not support her this time. Yes, it felt absolutely dreadful, she is my friend who was trying to start a business. I wanted to be able to help and encourage her, but I could not support her on this venture, and that is okay. I was looking after my own welfare. It is okay to do this.

I follow so many different people now on social media. There are so many body neutral pages and body positivity pages that I engage with regularly. A real sense of community with people celebrating their own bodies and celebrating other peoples too. All shapes, sizes, genders, races, all supporting each other and building each other up. I have found it to be a really supportive community and by joining in and celebrating all body types and also helping each other overcome the damage that the dieting industry and eating disorders has done to us, I have found it has really aided my recovery. Celebrating the fact that yes, we are all different, and this is a good thing, we are meant to be different, life would be pretty boring if we all looked exactly the same. I recognise now I was a victim of diet culture and as a result, I hate to admit I was indeed, fatphobic. I needed to undo all the damage society had done on my way of thinking and undo this awful thought process.

I have filled my social media with all body types, so I am not being directly exposed to one type all the time. Believing that only one type of body was deemed perfect and punishing myself for not looking like what I believed was the only good attractive body shape. Instead, now when I log onto social media, I am constantly reminded that it does not matter. The people I follow all do amazing inspirational things despite their own issues, my fellow tribe of warriors. These are real inspiring people, and people I look up to. Completely different to when I was trapped in my disordered ways, only believing my role models to be those in the adverts with the body I desperately wanted. Whereas now, my role models are strong, inspirational people, who have overcome body image issues, overcome eating disorders and are now living their best life. Diet and disorder free.

Fear Clothes

Anything tight fitting, jeans, things that showed too much of my flesh, things that completely covered me and that were too baggy, all swim wear… It seemed impossible to find clothes that pleased that ED voice, it was impossible to feel comfortable. Bikinis and crop tops were completely unimaginable and just a complete no! Body fitting dresses I would admire, especially on curvy woman, they looked great, but in my eyes, I was too fat to wear anything like that and would only embarrass myself and those who were seen with me, if I was to do so.

The worse item of clothing for me for some reason were jeans. They fitted my legs and waist, however all I could focus on was my rolls if I bent down or when I was seated. I was so paranoid of flesh sitting on top of my jeans and being on show. Everyone was surely laughing at me, pointing at how fat I was, teasing me again. I started to live in leggings and floaty dresses, it became my style, however in the middle of winter, floaty dresses and leggings were not the best clothing in the world. I wanted a nice woolly jumper to help keep me warm, but the more I told myself I could not wear jeans, the more I pulled myself down, convinced myself I looked truly hideous in them, the more my anxiety rose. Until I just could not do it. I could not wear jeans anymore. I was too fat for jeans.

Vest style tops were another massive fear, in my eyes the top of my arms were gross, massive and definitely should not be on show. In the middle of the summer, I was able to wear these things at home, and with those very close to me, but then I'd catch my reflection in the mirror, and stop in my tracks. *Zoe you look disgusting, look at your arms, they are massive, you should not be wearing this*, and more often than not I would end up changing. It was not just vest tops but any dress that had no sleeves or any sleeveless item of clothing. Regardless of what I was doing, who I was with, all I could focus on was how big my arms must look, and what I could possibly do to get them smaller.

Shorts and skirts started to become another fear too. Again middle of summer, paired with a vest top, I now had two "problem areas" on show, my tree trunk legs and my oversized arms. With shorts and skirts all I could focus on was my legs, if I caught my reflection or saw myself in the mirror my eating disorder voice zoned in on them and exaggerated their appearance. Convincing me that every laugh I heard as I was walking down the street was aimed at me. Every time I caught someone's eye, I assumed they were judging me, thinking, she is too fat to be wearing that. It continued to drive me to engage in unhelpful behaviours, and my unhealthy relationship with my body continued.

Holiday Abroad

YES! We were going to Crete, I love Greek history, so was very excited to explore. It was also a break, time away from all of life's stresses, laid on a beach with the warm sun and sound of the sea. And time spent just me and my amazing hubby. Time to unwind, we started to pack a day or two before our flight and this was proving an extremely difficult task. What on earth did I take to wear, what would keep me cool? A lot of my flesh was going to be on show, wearing shorts and little playsuits, in front of everyone? Suddenly this holiday I had been so excited for, started to make me feel incredibly anxious. So much so I started to fear it and did not want to go. I was so convinced I would be letting James down, he would be seen with me, this fat ugly woman, with legs the size of tree trunks, I couldn't do that to him, he did not deserve that. James realised I had stopped packing and was just stood in some sort of trance. He asked me what was wrong and I exploded. I told him exactly what I was thinking, told him I did not know what to pack, everything made me look fat, I was fat, everyone would laugh at me, especially around the pool and beach, surely he should find someone else to go with. I did not quite expect the response I got.

James literally laughed at me, which really angered that eating disorder voice, he reminded me how excited I was to visit Crete and explore the neighbouring islands. We had a trip planned to Spinalonga, which I had been desperate to visit, and reminded me how much we both needed to get away and have a break.

He was right, was I really going to let the way I looked and felt stop me from exploring this beautiful island? I continued to pack, accepting that I was going to have to wear shorts and strappy tops, embracing and packing so many of my fear clothes. The day came when we were due to fly, what I had packed was not a concern, I was just so excited for our trip away. The taxi arrived early in the morning and took us to the airport, we played a few games and talked about all the adventures we were going to have. I had agreed to try and eat the best I could, by this time I was collapsing often, and did not want to collapse in a foreign country and become unwell whilst abroad. However, we were not on holiday yet, so I managed to escape breakfast. I was convinced it would bloat me and therefore make the flight uncomfortable.

I was wearing a dress and leggings, which was standard for me, and I figured that before we landed I could just take the leggings off and I would be in a little summer dress, which would keep me cool until we got to the hotel. Everyone on the plane seemed to have a very similar idea, and about an hour before we were due to land people were removing layers of clothing to reveal summer clothing underneath their jumpers and long sleeve shirts. Straight away I started to compare, everyone around me looked so much better, I was too fat to be wearing just a dress, surely, should I keep my legs covered up? I did not want to let James down after all. The ED voice had somehow realised this was a massive fear for me on this holiday, and really took advantage of my body dysmorphia to keep me from enjoying myself. James asked me if I was going to get changed, as he had just changed into shorts, but I decided to stay as I was, he asked why and I just made up an excuse about air con on the bus always being a little chilly, luckily for the voice, James believed it.

We arrived at the hotel, it was stunning, and located in a small resort near the capital of Crete. We had unpacked and still had a few hours of sunshine left, we were both feeling groggy and decided to have a swim. We quickly got changed and headed to the pool. We laid the towels on a sunbed, James jumped straight into the water and looked around to find me. I was sat on the poolside, with my kaftan still on with my toes in the water and sunglasses on hiding my tears. He asked me if I was coming in and I just said I was happy with my feet in at the minute, it had been a long day and I just wanted to relax.

However deep down, the ED voice was finding new ways to tear me to shreds. There were so many body types around me, however as always, I zoned in on what I thought my body should look like. I focused on the women in bikinis, who looked like models, and that voice was just accusing my husband of wishing that his wife looked like that.

He was going to leave me, he would realise he could have someone fitter, someone he would be proud to have on his arm. Here I was in this beautiful paradise, lovely sunshine, cool water splashing my legs, I should have felt happy, I should have felt content, but I did not feel enough. I was not good enough.

We continued our evening and went to one of the restaurants in the hotel for a meal. I of course scanned the menu for a safe option and automatically started to wonder how many laps of the pool I should do tomorrow to compensate and if I could get away with getting up early and going for a run around the resort. We had a lovely evening despite the voice screaming at me, I was admiring the beauty of the island and tried to keep myself within the present moment, taking in each detail instead of focusing on my body, we got back to the room and fell quickly to sleep.

The next morning the sun brightened up the room, I woke up feeling fresh, and we headed down for breakfast, there was loads of fresh fruit and Greek yogurt which was my safe food, so I was able to eat a little breakfast. We agreed after a day travelling to just have the day around the pool then explore the town and book our excursions for the following day.

We got changed and headed to the pool. It started all over again, however the difference is this time, my husband seemed to have become a mind reader. He could see me looking around, and then see me tugging unknowingly at my own skin. He took my hands and told me he loved me, to stop looking and focusing on others and focus on the present moment, focus on the sensation of the water and how the sun felt. I decided to go for it and have a swim, my mind was racing, my thoughts were going crazy but I really wanted to enjoy this holiday, regardless of feeling severely insecure.

I wanted to please James and he was clearly getting a little annoyed that my body image issues were stopping me from enjoying this holiday. So instead of expressing how I felt, I plastered on a fake smile and vowed to remember how I felt about my body, so when I got home, I had something to work towards, remembering how amazing those other women looked. I suppressed all my thoughts and feelings and kept them hidden for the remainder of the holiday. Every time I was around the pool in my swimwear, I was pulling myself to shreds, every time we were on excursions and I was in shorts or playsuits, I was looking around thinking everyone was laughing at me, every evening when we were dressed up to go out, I secretly thought I was not good enough for James. As soon as we got home, I had the mental images of the beach model in my head, and I continued my path of self-destruction.

Changing Body Image

This Is The BIG ONE - Set Point Theory

My mind was absolutely blown when I was introduced to set point theory. It really did change my life. Hopefully by sharing this hidden secret with you, the secret that dieting industries do not want us to know, I will shatter all those beliefs you may be following and believing regarding your weight.

I was in treatment and my community support worker asked me,

"Zoe have you ever heard of set point theory?"

I said,

"No what is that?"

It was explained to me that set point theory, is the science as to why diets don't work! It explains why we lose the same 10lbs over and over again, why we get trapped in this vicious dieting circle and can become completely obsessed trying to manipulate our bodies. Set point was developed by Dr William Bennet and researcher Joel Gurwin in 1982.

This theory basically explains that we have a pre-determined genetic weight, meaning if we ate normally – (which yes, does involve overindulging, and yes, may involve not quite getting enough one day,) a balance – by eating intuitively listening to our bodies' hunger signals without thinking about it constantly, our weight is in our genetics, already decided. If you think about your body's height for example, that is in your genetics, if you feel you are too tall, do you spend so much time and energy trying to become shorter? No, so why do we do it with our weight?

Our bodies can cope with day-to-day fluctuations; we have this amazing thing called a metabolism which does all this for us! Let me explain a little further how. Our body's temperature for example, when we get too hot, our natural defences kick in to try and cool us down and we may sweat more, as our body adjusts, our weight works in exactly the same way.

If we overeat one day, our bodies will do things, naturally, like increasing our metabolism and slowing down our hunger signals to keep us at our set weight, our pre-determined genetic weight. However, what happens when we fight against our own DNA, try and lose weight for example below what our set point is?

Well, your body does not like this, at all. Your metabolism will slow down, making you feel colder and more tired as your body is trying to preserve energy, you will feel hungrier and think about food more as your natural hunger signals rise.

Also, another fact I found very interesting was that being below your set point and restricting like I said, can raise your hunger signals. What happens when we deny ourselves a bit of chocolate over and over again because it is bad food? We then cannot stop thinking about it, because our body actually needs it. So, what do we do? End up eating the whole bar. Then perhaps another one, resulting in a binge, which can then result in us actually gaining weight whilst trying to diet.

I was sat in treatment just thinking "*What? Why is this not being taught in schools, why is this not more talked about? It is the secret that the dieting industry does not want us to know, they are making money off us not knowing this?*"

And all of a sudden, the last 14 years of my life, the reason my weight was like a yo-yo and how I became trapped in this eating disorder made so much sense! I then saw the fact that I had two options, continue trying to manipulate my body into something it is not genetically designed to be, battling with my own DNA, constantly battling with all my issues, continuing not to enjoy my life, ordering the salad if I dared to go out, and obsess purely on how I look. OR, accept the fact that, OK, I am going to be bigger than what I like, live my life, be healthy, mentally and physically and be happy. It seems so obvious, but I was still engaging in many behaviours that kept my disorder going.

I was gaining weight, when going through recovery this happens. It is going to happen even if you were a healthy BMI to begin with. My journey accepting my set point was far from easy. I could tell I was getting bigger and kept trying to trick my rational brain. If I just eat a bit of fruit instead of a cereal bar I might not gain as much, if I make sure I am eating really healthily, that is looking after myself, nothing to do with ED.

However, every thought I had, I can now recognise it was indeed ED trying to find new ways to lure me back into its lethal trap. I had to stick to my meal plan from my dietician and trust the professionals. I felt like I was being torn in two, part of me wanted to quit recovery and just maintain, not fight with the voice anymore. The other part of me wanted to keep going, keep fighting and fully recover.

I finished an appointment with my therapist and had just got home, I had been weighed during the session and looked what my weight was. It was higher than I ever remember. the ED thoughts were running away with me, convinced recovery was just making me fat and I had to up my exercise a little and just restrict a little, that is what I decided to do.

It resulted in me only eating safe foods and doubling my agreed exercise limit. Within days the physical elements of the ED were returning, elements that had nearly completely vanished, back with vengeance. I was cold, could not think straight, I was snappy and irritable. It was not long at all before my husband noticed and one evening, he questioned me what was going on.

I fell to the floor in my exercise gear in complete tears, I looked up at him and said,

"My brain is literally being torn in two, I don't want to keep gaining, I do not like nor accept my set point, but if I

fight it, I just end up back here, in eating disorder misery. I do not know what to do."

He sat on the floor with me and cradled me. I spoke with my husband, who reminded me what was more important than being slim, reminding me that the perfect body does not exist, how this behaviour will only lead to an early grave and trusting the professionals, trusting my own body to reach its set point and then learning to accept my new body, my physically well body, then my mind would heal too. I had to trust my body and accept my set point. This was not an easy process but again what choice did I have? I knew if I wanted to be recovered once and for all from this eating disorder chaos I was trapped in, I needed to accept my set point.

Of course, I knew he was right, I wanted to keep working towards recovery. This feeling of being torn completely in two is normal and one of the hardest things I had to overcome. I had to unlearn everything I thought I knew from the diet culture and constantly remind myself about set point theory.

I laminated the printout I received from day programme and pinned it onto the kitchen cupboard and read through it every day, until I could recite it. I kept sticking to my meal plan, however also allowing myself to have spontaneous date nights, and meals with friends, trusting this theory that my weight fluctuates but my body will keep it in the range it knows will keep me healthy. After months of battling, I was weighed again, another jump, but this time I was not so freaked out. I reminded myself that my body knows what it is doing, I should trust it, trust the professionals.

Another few weeks later when I was weighed again, I was astonished, stunned, my weight had come down a little. But I was eating no less than before, exercising no differently, in fact I had eaten more than what was on my plan as I had gone out for a meal with friends. How could I have lost a little weight?

My therapist then explained to me that sometimes in recovery we overshoot our set points, it is common. Our bodies are just taking a little time working out where our weight needs to be and also by sticking to the meal plan, regular eating and not compensating, your body knows you are not going to starve it, your body also needs to learn to trust you again, so does not hold on to everything you eat. I had overshot my set point, however this was proof I had reached my set point and proof that this was a real thing and actually worked.

One thing I did find, which I will continue to share, is once I reached my set point, a weight in which my body was happy with, all of those symptoms of an eating disorder started to vanish.

I felt well again, my body image issues started to fade, as I recognised it was pointless trying to manipulate my body into something it is just not meant to be. My self-confidence grew, as I embraced and actually started to celebrate my body and the binge purge restrict cycles had stopped.

My body physically had healed and my mind was well on its way. And from that moment, I have never looked back. I will not eat numbers, I will eat food. I am now according to that BMI chart overweight, but for the first time in my life, I am living, not weighing out my salad, or saying no to going out for a coffee with friends, my heart rate has doubled and is now healthy, and all the other issues I had including fertility issues have improved. So much so in fact, that now I have stopped dieting and I have accepted my set point, allowed my body to get to the size it needed to be at. I'm eating well and exercising because I want to, not because I have to. I am now well enough to carry a child, and the healthiest I have ever been. That BMI chart told me that I was healthy, when I was stuck in eating disorder chaos, but those behaviours, the fact that my body was shutting down, does that really sound healthy to you?

So now I have explained set point theory to you, just think for a moment, have your views on the dieting industry changed? The diet circle is real and I was trapped in it for too long. I kept thinking, oh I need to lose weight, so I would go on a diet, lose weight, but then the second I ate a little more normally, I just put the weight back on (set point theory). So, I would once again try a diet, lose weight, then eat normally (set point), I would gain weight... do you see where I am going with this?

Diets do not actually work long term and your body will fight to get back to its set point. I can put money on this, just ask someone who next says they are doing one of these big multi-million-pound industry diets, how many times they have done it? Because I bet it's more than once. I used to, and yo-yoing constantly was a lot more damaging for my health and just led to me being a big eating disorder mess than if had just accepted that (according to the outdated and dangerous BMI chart) I was going to be overweight.

Please stop wasting your money and do what I have done. Accept your set point, accept your body, and live. Fully.

You see, life really is too short for self-hatred and celery sticks! All these diets, Cambridge, Slimming World, Weight Watchers, Slim Fast, you name it I've tried it, diet pills, detox teas, fruit cleanses, shake diets, and my new personal favourite, lifestyle change. I found that all of these were not sustainable in the long-term. Which encourages very disordered behaviours which can be deemed as normal in the dieting industry. Rebel and get your life back.

Changing Clothes/ Fear Clothes

I recognised it took me ages to get ready for anything as my need to constantly change my clothes was exhausting. The only way I managed to overcome this was simply once again, throwing myself in making myself feel anxious and riding the wave. I challenged myself one day to leave the house as soon as I got changed, not to get redressed. Simply pull something out of my wardrobe, put it on and leave. There was a reason each item of clothing was in my wardrobe, I liked it and bought it, therefore if I liked something and enjoyed wearing it once that should be enough.

I was already running slightly late, I was supposed to be meeting a friend for a coffee and a catch up. I pulled a dress out of my wardrobe paired it with my leggings and was about to leave the house. I caught sight of myself in the mirror before I left, automatically my thoughts turned distorted. *I looked awful, my friend would be embarrassed, I have to get changed.* Then I looked at the time, I was already fifteen minutes late, if I got changed again that outfit would probably not be right either and the ED would pick fault at that somehow. I then remembered I had worn this dress a load of times, it was one of my old faithfuls - colourful, floaty and just me. I said out loud:

"*No I am not getting changed again, I have worn this loads before, and it is okay and now go, you are late.*"

I got in the car and stated to drive into the city, I passed Tesco on the way and remember thinking, I could just pop in really quickly and see if there is something better to wear, something that looks better. I look awful. Again, recognising the thought I rode the anxiety wave and drove straight past it with gritted teeth, wanting to cry. I felt like I was about to burst but focused on what I was about to do, see my friend and have a good catch up. I reached my friend and we hugged as we greeted each other, at first, she teased me for being late and then she stepped back and said,

"*You always look fab, I love that dress.*"

Instantly, of course I assumed she was lying, then remembered she is my friend, I trusted her, she would not lie to me and all that chaos when I was trying to leave the house really was just the ED voice, trying to manipulate me.

I was so proud I had just gritted my teeth and rode the anxiety wave instead of giving in to the voice.

The next stage, once I accepted my set point and started to learn how to challenge my negative thoughts around my body and stopped constantly changing my outfit, was to face my fears. I had become scared of so many different items of clothing and so many different scenarios. The thought of going swimming had actually made me physically sick. And once I learnt to be body neutral this anxiety started to ease.

I put myself in so many uncomfortable situations in order to overcome them. I made myself go swimming. I was so convinced that everyone would laugh at me and so convinced that people would be grossed out by my disgusting body, but I made myself do it, because actually it really did not matter. I was entitled to swim if I wanted and if that is what people think, then it is them that has the issue, because what does it actually matter?

I used the step ladder approach which I explained in the restriction section. I would build myself up to wear something I thought was challenging:

Step 1 – Go swimming full swim costume with someone you trust.

Step 2 – Go swimming on my own, in swimming costume.

Step 3 – Buy a bikini – wear it in the garden sunbathing only.

Step 4 – Wear it swimming with someone I trusted.

Step 5 – Go for it, head to the beach in that item of clothing that is so terrifying.

Similar to the restriction element, I had to repeat a few steps on the way, but eventually I did it! I was anxious and a complete wreck the first time I wore it, convinced everyone was laughing and looking, judging me. I was too fat to be wearing this surely? However, the more I kept redoing this task, the more situations I put myself in, the better I could ride that anxiety wave.

We see it everywhere don't we? In magazines, across social media, *get bikini body ready*! What is this sort of thing actually saying? That you have to look a certain way to be allowed on the beach in a bikini, why? I had these issues at every size, when I was very slim, I was once told I could not wear a body fitting dress because I did not have the right shape. I am sorry the same rules apply to the bikini, why do I need to be a specific body type to wear this item of clothing?

I see this meme everywhere on a lot of body positive accounts I follow on social media and I love it:

how to get a bikini body…

step one, go to the beach.

step two, put on a bikini.

Boom bikini body done.

We should be allowed to wear what we like, if you enjoy wearing it, you do it! I used to be afraid of wearing shorts, or playsuits because I was embarrassed of my tree trunk legs, that is one phrase from the school bullying that haunted me the most. In the summer it could be 30 degrees (give or take as this is England), but I would still wear leggings, covered up, because I was afraid of what people might say, afraid of being called fat.

What is it with that word? It is at the end of the day just an adjective, and I am fat and what? As J.K Rowling once said,

"…is 'fat' really the worst thing a human being can be? Is 'fat' worse than 'vindictive', 'jealous', 'shallow', 'vain', 'boring' or 'cruel'? Not to me"

Calling people names and body shaming others, makes you these things, which again is the worst thing you could truly be.

I used the step ladder approach and started to wear shorts and playsuits more, when I was with trusted people, and when I was having therapy. I knew I could wear whatever I liked without judgement, so I started to challenge the voice telling me I could not wear them, putting myself in uncomfortable situations to overcome my fears, riding the anxiety wave and reminding myself it did not matter what others think, what do I think? Am I comfortable and cool? That should be all that matters.

We also get hung up on sizes, but, what does that size matter? I have been guilty of it, squeezing into a pair of jeans that only just fit because they are the size down, instead of actually buying the jeans that fit me and look better because they fit right.

I actually remember in recovery, when I was battling with my set point, I was sat in Debenhams with tears streaming, and I mean *streaming* down my face because this particular style of dress did not fit. It was the size I had worn for the past year or so, but as we know different brands can fit differently, and also my body was healing from the disorder as I continued my journey. I sat for a while like I said in tears, then I actually started to laugh, then I got the giggles. God knows what people must have thought, but was I really going to let this dress make me feel this worthless and rubbish about myself? Was I really going to let this bother me for the rest of the day, and start blaming myself for the fact this dress did not fit right? HELL NO.

It was just a piece of material; I refused to let that item of clothing ruin how I felt about myself. I kind of composed myself and got the next size up, and it fitted perfectly, lesson learnt, sizes in each shop really are different, and it does not matter anyway, if I feel good in it, if I like the item of clothing, I am going to wear it, regardless of what the label may say.

FAT IS NOT A FEELING!

This is possibly one of my favourite ever phrases, I was sat in day programme and I said the phrase, I feel fat. Within an instant my community support worker had shouted, "*fat is not a feeling, what are you feeling?*" It annoyed me to begin with, as it felt he had disregarded what I was feeling, but it really did get me thinking.

So many times, I would say, "*I feel fat*", we probably all do at some point. However, it's more likely that there's something underlying that's at the root cause. You can feel full, feel bloated, I understand and emphasise with that, however fat is not an emotion and you cannot feel it. What I was really feeling was often uncomfortable in my body for some reason. When I had my worst body image negative thoughts it was when my mood was low or something had happened to make me feel insecure.

Let me give you an example. I had been working loads of overtime, I had just found out I was pregnant, I had a few big media campaigns on the go for eating disorder awareness week, I had a body image workshop I was delivering I needed to prepare for, I was writing a few articles for some newspapers that had been in touch and I was also writing this book, as well as my normal caring duties, day to day chores and generally living.

I was slowly getting exhausted and struggling to keep up with everything, I felt like I was losing control. I got home from work and my husband said to me,

"*What would you like for tea we have not done the meal plan for today?*"

I sat and thought about it, and replied with,

"*We should have something healthy, I just feel really fat today.*"

He stopped, and looked at me and reminded me, what my community support worker had said, fat is not a feeling. He then spent some time with me working out what I was really feeling, I paused and reflected. I felt stressed, out of control almost, with so much going on, I was feeling frantic and overwhelmed. So, the next day when I was asked to work overtime I said no, which is amazing and novel for me. But I went home and took some much-needed time out for me, practiced self-care. I just felt like I had hit the reset button. Then all of a sudden, the feeling and subconscious body shaming had stopped, because I felt better within myself.

I jump on others now as well, when I hear them say "I feel fat". I literally find myself shouting, fat is not a feeling, what are you feeling? And between us we always manage to find out what is actually causing them to feel this way. Stressed, tired, burnt out, or they have been comparing themselves to others. There is always a reason behind saying this, again using myself as the example, I felt fat whenever I was experiencing a negative emotion. It came down to emotional avoidance, I was taking out whatever was happening, my negative feelings and frustrations, on myself instead of actually dealing with them.

Key points to take away

- Please go and check out my TEDx talk on YouTube and educate yourself further on set point theory. It is called 'Healthy weight unhealthy mind – embracing your set point'.
- Being stuck in a never-ending dieting circle is no way to live your life.
- When you step away from diet culture you actually have so much more free time to do things you enjoy. You start living. Your quality of life all of a sudden improves.
- A life counting calories instead of memories is not the life I want.
- The BMI chart cannot tell you how healthy you really are.
- You cannot cure negative body image by changing your size. The work needs to be done on your mind, how do you perceive your whole self, and why are looks important to you?
- Our bodies are meant to be different, we are not all the same shoe size or height, so we are not all going to be the same weight.
- Your clothes should fit you, if they no longer fit, then they are not fit for purpose. Get rid of them and find clothes that represent your style and you feel comfortable in.
- You already have the bikini body, you do not need to look a certain way to wear certain clothes. Unrealistic beauty standards and diet culture is the problem. Not you.
- You may feel "fatter" but please dig a little deeper and explore what else could be going on for you. Is there a reason you could be feeling this way?
- I realised I was fatphobic, I was scared of fat or getting

fat. How society treats those in larger bodies is unacceptable. Learning the root of my phobia and realising I was wrong helped me. Fat is not the worst thing a human can be.

- Exposure work is difficult, but it does get easier. Log your experiences and journal along the way to help channel your thoughts.
- No one that matters cares what size you are, they love you for the size of your heart, not the size of your jeans.

Chapter 12
Checking Behaviours

Self-Weighing

I needed to know, I needed to know if my weight had changed since this morning, I ate breakfast, how on earth could I have been so stupid? I ran upstairs and stepped on the scale, it was one pound more than what I weighed in the morning, and I felt what seemed like my world, collapsing around me. How could this be, it was just natural 0% fat Greek yogurt and some blueberries, how could I have gained, this cannot be possible? I needed to exercise now, I needed to restrict more, I needed to lose that weight quickly.

I used to only weigh myself once a week, on a Monday morning as soon as I woke up. However, as the years progressed and the ED took more of a hold over me, it became twice a week - Monday and then a check mid-week.

Very quickly, it was not enough and I started to weigh myself every day. Every morning, very quickly this still did not satisfy that eating disorder voice, and I started to weigh myself twice a day, morning and then again at night. Obviously, it was going to be different, our weight fluctuates throughout the day, but my rational mind could not see this. I was heavy at night, I had gained weight throughout the day, I needed to restrict and exercise more, it was the only way. I was somehow getting fatter throughout the day.

Very quickly weighing myself twice a day was simply not enough, I needed to know at all times of the day what my weight was. Whenever we went out, I would weigh myself just before we left the house, and as soon as we got home, I would weigh myself again. So, I could keep track of exactly what I weighed. If we were out and I saw some scales, the temptation would be too much, and very often I would jump on them just to see what they said. If we were visiting friends and family and they had scales, again I'd give in to temptation and use them. There was also a set at the gym which I would use, before and after each workout. I constantly had to know what my weight was. It became one of the first things I could think about every morning, and my weight would play on my mind before managing to fall asleep. I had become completely obsessed with yet more numbers.

I kept a notepad of my habits and every day I would make sure I included my weight at the top of the page. Then every week I did an overview, I could see I had lost weight, I could see the number going down and I seemed to have a sense of achievement. I was still getting praised and compliments for losing weight, so this just encouraged me.

When I was at work, I found it very difficult, as I worked ten-hour shifts, if not more. I would weigh myself every morning just before I left, but then the second I got home or to the gym, I would weigh myself again, then before I left the gym I would weigh myself again, then just before bed.

When I ate a meal, I would have to weigh myself afterwards too, so I knew how much weight I had gained from eating. My rational brain was gone, it knew that this was not how it worked, but my ED voice was in full control when it came to the scales, and it constantly had to keep tabs. This became my daily routine. At the weekend it would be so much more, every few hours if I was at home, I needed to remind myself just how fat I was and remind myself why I was restricting and engaging in all these behaviours. It would be worth it surely?

I came home one day after work and my daily gym venture, went to use the scales and they did not work. How could this be? Normally they warn me if the batteries are going. I checked the batteries and discovered they were missing. I stormed downstairs and confronted James, he was very honest and told me he had taken the batteries out, as he believed what I was doing was completely ridiculous. He had recognised how I would not eat if that number was not where the ED believed it should be, he wanted me to eat something that night.

His plan completely backfired. If I could not weigh myself I could not eat, I could not risk it. It caused another almighty row, as once again I could not see his point of view, I could not understand why keeping track of my weight was such a terrible thing to do, everyone did it. He tried explaining that a lot of people may weigh themselves once a week, not five times a day, but I was just being extra cautious, extra careful, nothing more. I threatened that if he did not give me the batteries back, I would drive to the supermarket and replace them, he told me where he had hid the batteries and I quickly put them back into the scales and weighed myself, feeding the anxiety.

My weight did drop, a significant amount, I was larger before the ED took full grips of me, so my weight still did not seem too drastic, but it was the speed and how I was losing it which was very dangerous. I could see on the scales that it was going down, and I swore, just a few more pounds and I would stop, once I reached my target weight, I would be happy. However, once I did reach that target weight, I would set myself a new target and it would start all over again.

The number kept getting lower and lower. My target kept decreasing, no matter how many times and how quickly I would reach my new target. It would not be enough for that ED mind. It would not please that the ED voice, it continued to push me.

We were camping in Newquay, we both surf so we go there a few times a year to blow off some steam and spend all the time in the calming waves. I did not pack the scales. James point blanked refused to take them with us, and even I thought it was a bit daft taking them camping with us, but how would I know what my weight would be throughout the week. I couldn't possibly go a whole week without knowing, I debated trying to sneak them in my shower bag, but they were glass and I knew they would get smashed amongst all the camping equipment we had. So, my rational brain knew I had to leave them behind. The first day I was okay, I weighed myself in the morning before we left and when we stopped at the services, as it was a seven-hour drive from where we live, there were some scales in the services, so I was able to weigh myself mid-day and see my weight again. I was not too anxious in the evening, as we had spent the whole day travelling then putting up the tent and setting up and had a swim. By the time we had done all this we went to sleep.

The next morning, I searched each of the campsite facilities for some scales. There might be some somewhere, there must be - there was not. It had been the first time in ages I had not weighed myself in the morning and the anxiety was getting too much to bear. I tried to carry on with the day, and when we walked into the town after surfing all morning, I searched the shops for scales. However, it was a tourist area we were in that day, so there was none, nowhere. I wanted to cry. I needed to know what my weight was, I had to know! My ED voice was screaming at me that it was going to be double if I could not keep track of it. We needed to pick up some groceries from the supermarket for tea, I had agreed to try and eat one meal a day while we were on holiday, as I knew I would be in the water a lot and knew actually I needed to be clear headed and focused. One meal was not enough and I was foolish looking back, but we found a local ASDA. I walked towards the toilets and my heart skipped a beat, there was a BMI checker near the facilities. Finally, I would be able to keep track, just a little. Without hesitation I paid and jumped on them and waited nervously for it to print out my weight, height and BMI. I was mortified it was different to when I'd set off the day before, again ignoring the fact I had layers of clothing on, wet hair and also had drank a lot of fluid throughout the day, as we were active.

Every day on the holiday, I made us visit that ASDA for some reason. Every day I would find something that we needed, just so I could weigh myself, it was only once a day, but I kept telling myself, as soon as we got home, I could keep track better. I just needed to get through the week, I just needed to persevere. Between all the number checking, calories in and out, weight and focusing on my size, ED had completely ruined yet another holiday. Another bunch of memories tainted by that ED voice and the needing to please it constantly, even though it was never possible to please, it would never be happy.

I was ashamed of my weight, embarrassed. I had spent so long losing it and worked so hard to get to where I did, I did not want my weight to go up, I did not want to gain. Every time I got weighed in treatment, I felt sick, my anxiety would skyrocket and it would set me back a little for a few days afterwards.

According to the BMI chart I was healthy, so in my eyes I struggled to see why losing weight was a bad thing. I needed to lose the weight, I was in the overweight category before, and for me that meant unhealthy. I did not want to gain, I could see my BMI lowering and knew I would reach the underweight category, however part of me wanted that. I wanted to be underweight, I wanted to be tiny. I did not care about the consequences or the effects that losing all this weight was having on body, I was healthy, the BMI chart told me so, why should I listen to my treatment team?

As I continued treatment my rational brain could see what I was doing, and knew even when I did reach underweight, it would not be enough to please the ED voice. I had already damaged parts of my body beyond repair, but the thought of gaining, even though I was healthy, was torture. My weight never leaped up dramatically, of course it went up throughout recovery, it needed to, but it made my eating disorder voice scream at me. I could not seem to get the balance right for self-weighing. I needed to be ok with that number, so I would weigh myself every now and then at my parents, and then have to challenge all the thoughts. I knew I could not completely avoid the scales all my life, there was going to be times I had to be weighed and I needed to be OK with that and not be triggered. I had to learn to accept that the number is just a number.

One morning, I weighed myself. Of course, I was not happy with that number, I never was. So as a result, I skipped breakfast and headed straight to day programme. The session that day was contributing and maintain factors, what was keeping our eating disorders going. We discussed as a group pros and cons of getting rid of the scales, I knew I had to, I could see how they were maintaining my disorder, and yet still something was holding me back. Our community support worker empathised with us, he had been in our shoes and completely understood. He then told us, he smashed his with a sledge hammer, he was furious with them and how he felt controlled by this number, unable to move forward because he was too obsessed with this number. I sat there and realised; this was me.

I thought hard about what both my therapist and our community support worker had told us, my husband and I were supposed to be having a nice meal together that evening, however already I was fretting over how much weight I was going to gain. I had to get out of this somehow. I went upstairs and weighed myself, then I could weigh myself after the meal and figure out how much exercise I needed to do and how many laxatives I had to take.

Then I stopped. I remembered what our community support worker said, these scales had complete control of me. They controlled my life. I was fed up with constantly obsessing and realised I had been missing out on so much - meals out with friends, Sunday dinners with the family, days out with James, drinks with the girls. I had missed out on a chance of happiness; I was missing out on life. If I dared to go out, dared to enjoy myself, I would come home, stand on the scales and they would tell me I had failed. This was not what I wanted out of life, this is not how I want to live.

In that moment I grabbed my husband, wrote down all my feelings and frustrations, grabbed my scales and headed outside. I was shaking, furious as I had realised just how much of my life had been given to this object, just how much I believed they measured my self-worth. I got James to record what I was saying, reiterating how much of my life I had wasted, obsessing on this number, how many missed memories because I was too frightened of what a number would tell me. I wanted my life back and I could not do that if this number checking continued, the scales were denying me a chance of recovery, and in that moment I decided, enough was enough.

I raised the scales above my head and smashed them on the floor, the glass shattered everywhere and I wanted to cry with relief, and then just for good measure I got the hammer to the mechanism as well, just to make sure and to release the last of the frustration I had left. The rush, the exhilaration, the freedom. In that moment I realised I had committed myself to recovery.

Once I did this, I found the constant obsession over my weight did start to decrease. Of course this did take time, just because I had got rid of the scales at home, did not mean I could not weigh myself, there were still scales at the gym, at my parents' house, friends' houses, supermarkets. I got rid of mine but then my mind would fixate on them whenever I saw them. However, I had this new sense of stubbornness, I had gotten a taste of what recovery could mean and it helped my rational brain fight.

I kept reminding myself of how I felt when I finally got rid of the scales, how that number had controlled me and life was more than that number on the scale. I of course did slip up now and then, it is unfortunately part of recovery, hiccups happen, and what I have found so interesting is every time I weighed myself my thoughts would come flooding back, and I would end up engaging in unhealthy and unhelpful behaviours.

Measuring

Monday already! Time to retake my measurements. Every week I would write down my measurements and keep a record in my notebook, similar to my weight, I could keep track on what my body was doing.

I would measure my stomach, hips, chest, bum and thighs. All of my major problem areas. Which looking back, makes me chuckle as I saw my whole body as one big problem. This is something I have done for as long as I can remember, since the age of fourteen I would measure myself every now and then, but as the ED progressed it became a weekly check in.

I could monitor my progress. More numbers to become obsessed with. I kept the tape measure in my top draw along with my laxatives, diet pills and notes on progress. Once again, my husband did question my unusual habits, but my eating disorder mind could argue with anything he said. He would remind me that sometimes our bodies can bloat, and our bodies can change, but I saw any slight change, any slight increase, as the absolute worst-case scenario. When I did measure weekly, when the ED was in full force, it only went up very slightly once. And when I say very slightly it was the case of a millimetre.

It was my best friend's wedding, I was bridesmaid and we had planned to spend the whole day and night before the wedding with fellow bridesmaids in this cottage near the venue. There was a BBQ for my friend's families and other friends, fellow bridesmaid and partners, to join us to celebrate the events the next day. We had a few drinks, it was relaxed good fun, so I joined in and had a few things to eat at the party, very consciously picking things I thought might have less calories.

The next day was incredible, but lots of fears to overcome, however, I was not going to make a scene on my best friend's wedding day! There were ten bridesmaids in total, the morning of the wedding was chaos, we had some pastries and prosecco first thing in the morning while we were getting ready. Then of course arrival drinks after the wedding and we had an incredible two course meal followed by more drinking and celebrating. ED was very much screaming at me, but I was adamant not to let this ruin the day, I did not want anyone to know or guess what was going on, not today, this was my friend's day.

The next day my husband cooked everyone in the cottage a fry up, and we sat down and reminisced on what an incredible day we'd had. As soon as we got home, I of course had to weigh and measure myself. Despite my husband pleading with me, reminding me that my body might be bloated, we had drank a lot, eaten a little more than usual but to remember how much fun we had, my eating disorder brain saw no truth in his logic, I was fat. I had gained a lot of weight and my measurements had gone up very slightly, I clearly could not have fun, this was what happened when I did, I had failed once again. The same day I went for a really long run and refused to eat anything. It took a few days for me to calm down before I could eat anything again, and my exercise spiralled.

Once I had stopped my scales obsession, I realised this was my next step. I was still writing down my measurements and focusing in particular on my stomach, thighs and biceps. I thought if I could shrink them smaller, I would be happier, if I was smaller, I would be happier. It gave me a focus, something to pour my negative emotions into. However, it turns out the smaller I got, the more depressed and obsessed I became, being smaller did not make me happy, I was not living, I was existing.

One morning when I was about to engage in my weekly measurements I stopped and realised I could not do it. I had gotten rid of my scales and this needed to be next. Before I could change my mind, I grabbed my tape measure and binned it. There. Gone. Again, I had a sense of achievement and felt somewhat rebellious. I was rebelling against that eating disorder voice, of course it was going to scream at me for doing this, but I wanted to recover. As the week went on, my mind was whirling not knowing what my measurements were. *What if they all of a sudden went up? What if I was getting obese and did not know?* These thoughts seemed so logical however I was able to challenge them, just because I did not know my weight or size. My team did still weigh me, they would be able to intervene if I was gaining too quickly, recovery is a process and it takes time to heal.

I realised even though I had stopped self-weighing and measuring my body, I was still finding ways to keep track of my body. I had starting using my hands to measure my body instead, however, this is so inaccurate and was only fuelling and contributing to my disorder. I spoke to and was honest with my therapist about this and we had a discussion one day about these behaviours in a session. We discussed how I still felt my self-worth was based on how I looked, how others would see me differently and even dislike me if I was bigger. We talked about how long I had struggled with eating disorders for, and how I had already been every size possible due to restricting, binging and just being stuck in an eating disorder whirlwind.

I then realised my friends have always been my friends and have never treated me any differently regardless of what size I was. My friends love me for me, not for the number on the scale or the size of my jeans.

I was then tasked with a very cringeworthy piece of homework; I had to ask my friends why they actually liked me, what they liked about me. I hated this with a passion, but after I sent the message to a few friends I was overwhelmed with the responses.

They were telling me that I was a kind, loyal friend, who could always make them laugh and even though I was a party animal, I was still trustworthy and they knew they could count on me. As the responses continued to flood my inbox, I was completely overwhelmed, but what struck me the most was not one of my friends had mentioned my size or how I looked. They were all comments about my personality, nothing else.

I remember a tear trickling down my cheek and thinking, "*this is why my friends love me, this is why they want me in their lives, and it has nothing to do at all with my size*". For years I truly believed they liked me less when I was bigger. That they made fun of me and would turn their backs on me if I got bigger again. But these amazing people in my life have always loved me, regardless of my size. They love me for me and my personality, nothing more. I started to focus on my inner qualities instead of being so obsessed with numbers, started to focus on who I was, and accepting I had good qualities. This seemed to catapult me forward in recovery and aided so much in me stopping these checking behaviours.

Every inch of our bodies is beautiful inside and out. Why we are so focused on numbers, do numbers really measure our self-worth? We are not a number; we are human beings with strong fierce personalities. Society and diet culture have us believe our self-worth is based on numbers, the number on the scale and the size of our jeans.

No, I say no more. I refuse to be judged on who I am based on these numbers. I will be judged however, on what I do, my personality and the way I treat others, because this is what measures our true self-worth, this is what makes us truly beautiful.

Fitness App

We live in a world now where we have access to a wide variety of apps, and ways to monitor our health and encourage weight loss. I had every app available, the one I had become completely addicted to was my fitness tracker app. I wore a smart watch around my wrist and as previously mentioned it allowed me to track my calories in and out. I wore it all day and night and only took it off to shower. Every opportunity I had I was on the app, looking at how many calories had gone out already that day and how many steps I had done. I was constantly looking up food on the database to research what had the least calories in certain food groups, and what exercise routines it suggested for me in order to burn the most calories.

I could also track how many minutes of exercise I was doing each day. It would auto recognise when you had been moving for a set amount of time and track it as exercise. My new challenge, keep moving all day, keep my heartbeat up from the moment I woke up to the minute I went to sleep. Of course this was completely impossible, however, I kept trying. Every day I would monitor how many minutes I had exercised each day and compare it to previous days and see where I could improve. The app also allowed you to invite friends to a step challenge, who could do the most steps in a week. I took part in these challenges with everyone and anyone who would accept the invitation. It was another way for me to keep focused and also it became a mask for my ever-increasing disorder, a way to hide how out of control I had gotten.

I was asked all the time why I was pacing. I was able to say, oh I am doing a step challenge with, whoever, and just like that, it was acceptable. It was quite common in our workplace to do these challenges, so no one became suspicious. I was praised all the time for my determination and drive to beat my fellow friends, it became a joke and a bit of fun. I was laughing about it and others would remind me to keep walking to get my steps up, they were actually encouraging me in this unhealthy competition, no one knew it was not just a competition with them I was in, but a competition with myself.

It had very quickly become another fixation, from the second I placed it on my wrist, I had more numbers to focus on, more ways to feed my disorder and more ways to completely waste my time. It also had a weight section within the app, where you could enter your weight and enter your goal weight, it would then give you a maximum amount of calories you could eat each day in order to reach your goal. I followed this well, until of course it was not enough and I needed to go lower and lower. A much occurring theme with ED. It seems to start off okay and then very quickly you can spiral. I loved the graph on the app. I could see my weight going down, and again the app gave me affirmation, it kept congratulating me when I had reached my goal and encouraged me to set a new one. It never questioned how quickly I was losing the weight, how could it? It was just a piece of technology.

This particular fitness app could also monitor my heart rate, which actually became quite useful. When I first began to realise something might not be right, it was because of this fitness tracker. It would monitor my heart rate throughout the day, and through the night and tell you your resting heart rate. Mine to begin with was 60 beats per minute, which is normal, then it started to get lower. I researched it a little bit and apparently people who are fit and healthy and exercise regularly can have a lower resting heart rate, so mine was now 50 beats per minute and I figured that was fine. However, as I continued to engage in more and more eating disorder behaviours, my heart rate dropped lower and lower, until it reached 35 beats per minute. I knew this was not right and for the first time actually questioned if it could be my excessive exercise that would cause this.

I noticed my heart rate was very high whenever I exercised, it could have been a very short walk and my heartrate was through the roof, but when I was resting, it was dangerously low. I knew this was not right and actually decided to visit the doctor. The thing that very much fed my disorder and enabled it to run riot was also the piece of technology that made me think and realise maybe something was not quite right here. As soon as I entered treatment and my resting heart rate rose to a stable beat, I knew I needed to get rid of my tracker. It was too easy to look at calories, and even if I turned the calorie counting bit of the app off, it was too tempting. I knew it would continue to feed my disorder, so after much persuasion from my treatment team I decided to change this habit.

I started by not charging it. Once it had run out of power I would take it off. Gone. Originally this did work for a few months, however I found myself being drawn towards it every time I opened my bedside draw. I was feeling a little stressed due to starting a different job and felt like I needed a sense of control. Opening up my draw, there was my answer, a way I could have control again. It was lying there, my fitness tracker.

I could just put it on and see how I was doing, see how many calories I was burning with my new exercise regime and log my meals to see what my intake and outtake is, what harm could it do? I decided to charge it up and put it back on, instantly pleasing the ED voice, giving in to its demands. Within hours I had become hooked again, logging everything and exercise became about burning calories again instead of celebrating what my body could do. My meals became smaller as I tried to keep my calories under a set amount and keep my outtake higher than my intake. A few days had passed and I had gone backwards in my recovery, engaging in old behaviours and losing things I had worked so hard on.

I had a community support appointment as I realised, I was falling and reached out for help. We sat in Costa and I was adamant I did not need or want a snack. After a discussion I was able to see it was because of calorie content and this would not help me recover, we sat at the table and were talking about my recent lapse. I was honest and told him I was tracking intake and outtake again.

He asked how I knew exactly what I was burning through exercise and I revealed I had put my fitness tracker back on. He did not need to say anything, he simply looked at me, with a slight smile and raised his eyebrows, I laughed and said,

"*Don't.*"

I knew what he was going to say, but he still said it.

"Is this behaviour helpful Zoe, is wearing that thing helping you recover or hindering it?"

I of course knew the answer, but I needed to know again, I needed to know what was going in and out of my body. However, did I? How did we manage without these devices? And was this behaviour helpful to me?

After doing some thought challenging and questioning the ED voice, I realised of course my community support worker was right, it was hindering my recovery. I could not and would not recover if this number checking continued, I needed to get to the root of what was bothering me, and at the time I was trying to avoid admitting I was feeling overwhelmed with this job, and obviously turned to unhelpful coping strategies. I decided that night to sell my tracker. It sold instantly and I delivered it, I then donated the money to BEAT.

The tracker was gone, out the house and out of temptations reach. Do I miss it? Not at all, I knew if I had kept it in the house, I would have fallen again, the temptation would have been far too great, it needed to be gone for good!

Once I had got rid of the tracker, I then had a good long hard look through my phone and was overwhelmed with shame and realisation. The number of apps I had, fitness apps, exercise apps, log my calories apps, was a little ridiculous and somewhat embarrassing. My phone was getting low on storage so I needed to delete something, but all I had on there was social media and fitness apps. Looking at my options, I could isolate myself even further from my friends and let the ED continue controlling me and falling.

Or I could focus on what really mattered, keeping in touch with those closest to me, and recovering. I was angry at the time as I remember I did not want to delete anything. It was my phone's fault, my memory card's fault, everything else's fault but my disorder. I realised I was shielding it but could not figure out why and then I snapped, deleting all my fitness apps, every single one, gone.

I did not need them on my phone and once I got rid of all these triggering apps, I realised that my exercise did not need tracking. I was able to enjoy exercise without focusing so much on calories, I was able to be more involved in my Zumba class and have a laugh instead of being glued to my tracker and my apps, checking how many calories I had burnt. I was able to take my time when out for walks, and actually appreciate the beautiful countryside in which I live, instead of again tracking my walks working out how far I had gone and once again being obsessed with how many calories I burnt.

My husband would often come for a stroll with me in the summer, and we walked hand in hand at a steady pace in the summer sun, getting completely lost down different routes we had never taken, exploring our local area and discovering the hidden beauties and scenic places on our doorstep, we never even knew existed. Walking seemed calming, enjoyable again, not a punishment and not driven by the need to burn calories. It was even the little things I noticed, walking to the shop I was not tracking my calories, simply enjoying the walk. I had more time in the evening as I was not going over every detail of activity during the day on the apps but actually spending time with my husband.

Seeking Reassurance

"Are you sure I don't look fat in this? You can be honest, please tell me the truth."

I was constantly asking James these questions, however no matter what he said, I would accuse him of lying to me. Nothing seemed to please that eating disorder voice. I truly believed he was lying to me every time he complimented my appearance. This of course would lead to more arguments, I did not understand why he was lying to me. I looked hideous, in everything, why would he lie? Eventually he stopped giving me compliments to avoid the arguments. ED then twisted this around, we would argue about how he never complimented my appearance - he must think I look awful, he must hate my body, he never says he likes it. The poor man could not seem to do anything right as far as he was concerned, and as far as ED was concerned, everything he said could be twisted, manipulated and turned into a negative.

It was summer, we were in town, enjoying the summer's day together and about to meet some friends, I was wearing a strappy top and some shorts, James complimented my chest, he loved my assets, he told me they looked good in that top, my brain managed to twist that into, he thinks they are big, big means fat, he is calling you fat. I of course felt hurt and ashamed so suggested we went shopping, I bought a new t-shirt with a higher neckline and short sleeves and changed into it before we met our friends,

I must have looked hideous. Truth is he just thought I looked nice, but ED can turn any compliment into a negative.

I had this habit of ignoring any positives. Any compliment I received about my body I would disregard, despite seeking it out in the first place. I knew my husband would not lie to me and my friends would in fact tell me if I looked awful in something. Whenever I went shopping, they were always so good at saying what suited me and what did not, so I could trust them. But how could I start accepting compliments on my body, and actually tune in and listen to what was being said to me?

This was extremely difficult to do, my ED brain had an argument and answer for everything, and every compliment could be twisted. However, I started using two very simple words whenever someone commented on my appearance or when I was indeed seeking reassurance. Instead of brushing it off or seeing it a different way, I would pause, re-play what they had just said to me and simply reply with, *thank you*. It felt wrong and uncomfortable, unnatural even, but as time went by I was able to start challenging the thoughts that everyone was lying to me, as I had started to absorb and listen to some of the complements on my appearance.

I had to stop seeking the reassurance; I had to learn to trust myself and not care so much what others thought I may or may not look like. I wanted to wear whatever I wanted to, without the fear of what others would think. When I got dressed in the morning, instead of asking my husband if I looked okay, I started asking myself, *do I like this outfit, is it me? Does it show off my true personality*? At the time I started doing this I still did not trust my own opinion, as I thought I looked dreadful in everything thanks to the ED voice, so when I did seek out reassurance from my husband and ask his thoughts, I had to learn to accept his first answer.

Sitting with his opinion and not trying to change it, this was his opinion and everyone is entitled to their opinion. It was painful and trying to fight with the voice telling me he was lying, recognising that these thoughts were not helpful and moving on to a different task, not focusing on what I was wearing or how I looked. I made my husband aware of what I was trying to do, so when I was seeking reassurance over and over again, he would not engage in the conversation, he would reply once and then the other replies were simply, I have already told you my opinion, and leave it at that.

This infuriated me, or rather, it infuriated ED. He would not give me the needed feedback over and over again, I had to learn to trust his first answer and not try and pull it apart and twist what he was saying.

Mirror Usage

Every day I would get into the habit of examining my body in the mirror. Every single morning, I would stand in front of my floor length mirror and allow my disordered brain to tear myself to shreds. Starting with the top of my body, my hair was a mess, it was a weird colour, my eyes have massive bags under them, I look pale. Scanning all the way down to my feet. My ankles are fat, why did you get a tattoo there it looks awful, you have masculine feet. Picking and pulling parts of my body as I scanned it, that was not toned enough, not slim enough, not muscly enough. I was not good enough.

I would pay particular attention to my stomach and legs, these were my main insecurities. I had uncertainties about all of my body, however these two parts seemed to be my worst, I had labelled them my "problem areas". I would have to do this routine every single morning. Reminding myself daily why I needed to continue my quest to shrink, why I needed to keep restricting and exercising. Every morning getting myself in the mindset that I was a fat ugly waste of space.

It was every time I glanced in the mirror, my mind would automatically pick out a flaw in my appearance, I would glance in a small face mirror in the bathroom and automatically think, your hair is a mess. A mirror could be anything that involved my reflection, from walking past shop windows and pausing to remind myself how awful I looked, to simply catching a glimpse of my reflection in the car or a bus, automatically I would pull myself down, bullying my own self esteem.

Shopping slowly became my worst nightmare purely because of the amount of mirrors in a changing room. I went shopping with a friend and I had picked up a dress on a sale rack and decided to try it on. It was a black skater dress with some butterflies on. I adore butterflies and it looked a really pretty dress. I stepped into the changing room to try it on and my heart started to race, I started to feel sick, all around me in this cubicle was mirrors. I could see my body at every angle and instantly my brain started screaming all these different insecurities at me, from every viewpoint of my body. I just stood for a few minutes and let my disordered mind take over, I then just sat on the floor and tears started rolling down my cheeks. I felt disgusted in myself, ashamed of how I looked, totally lost. I eventually calmed down, put the dress back and told my friend I did not feel great, so I had to leave, I went home and as soon as I got in, I got changed and went for a run, I had to. The ED voice was screaming at me, I was being haunted by my experience in the changing room.

Then when I got back from my run, I went straight back to the floor length mirror to see if I looked any different, to see if I had changed. Of course, I hadn't, so I spent the next ten minutes scanning my body picking out all my flaws.

Also, I would engage in this unhealthy habit whilst at the gym, there was a huge mirror across the wall so you could check your posture and check you were doing the exercises properly. I used it to push myself harder. Every circuit I did, I could see myself and my mind would instantly criticise my body and I would tell myself how fat I was, how I needed to keep pushing. Keep going. When I was on the treadmill, I could see my reflection in the windows in front of me, and again this would push me to work beyond my limits. I did not recognise how toxic this behaviour was, until my treatment team spoke to me about my checking behaviours and it was highlighted.

It became so obvious that mirror usage and my morning routine of pulling myself to pieces would set me in a bad mood and disordered way of thinking for the rest of the day. I knew it would affect what I ate and my exercise for the day but I could not stop. It had become my routine; a terrible habit and it was chipping away at my self-esteem every single time I looked at myself in the mirror.

The first thing I did was cover my mirror with Post-it notes, with quotes on them about body positivity. Random affirmations I found on the internet, such as, *life is too short to spend another day at war with your body* and *imagine what you could have done with the time you spent trying to shrink your body, you could have got shit done!* I also had quotes of what my husband liked about me, not just my body, such as he loved the fact I always painted my toenails stupidly bright colours and he loved how playful I am. Things reminding me of my real worth, and not focusing so much on numbers or my size.

I discussed my mirror usage in therapy and something I found particularly interesting, that was brought to my attention, was that the mirror only shows you a squashed version of yourself. If you stand in front of a full-length mirror and get someone to mark where your feet are and where your head is, then go and stand next to those marks, that is not a true representation of how tall you are, nor your size. It's a squashed mini you, not at all accurate. So, focusing on how I looked and appeared really was wasted time. Another thing I learnt to do was to start praising my body for all the amazing things that it can indeed do instead of criticising it.

When I looked in the mirror and started my self-criticism, I recognised the thoughts, and stopped myself and asked, *is this pattern of thoughts helpful? Is this a healthy way of thinking? No, what is a better way of seeing this situation*? I learnt to start praising my body, and again this is painful and uncomfortable to begin with, because we are not used to praising ourselves, but I encourage you all to do this.

When I hear myself saying things like, *oh my gosh my legs are like tree trunks*, I recognise the thought and think of how amazing my legs actually are. My legs may not look like how I want them to be, but I am thankful for them. Without them I would not be able to dance and jump for joy, I would not be able to walk or go swimming. Another thought might pop up, particularly for me I had an issue with my stomach area. Stop. Recognise the thought and give thanks to it. My stomach actually protects my reproductive system, it is there for a reason, it is doing a job, thank you.

I was teased relentlessly for being broad, but actually I am thankful for that, as it means I am strong. I am able to lift the kids up at work with ease.

I hope this makes sense to you. I delivered a workshop a few months ago teaching this technique, and I got each person to tell me their biggest insecurity and then flip it to a more neutral thankful approach. Here are some of my favourites:

- One young gentleman told me, he hated his unruly hair, but actually he accepted that there is nothing he could do with it. His friends actually love it and it's great if he is running late, it saves time.
- A young lady told me she hated being so short, this is my favourite, her spin on it was actually it is okay to be short, and it means she can be carried home easily when she has had too many drinks.

- A young man hated the fact he had small arms, no muscles on them, feminine arms. His positive spin; he could have muscles and spend all hours of the day at the gym or he could continue spending his free time with his girlfriend, who loved him anyway.
- An older lady who always hated her wrinkles, she struggled to see how they were a positive and then came out with, well, I suppose these are actually known as laughter lines. I am thankful for them as they remind me all the happy memories I have had.

I continue to thank my body and put a spin on all my insecurities, and by doing this every day, I have learnt to accept my flaws, they are not flaws, they are part of me, and the mirror does not seem such a scary thing anymore.

Key points to take away:

- Your weight will fluctuate throughout life, your worth however, will not.
- Smash the scales, get rid of them. What is the actual point in them? Your weight is the least interesting thing about you.
- No matter what the number on the scales say, it will never be low enough in the eyes of the eating disorder.
- Refuse to be judged on who you are based on numbers.
- You cannot cure negative body image by changing your appearance. You need to work on your mind, how you perceive your whole self.
- You deserve to take up space in this world.
- Think about what you love about a friend. I bet it has nothing to do with their weight. Same rule applies to yourself.
- Your fitness tracker or smart watch is not your pal.
- If you are using apps or a fitness tracker, ask yourself honestly. Is this helping or hindering my recovery? If hindering, bite the bullet and get rid.
- Mirrors cannot tell you how loved you are, putting positive affirmations from loved ones around your mirror can help you see the real beauty that lies within you.
- Our bodies do the most amazing things for us. Instead of hating them for what they are not, let's celebrate them, thank our bodies for all the amazing things that they can do for us.

Chapter 13
Implications On Those Who Care

Many people seem to forget the impact an eating disorder can have not just on the person struggling, but it has a domino effect, and everyone trying to support someone with this illness can feel overwhelmed and lost.

I found that everyone kept blaming themselves. My family for example kept saying, *"we were bad parents."* Truth is, it is no one's fault. I slightly detest that people were trying to take blame. I kept having to explain to loved ones that it was no one's fault, it was such a variety of different things and a way for me to feel in control and numb out negative emotions and traumas.

However, I can explain this until I am blue in the face and yet, people still feel the need to blame themselves, which makes me feel awful and somewhat guilty that I have made them feel this way, when again it is just not the case. Before entering treatment, I had isolated myself from so many friends as I refused to do anything other than exercise. I self-sabotaged many relationships to try and protect my illness. I have always been good at wearing a 'mask' if you like. My mask became very handy, and I learnt to wear it well. Whenever anyone asked if I was okay or started to get concerned I was able to throw them off the scent by appearing my bright bubbly and jokey self.

No one knew the war I was raging within myself. I looked so happy and cheerful whenever others were with me, how could I possibly have a problem? However, no matter how much I tried to hide and how well I wore my mask, a few had started to see what was going on, and I started to struggle to hide my behaviours and my mask slipped.

During this section I have asked some of my nearest and dearest to write their experiences down, what was their experience supporting me through this illness? From recognising that all might not be as well as I was trying to make out, to me entering treatment and relapse prevention.

Thank you to all those that loved me when I could not love myself.

Friends

Some of my closest friends struggled to come to terms with my diagnosis. I looked healthy, I was able to eat in front of them, I did not seem to have a problem. They did not see the aftermath of that meal or the anxiety building up beforehand. But then the more they thought about it, the more they realised it was there, it had always been there. Always dieting and exercising, talking about calories, and I always seemed to be busy.

My closest friends had no idea what was really going on, and during recovery it was suggested by my psychologist that the more open and honest I was with others, the less power the ED had. I was terrified about opening up, but the people I wanted to let in the most were my closest friends. How could I tell them I was in treatment for this illness, how were they going to react? Surely, they were going to disown me or dismiss my illness.

I was petrified of being pushed away by the people I loved and thought they would not want to be my friend once they found out I was struggling with an eating disorder. These were my husband's friends as well as mine, so by opening up to them, we thought it would give my husband some much needed support. We had started to see them less and less, in particular around mealtimes. I would make excuses to go home or cancel plans. At the time I could not see what I was doing, the ED masked my true feelings and I wanted to do anything to please that voice. Whenever we did see them, I felt not really present, as the thoughts about what I should be doing consumed me. I should not be here,

I should be exercising I could be burning calories, you are failing Zoe.

This of course was not the case, I found my friends still loved me and wanted to encourage me to get better. I was able to talk them through all of my thoughts and feelings despite the ED voice screaming at me to stop. They reminded me that they would be there and actually the thing that upset them the most was that I could not tell them sooner what was going on. Truth is though, I was not ready to open up as I could not explain what was going on. I had to understand the illness more myself before trying to explain to anyone else what was going on.

Emily's Story

I first met Zoe through my now husband. They went to university together and had become good friends during that time. My first memory of Zoe doesn't exist if I'm honest, I don't remember an initial meeting point. I was going through a few problems personally at that time, which has most probably removed the first year or so of our friendship from the forefront of my mind.

It wasn't until my husband and I were getting married that Zoe and I entered a strong friendship. I guess we began spending more and more time together as couples. We would often go out for meals together, have spontaneous trips to the zoo and Eurovision song contest parties. Not to mention the many BBQs we enjoyed together. We were a group who loved food and many of our gatherings seemed to be based around food or drink.

By the time it came to Zoe and James' wedding, I no longer felt like Jonty's wife. I actually could call them my friends too and not just Jonty's friends. I see them as family, and we were so excited to be a part of the wedding. Zoe had started a pre-wedding diet and was exercising lots, but I saw this as normal. At this time her personality was the same and she was still that bubbly person we love. It was the year following this that my concerns began.

In October 2017 I gave birth to a healthy baby girl and the first people at the hospital were of course Zoe and James. By May 2018 I was wondering where my friend was. We went from seeing them every week to rarely spending time together. I thought it was me and that now that I was a mum I wasn't as fun to be around. I always had my daughter with me, I had sleep deprivation and I didn't have as much freedom so maybe they wanted to spend more time with their other friends. My husband continued to have boys nights, which only upset me more as I was left alone.

I knew that something was wrong from looking at Zoe. Her face was gaunt, arms tiny and she didn't look well but she had told me the issue was with her heart. She wasn't lying but that wasn't the whole story. I had no reason to doubt what she was telling me as she is my best friend. I couldn't get much information from her and when asking my husband to 'check in' with James we didn't get much in return there either.

September 2018 arrived and I'd given up. By this point I had spent many an evening crying to my husband. I felt alone and I had lost my best friend. I'd made the decision that I was no longer asking to spend time together as I knew the answer would be no. I made my final attempt for normality and invited them for a meal and to my surprise they said yes.

The night arrived and everything seemed tense. We sat down to eat and I noticed Zoe was taking more time than normal. I thought *Oh no she might not like it, I should've cooked something safer.* About halfway through the meal Zoe looked to James for reassurance as she told us she had an eating disorder. My heart sank as I suddenly felt completely selfish for the feelings I'd been having. She then proceeded to tell us that she wouldn't make it to Christmas if she didn't change and I began to cry. I had already thought

I'd 'lost' my friend, but this could have become a reality. Why hadn't she told me sooner? I wouldn't have force fed her, I could've helped. I'd grown up with an unhealthy relationship with food myself and used to be watched by my teachers at school to ensure I was eating.

I already knew a fair amount about anorexia but I'd never heard of Atypical Anorexia. I went to the BEAT website to try and clue myself up a bit more and remind myself of what not to say if she had a wobble.

Recovery is a long bumpy ride and not one to be rushed. We took Zoe on a self-catering holiday in the January. We chose to stick to home cooked food to allow an easier trip but also planned one meal out to try and push her out of comfort zone. Jonty (my husband) never fully understood the emotion behind an eating disorder and still to this day, I have to remind him. She enjoyed a full 3 course meal and things were starting to look better.

We knew it wouldn't be straightforward and that relapses would happen, but we knew Zoe could now handle this. She has a support system, and we were there to give her a little kick of encouragement when needed. To an extent, I try to sit back and let her do her thing but there was no way I'd let her get to the stage she was at in 2018. I created some envelops of encouragement to remind Zoe of the reasons we love her.

So, what's next for the Zoe and Emily dream team! Well tackling motherhood together for one. I'll be sorting out sassy toddler tantrums while Zoe battles new-born sleep deprivation. Our friendship is stronger and I'm so grateful that Zoe now pops me a text if she's struggling and all I need to do is listen. I have been able to understand and acknowledge when my own mental health needs some attention. I wouldn't wish this experience on anyone but I'm so thankful I can spot the signs and help others. Here's to becoming old ladies together and embarrassing our kids together for the rest of our lives.

My Darling Husband

James. The man who refused to give up on me when I had long given up on myself. I know I said some of the most hurtful things to you, however we both knew deep down, that it was never me saying these things, it was very much the ED voice. I tried to push you away and convince you that you would be better off without me. I lied to you about my behaviours and tried to hide my illness from you as much as possible and was not honest with you when I started to really struggle.

Truth is I have always struggled, we just did not realise how much. I was constantly pulling myself down and tearing into my body image, but it became the normal thing for me to do, so we never questioned it. The constant dieting was again just something I have always done, something I could do well, so my weight constantly changing masked the illness form us both, not just you. I had no idea what was going on, but you started to realise, you noticed me changing quickly and spiralling. You addressed it instead of burying your head in the sand. Thank you, for all you did to try and understand my illness. At times I know it was frustrating and you severely struggled, but you always tried. Yes, at times you said the complete wrong thing, but you tried. At times you felt lost and did not know the right thing to do, but again you tried.

During recovery we argued more than what we have ever done. We both knew what I should be doing, but the ED voice was strong and trying to keep me trapped, you tried to help me during mealtimes and encouraged me to reach my targets and goals. You knew my coping strategies and encouraged me to use them when you could see I was struggling. You accept sometimes I need help and sometimes I need time on my own to work through my thoughts and feelings and understand this. I really cannot put into words how much you have supported me throughout my whole recovery rollercoaster, and I know you will continue to do so.

James' Story

Zoe and I first met when we were at school together, with our surnames following each other in alphabetical order, we were sat together in several classes. So, how could I not notice this wonderful woman, singing away to herself?

Zoe was such a kind person with a bubbly personality who brightened up my day and still brings joy to my life. I remember noticing that she never seemed to eat much at school, but I didn't think much of it as she didn't seem unwell.

There were times when she would have a chocolate bar and break off squares giving them to other people until she was left with one, or even no squares left for herself. Maybe you could think of this as being over generous, however looking back at it with what I know now this was clearly an excuse to avoid eating. I never knew what was going through her head at the time but looking back I imagine in her head the ED was saying "you don't deserve this chocolate, everyone else deserves it more than you do."

At the time I was frustrated by these behaviours. I knew it wasn't right, and it concerned me, but as Zoe didn't seem poorly, I didn't realise the extent of the disorder. When we started dating if I complimented Zoe, she would never accept it, instead dismissing it. Instead of: *"you're beautiful"*, *"oh, thank you"*; it would go more like: *"you're beautiful"*, *"no I'm not!"*. Again, it never made sense to me why she would always have a negative view of herself, and at the time I never realised what was going through her mind, not knowing how this was just one part of a much larger complex problem.

I fell in love with this wonderful woman and we've now been together for 14 years, and over that entire time there have always been eating disorder behaviours. During university these would vary, usually related to her emotions. If she was busy, stressed or unhappy it would get worse, but when she was happy and enjoying what she was doing it would get better.

We would go away on holidays and I found it bizarre to not eat any lunch because "we had a buffet breakfast", a thought process that could make sense to me if we were eating 5 full English breakfasts, but we weren't and despite my protests Zoe was adamant. I remember one holiday in particular where we sat in a cafe near lake Windermere and had afternoon tea together for lunch for the first time ever. It was strange and also quite saddening to realise that such a simple thing as sitting together on holiday, taking the time to have a nice lunch brought so much joy to me because it was something we had never done before.

I had known for some time that I wanted to spend the rest of my life with Zoe. She brightened up every single day, bringing joy and happiness into my life in a way that only this unique woman could. I wanted to marry her so I wanted to plan a proposal that she would love. Zoe loves Greek mythology and had always wanted to visit Greece, so we booked a holiday to Rhodes and it was here where one beautiful night at sunset, we walked along the beach and I went down on one knee and asked that all important question. I was expecting her to say yes, rather than burst into tears, hugging me and then trying on the ring, but eventually she answered '*yes, of course I want to marry you*'.

I was overjoyed to be planning our wedding, looking forward to the day I could proudly call Zoe my wife. What I didn't realise was that 'the wedding diet' was the start of a slippery downwards slope for ED. Small breakfasts, nutritionless lunches and unreasonable tracking of ingredients were all behaviours which I found absolutely ridiculous, but 'the wedding diet' seemed such a 'normal' thing because, well, that's what all women do, isn't it? Zoe didn't need to diet for our wedding, and especially not for me. I loved her with all my heart and she was beautiful just the way she was. I am ashamed to admit that I even agreed to weigh out ingredients, even down to onions or lettuce, when I was cooking meals, because I knew if I didn't, she would refuse to eat it.

In a very short space of time, several people very close to Zoe sadly passed away. Something that would be very difficult for anyone to deal with, and for Zoe it meant resorting to her eating disorder behaviours to cope. But it wasn't coping, it was masking and distracting from emotions by focusing on restriction and exercise instead of dealing with these emotions.

It left Zoe steeped in a sadness and subdued that bubbly personality I have always loved. The behaviours of Zoe's pre-wedding diet were still there but worsened. I would come home from work to see that half of Zoe's pack-up was left uneaten. The dieting had happened for so long it started to seem normal, so these extra restrictions didn't seem as bad as they were.

Zoe was already visiting the gym, but it had increased from a couple of times a week to every single day. She would get up in the morning, go to work, go to the gym and I wouldn't see her until the evening. We were married and had created a wonderful home together, but I would come home from work and feel lonely, lost, waiting around to spend time with my wife.

It kept getting worse. Zoe started missing lunch and breakfast. These were easiest to hide from me because I would be at work, but I knew something wasn't right. I remember finding out from her work colleagues that she wasn't eating at work. We were all very concerned but no matter what we did or said we couldn't get Zoe to understand that she needed to eat properly. I hated the secrecy, my wife who I share everything with hiding this from me.

At this point I am still horrified that I didn't realise this was an eating disorder. So many behaviours that are actually terrible are promoted on social media as 'healthy' and fasting diets are advertised on TV. These dangerous behaviours seem to have become part of our culture and make it harder to see the signs of an eating disorder which could cause major health issues.

But then Zoe started to miss dinner. I would still cook a meal for two not knowing if we would sit down and eat together or if Zoe would refuse to eat it. I was extremely concerned for her health but didn't know what to do, I couldn't convince her to eat and she didn't see it as wrong. I felt miserable as I sat alone eating dinner, knowing that Zoe was wasting away and there was nothing I could do to help her.

It continued to escalate, turning into "I only need to eat every other day" and then "I only need to eat a couple of times a week". It was horrible to see my wife slowly killing herself, whilst she was adamant that she should eat less and less.

As part of this, Zoe became obsessed with her weight. Obsessed with the scales, weighing herself all the time. I knew it wasn't healthy to do this, so I decided to remove the batteries from the scales to try and stop this obsession. However, it didn't help. Zoe was furious with me because the ED thrived on knowing that number, and me removing the batteries just caused an argument until they were put back in.

Everything that Zoe was doing was eventually going to take its toll on her body. she started collapsing frequently, had chest pains and was tired with no energy, but Zoe couldn't sleep properly either. All of this meant that our lives ended up being preoccupied with avoiding social occasions if food might be involved. Zoe was tired and wouldn't be interested in us spending time together. Instead, her thoughts were reduced to food, exercise and calories. Not much else.

We have two young nieces, but at this point when we saw them Zoe didn't have the energy or interest to spend time playing with them. It was heart-breaking to see someone who loves her nieces so much not have the energy to spend time with them.

With all of this happening I knew that something had to be done about this. Zoe had already been to the GP numerous times, but none of these visits ended with a positive outcome. The GP never fully considered an eating disorder and dismissed Zoe's problems and behaviours. After doing some research and using the charity BEAT, I was convinced that this was actually an eating disorder.

I arranged a call with the coordinator of our local specialist adult eating disorder service and discussed all of Zoe's behaviours. Everything I said; restricting, exercising, obsessing with weight and calories, collapsing, were clear signs of an eating disorder. It was relieving to know what this was and that there was a path to recovering, that we could have our lives back again. I was advised to request for the GP to refer Zoe through to their service and that is the best thing we could have ever done.

Accessing this invaluable service was relatively easy, however, getting the referral would have never happened without our own research, advising the GP to refer Zoe and directing them where to refer Zoe.

It was a tedious journey through recovery. When we were finally sitting down and eating meals together it felt like it took forever to finish a meal. I think the longest one was a stir fry which went in the microwave to reheat one too many times, but after 50 long minutes we got there. The meals are so difficult, as you sit there thinking '*is she okay*', '*is she going to eat it*', '*what's going through her head*', '*what should I do*'. A stream of concerns which all get in the way of the one thing I should actually be doing, talking to my wife, making a relaxed atmosphere and distracting from thinking about ED.

I was always terrified of losing Zoe throughout this. When Zoe was engulfed in eating disorder behaviours which were worsening and things were tough, I didn't even know if recovery was possible, I thought this was a battle which we could never win and I remember lying awake at night thinking how could I explain to our young niece that Aunty Zoe isn't around anymore. Thankfully, being as stubborn as she is, once Zoe started recovery, I could see that she wanted to recover. She was motivated and determined and I'm so thankful to see my wife recovered.

Now I am able to look back on the whole experience I wish I had the understanding I do now, as we would have sought help years before we actually did. I also wish I had done and said the right things at the right time to help Zoe's recovery, although I'm still not entirely sure which were the right things to do or say at any point.

It's fantastic to have the bubbly Zoe back again and to see her happier than ever. The process of recovery has given her more confidence and an ability to recognise and understand her emotions. Overall, it's fantastic to see that she has come out of the other side of recovery happy and with new skills which will give her the best opportunity for the future, not just for eating but that can be applied to all aspects of life.

I'm now looking forward to the future, with Zoe and our baby girl there is much excitement in the future. I know it will not always be easy and I know there is a chance that Zoe could relapse. If she does, I still don't have all the answers, but I understand eating disorders better than I have before, so I will be able to have productive conversations which means I might be able to help set Zoe in the right direction.

Chapter 14
Relapses

Relapses happen, it can be a normal part of recovery, and each time I have fallen, I have learnt something new. Eating disorders are clever and will find different ways to pull you back in. Each time I did fall, I was overwhelmed with guilt. I was letting everyone down and I felt like a complete failure. I was always scared to admit when I had fallen as I wanted to make people proud of how well I was doing and relapses meant failure. I did not want people to worry about me and tried my best to hide when I was struggling. This of course added to the feeling of worthlessness and the secrecy which only made the ED voice stronger.

The one thing I struggled with was recognising when I was just having a difficult few days and had lapsed temporarily and when I needed extra support because I had relapsed completely. I never wanted to reach out for support in fear that it was just a hiccup and I did not need any more intervention, however even a temporary lapse in behaviour can snowball incredibly quickly, as I found out.

Christmas & January

Every year at Christmas I still struggle. The amount of food we have in the house, the amount of parties I go to, Christmas drinks every weekend. Christmas dinners and everything about Christmas screams indulgent. It is always in January that I struggle. Everywhere you look there are diets advertising, people recommending how to lose the Christmas pounds, people engaging in weight loss challenges and it is everywhere, following me taunting me.

Even on the television there are adverts selling a variety of weight loss shakes, in the high street people are handing out leaflets for gym memberships and of course it is all over social media, spreading quickly like a plaque.

I was five months into my recovery journey and doing somewhat well, I had been discharged from my day programme, engaging with my therapist and dietician and eating regular meals and snacks. I had even managed to try to enjoy Christmas a little, engaged with all the parties, went out with friends and realised the festivities were not all about food. It then came to January and the New Year's resolutions were pouring in. Everyone around me wanted to lose weight, wanted to lose their Christmas pounds. By now I had learnt about set point theory, so knew that yes, I had gained weight, it was okay and part of living, however when I return to regular normal eating, the weight will come back down naturally without dieting. I remember trying to explain this to a friend however she was having none of it. Completely dismissed the idea of it and adamant to diet. It seemed everyone I spoke to was dieting and it was all anyone could talk about.

Within days the constant talk of dieting and exercising had started to rub off on me. I found myself restricting a little. I started eating only 'good foods' again, adamant it was not a diet and I was just eating healthier after all the rich food. My husband believed this and I managed to get away with it, I believed it as well. However, it was not enough for that eating disorder voice, very quickly I started skipping meals again. I would eat a safe meal such as stir fry or fish and vegetables at teatime, to avoid my husband suspecting anything, and avoid eating my other meals. But once again that was not enough for that ED voice and then the exercise started to creep back. I very soon and very quickly spiralled, it seemed I had forgotten everything that I had been taught. I was due a community support appointment the following week and my therapy was starting soon again after the Christmas break. If I recognised I was struggling I would have reached out to BEAT's online support, but I did not even realise what I was doing. I was just copying everyone else, fitting in with what others were doing, I was doing nothing wrong.

Within a week of starting to eat healthy and exercising more, I was gone. My disorder had completely consumed me again, I was taking laxatives, exercising hours every day, restricting heavily, skipping meals, and my checking behaviours had started to creep back in.

I had started weighing myself again at the gym and tracking it by writing it down. My husband did realise what I was doing and started to argue with the voice and question my motives. He told me I would end up in A&E if I carried on letting the ED win. Evening meals had become problematic again and I severely struggled to justify why I needed to eat.

I had gotten fat over Christmas and was simply trying to lose a little Christmas weight, everyone else was doing it, so why shouldn't I join in? I believed the lie ED was telling me, and I was engaging with it, letting it take over. The ED voice screamed at me every minute of the day. I was a fat waste of space, I had overindulged at Christmas and I was now disgusting, I had failed by enjoying myself and all my hard work over the last few years was pointless, the negative thoughts came flooding back along with the ED voice. I had eaten extremely little all week, which contributed to me not being able to think clearly. I was preoccupied with food thoughts again, I was going for a long run twice a day as well as going to the gym and engaging in other exercises, taking multiple laxatives instead of eating. Eventually this level of abuse had a negative impact on my body. I started to get chest pains again, became extremely lethargic but kept pushing. I came home from a run, went for a hot shower as it was cold and it had been raining outside. As the warm water soothed my aching muscles I started to feel dizzy, I stepped out the shower and felt extremely light headed. I hit the floor. I ended up passing out; it took a week for my body to stop working again, that was it. I came back around and my husband insisted I get checked out as I was extremely spaced out and still dizzy. He helped me get dressed and took me, reluctantly to the hospital.

I waited in A&E and the doctor explained I had become dehydrated. My husband explained what had happened and the doctor agreed if my blood pressure rose and dizziness went, they would discharge me, as long as I informed my eating disorder team. I agreed. I felt extremely ashamed, once again I had let the ED rule and very quickly, I had become unwell. I was on an IV drip, my husband sat opposite me, we were in a little room in A&E waiting for it to finish and he looked at me and smiled. We had been together for twelve years by this point, so I could read him like a book and knew what he was thinking and about to say, I said to him,

"Don't you dare"

He shrugged and then replied with,

"Well, I am going to anyway, I told you so."

I hated him at that point, but he was of course right. I had let the ED completely rule and over did it big time, I had barley eaten all week, exercised to the point where every bone and muscle in my body ached and severely overdosed on laxatives. He then told me to smile. I looked up and realised he was taking a picture, I pulled a face and thumbs down. I was beginning to feel better and some colour had returned to my cheeks. I asked him why he did that, I had an eating disorder recovery album on me phone, full of video logs, quotes and pictures of my flash cards in case I needed them. He said he was adding that picture to the album, and next time he noticed ED creeping back, he would refer to this photo as a reminder of what happens, a reminder to listen to your husband as he was right!

I was able to leave the hospital once the drip had finished, my blood pressure had returned to normal and I was advised to keep hydrated and rest for the next few days.

I did as I was told and I also had my community support appointment a few days after I was in hospital. I told them what had happened. I felt ashamed I had let it back in and was confused at how quickly I snowballed, one behaviour turned into four so quickly and I did not even recognise it. How could I not see what I was doing?

After a chat with my support worker, we recognised how January is always difficult for those in recovery, the constant diet and weight loss talk, it is hard not to get drawn in. We spoke about what happened and I was still severely upset with myself. I had let my husband down, he knew what I was doing and I felt guilty for putting him through the stress again. It was suggested we put what happened behind me and had some self-compassion. I was still in early recovery, I had not failed as I was still in therapy and still trying. If I failed, I would have quit the service and would not want to get better. I did want to recover, the thought of my long-term goal kept me going, I did want to get rid of this vile voice, and as long as I had hope and a little fight in me it was still possible. Hiccups like this happen; it did not mean I had failed at recovery.

Summer

I had started a new job, eating well, still exercising but not excessively, things were mainly going well. I was working on my PTSD symptoms in therapy which involved a lot of work; we went over the events that led to me developing this and were working on re-scripting techniques. However, recalling all these horrible memories was exhausting. I was experiencing horrific nightmares every time I closed my eyes, I would see him again, re-live the trauma, and re-live the past. I had once again become scared of sleeping. I was also having more flashbacks as I was thinking and confronting the trauma, working on my triggers and allowing myself to be exposed to them to overcome them. It was intense and exhausting work.

Things at my new job were not what I had hoped. I applied for the job as it was fewer hours and closer to home so I could focus on recovery and continue to heal, however I ended up working a lot more than I was contracted and I just did not seem to fit in. I missed my old place of work, my colleagues who had supported me. Here I felt I could not seek the same support as I did not know them yet. It was a mistake changing jobs, I regretted it and wanted to go back but was embarrassed to ask for my job back. I was miserable at work, not sleeping and reliving the trauma daily.

I had been eating well for a while and managed to have one normal menstruation cycle since January, however that was it. Worried I may have caused long term damage I visited my nurse practitioner. We spoke about my issues and it was agreed I needed to see a specialist. I was referred to a fertility specialist to investigate what was going on in my body, as a family is what my husband and I both wanted when I was further along into my recovery.

My first appointment with the specialist I was diagnosed with polycystic ovary syndrome. They also wanted to do some tests to see what damage I had done to my body. I asked outright if I was infertile, the specialist looked me in the eye and said, *"there are things we can do for you, we can look at IVF once you are more recovered."* That did not answer my question, however I knew what he was saying. We arranged for me to have an x-ray of my tubes to see what else was going on. I was heartbroken. *Had my eating disorder left me infertile? I felt flooded with guilt, what if I was infertile? I couldn't give James the one thing he wants too, I would be depriving him, he could do so much better than me, he could be happier with someone else.* Having our own family had become my focus in recovery; for this was my main goal, to be well enough to carry a child. What was the point in carrying on if this was not even possible? I felt like my heart had been broken into millions of pieces and all hope I had for recovery was lost.

I felt I had no control over the flashbacks and nightmares anymore. I was unhappy at work, and the thought of being infertile was too much. I needed some control back in my life, so once again I found comfort in my eating disorder. I started restricting a little and counting calories, setting myself a limit each day, then obviously this was not enough for that voice and I started to snowball back into old habits.

James had realised my behaviours and was trying to nudge me back in the right direction. He had noticed what I was doing and was growing concerned and every day hinted that I was letting the disorder back. However, I was pushing him away, he could do better than me, I could not give him what he wanted and he deserved better.

One evening we had a massive argument. I could not eat; I was done with recovery, too tired to fight, drowning in negative emotions I struggled to deal with. I walked away from the dining table into the kitchen, James followed me and began to get angry, I accused him of not caring and wanting someone better, shouting back at him. I began to disassociate as arguments and these sorts of environments reminded me of the abuse. Trying to stay in the present moment I was not answering James back, he thought I was ignoring him. Angry that I was trying to block him out ignoring what he was saying he grabbed my wrists and forced me to turn around.

In that moment he knew he had done wrong. I fell to the floor screaming as I entered a full-blown flashback. Reliving one of the times I was grabbed by the wrists pinned down and abused. I was re-living it, in detail, screaming out to stop unable to bring myself back to the present moment. Eventually I came around, my husband was sat on the floor next to me in the kitchen in tears and apparently, I had disassociated and had been out for around twenty minutes.

I was crying, shaking and unable to move. He came towards me to comfort me, but I had become scared of him. I was frightened of him grabbing me like that again, scared what it would lead to.

I stopped at a friends for a few nights, however did not like to impose on them, so found myself sofa surfing. Every night I did not seem to know where I was stopping, the uncertainty of not knowing what I was doing one day to the next drove my anxiety insane. I was not sleeping due to horrific nightmares, convinced my husband no longer wanted me due to being infertile and I had also become afraid of him thanks to my PTSD. I was not eating and really was not enjoying work. I had no reason to live, I went home as I needed more clothes and toiletries. I had spoken to James on the phone and it only resulted in another argument. He wanted me to come home, however I was adamant he could do better than me and I was also still somewhat cautious around him, the flashback was so intense I did not ever want to experience that again and he had made that happen. I had been prescribed Zopiclone to help me sleep. I could not take them the nights I was at work the following day as it took me ages to wake up in the morning and made me drowsy. I decided I really needed some rest in my own bed; I fiddled with the Zopiclone as my mind started to wonder.

I wonder what happens if I take too many of these? Will I drift off to sleep and never wake up? I had previously had suicidal thoughts. I knew these alone would not end my life, I had researched it. I thought for a few more moments, what I wanted out of life - my job was a mess, I had no relationship, and I couldn't sleep without awakening from horrific nightmares, living in a heightened sense of anxiety with uncontrollable flashbacks. I couldn't even eat properly, relapsed and unable to recover, trapped in this misery with no hope to cling to anymore. I was fed up of fighting; I did not want to end my life but wanted desperately to end this pain. I grabbed a bottle of wine, some paracetamol and my zopiclone, and popped them into a small bowl, completely numb from what I was doing; it was like I was on auto pilot. I started to take them, eating them like sweets and drinking the wine out of the bottle. I needed to sleep, and in that moment, I did not want to wake up again.

I can honestly not really remember what happened over the next few days, all I remember was waking in a hospital bed. Confused, dazed, receiving treatment through a drip and not sure what was going on. I looked at my phone, I rang my friend as it seemed we had spoken on the phone a few days ago and he was able to fill me in with how I got there. It seemed he played a big part and managed to get me to the hospital after recognising I needed help. I lost a few days of my life as I battled with my suicidal thoughts, not wanting to be there. My friend told me I was discharged apparently when I was still unwell. He put me up for the night as I was adamant I did not want to go home, then when I left his to return home thanks to a taxi, I took another overdose. I literally have no recollection of this, just vague memories. I remember after being discharged I was referred to the crisis team and put on a 72-hour plan. Every day I had to attend a centre for a check-up and talk. I had missed my first appointment after being discharged originally and they rang me. I'd answered and admitted I had taken another overdose, the next thing I remember was being at the centre in floods of tears with a woman, and then once again collapsing. Then the next thing I remembered was waking up on a ward. That is all my friend could tell me. In that moment I was too exhausted to try and gather my thoughts. I allowed myself to rest and continued receiving treatment for my overdose. Looking back, they should never have discharged me, I was clearly very unwell. However, they sent me away only for me to make another attempt and end up back in hospital.

My husband came to visit me. However he could not fill me in with what happened either, he just said he got a call telling me I was in hospital, I was safe and that is all that mattered. He sat next to me holding my hand and the tension in the air was unbearable. I was still feeling scared of him, I still needed some space to learn to trust him again, and he was heartbroken and unable to comprehend what had happened.

He insisted he loved me regardless and would continue to work at our relationship and give me space while I heal and work on my PTSD symptoms. When I was well enough, I returned home. We agreed to sleep separately while I worked hard on re-scripting my trauma. I was working hard with ED service to get my meals back on track and engaging with the crisis team. However, returning to work with all of this was impossible, it became obvious to the crisis team that I was still struggling and I needed a little more support. My home had become a trigger for me and I felt unsafe there. I spoke openly about my PTSD with my psychologist who suggested one way for closure is to report the incident to the police.

So that is what I did, it was time. I had suffered long enough. Once again though, by reporting the incident and going through the process and going through the details it only heightened my symptoms. I needed to be somewhere I felt safe so I could work on my nightmares and getting my eating disorder back under control, whilst in a safe and managed environment. It was agreed I would stay in a crisis house for a week in order for me to heal.

Most importantly though it gave me time to myself, away from everything. Time to really focus on my mental illnesses, getting myself better and engaging in proper self-care whilst doing so. It was while I was in the crisis house that I actually wrote my TEDx talk.

My first day in the crisis house was strange. I had entered this house with other patients all there for different reasons and around the clock staff support. I was shown my room for the week and left to unpack and settle. We had a shared kitchen space and it was agreed I could have set times where I could prepare my meal alone, without other patients, so I could work on my eating disorder. At nights there were staff around to help with my nightmares and help ground me until I became better at doing this independently. During the day I would have a meeting with the crisis team and also intervention work, where we could focus on specific things that had led to me being there. It all seemed so much to take in, but I had to accept I needed extra support; I could not tackle my eating disorder while I was living with extreme hypervigilance and tension.

I worked a lot during the week around relationship issues and self-esteem, we resolved the issues I was having with James and I learnt he is nothing like my previous abuser. The flashback incident was an accident and he is not a bad man.

I was able to communicate with him again with the support of staff, learning how to become less passive too and voice my opinions more without being afraid. I realised I was miserable at work, so once again with staff support, I contacted my old place of work and I was offered an interview. However, I was assured the job was mine, the interview was just a process, they had missed me and would welcome me back.

My self-esteem took a lot of work. I looked back at old resources I had been given and every day we discussed ways in which this could be further secured. I was working with a specialist while giving anonymous intelligence information to the police and once again the crisis house was able to support me through this, having that extra support was crucial. That finally left my eating disorder, however now it was not that difficult to get back under control. I had been trying to juggle too much, self-loathing, infertility, relationship breakdown, PTSD symptoms, work stresses and reporting the trauma to the police. One by one throughout the week, these issues dissolved. I just needed help prioritising the tasks and help sleeping, once all these things were sorted my head was clearer. I was not tired and I could tackle ED again.

It only took a few days to get my eating back on track, and within one week I had transformed. By the time I was discharged from the crisis house my trauma had been fully reported. I had done something about it, no longer afraid and somewhat proud I had spoken up. He no longer had power over me.

With that my PTSD symptoms eased. I still had flashbacks and nightmares, but they were manageable and thanks to my nightmare management plan we had developed whilst I was in there, and help and support all week from the staff, I was able to get some proper sleep again. I was excited about going back to work where I used to, being back with friends and in a supportive environment. I had learnt I can trust James and be honest with him, I was able to open up and tell him why he had frightened me and what was happening inside my head. We learned how to communicate.

But most importantly I learnt that my eating disorder provided me with a distraction. When all of this was going on, instead of dealing with it, I tried to mask it by using the disorder to numb everything. I learnt I entered a crisis stage by not dealing with my emotions and trying to just carry on, even though I could not carry on, I needed to stop and deal with what was going on. I learnt my disorder really was an unhelpful coping strategy and realised just how pointless it was turning to it as a way of coping. I needed better coping strategies and also, I had learnt it is okay to speak up when I needed help.

It frustrated me that it took an attempt on my own life to be taken seriously. So many occasions I would sit with them in A&E and be told to go and practice mindfulness or take a bath to calm myself down. While self-care's great, what I needed was intervention, help and support. However, each time they saw me in crisis, I appeared calm, as I wore my mask too well. I should have been more upfront with my emotions and been more forceful when asking for help.

Support Networks

The one thing I was still severely struggling with was letting people in and asking for help, however people were now very much aware of my eating disorder. I noticed when I returned to my old place of work, my colleagues knew about eating disorders and knew the signs and symptoms. They knew what to look out for and I found myself surrounded by support, whether I wanted it or not. Starting back at work shook my nerves, I had left here and now I was returning. When I left I was severely unwell, a shadow of myself and all my personality had been taken. I wanted to start afresh, however the anxiety was making my eating disorder pipe up. I remember one week I had started to struggle a little and my colleague had picked up on the fact I was quieter than normal. I just said I was tired and just was not really with it today, instantly she asked what I had eaten for breakfast. I felt shamed, I did not want to admit I had skipped breakfast but also as annoying as the prompt was, I realised just missing that one meal had already affected my work.

I found it harder to hide my lapses from friends as well as colleagues, as they were aware and had seen me deteriorate. They were quick to question me if I turned down food or parties, questioning why. It became irritating and suffocating, however I had to remember they had my best interest at heart. They did not trust me to reach out and ask for help, as I had proven multiple times I would not and instead try and tackle everything on my own. I would become irritable with them and often snap when they called me out on my behaviours, as much as it pains me to admit it, the fear of letting them down and relapsing has kept me on my track a little. I had all these people supporting me, I did not realise at the time, but I did have support.

Lapse Compared To A Relapse

I adore my friends and colleagues, however I do have to try and speak up when they are talking about diets around me. I find it hard to ask to change the subject and find my thoughts drifting towards eating disorder behaviours, I get worried about what they may say if I speak up and how they may act. If they want to diet, it is their choice, I cannot ask them to stop just to spare my feelings. I needed to be stronger and start voicing when I was getting triggered.

It was approaching Christmas again, a lot had happened in the year, and I had learnt to become a little more vocal, it was Christmas Dinner Day in the nursery and all the staff and children enjoyed a Christmas Dinner. I decided I was going to join in, I was due to be discharged from the service and I adored Christmas Dinner. We served it all out and we sat amongst the children whilst we ate. After we had finished and tidied up, I remember my colleagues talking about how many calories were in a pig in blanket and how they would have to exercise because they had enjoyed this meal and indulged. I tried to tune out, but was struggling. My eating disorder had picked up on the conversation and I was being dragged in.

The talk of the carbohydrates and how fat they all felt were music to my eating disorder's ears. I was due to finish at half twelve as I was on a half shift; I went home and immediately put on my running shoes and went out for a run. I could not eat tea and the next day could not face breakfast. I went to work and realised I had engaged in behaviours, I was having difficulty fighting the voice and had started to engage with the voice again. I realised I had

245

lapsed and recognised I needed to pull myself back round, so when I found the conversation turning to dieting again, I went into the other room. A lapse was okay, but I needed to turn it around, if I continued to engage with these behaviours I would relapse, and I did not want this. I focused hard on the following week and forced myself to stick to an old meal plan while I worked to get back on track. I challenged my thoughts and found within a week I had managed to pull myself back around, without any help.

A temporary lapse is not the end of the world, if I had ignored it and relapsed that would have been a lot harder to challenge and recover from.

Lapse vs Relapse

Throughout the whole of my recovery, I kept fretting I had relapsed completely every time I engaged in behaviours, when this was simply not the case at all. A lapse means a temporary return to old behaviours, a slip if you like. You have engaged in the ED voice, fallen but got straight back up again, ready for the battle to continue. Losing a few battles does not mean you are not going to win the war.

Lapses are completely common in recovery, for me the craving to buy laxatives or run off my calories were very hard to just stop. I had been engaging in these behaviours for over fourteen years on and off, it was always going to be hard to just stop. However, now I had been through treatment I was aware of the dangers and when I did return temporarily to behaviours, I learnt from it.

One lapse happened when I thought I had eaten too much, the reminder that I was a now overweight, thinking that it would not harm me this once. I needed laxatives; I needed to get this out of my system. I lapsed and took them and that night when I was in agony with my stomach, clutching it as I tossed and turned unable to sleep because of the pain, it reminded me - oh yeah, this is what happens Zoe. This is why this behaviour is dangerous and just not worth it.

I would journal my lapses, make a note and then next time I could hear the voice tempting me I'd think back to my lapse, read back on my journal and remind myself of that lesson, remind myself of the pain, remind myself why I was recovering. Then take some time to practice self-care, look after myself after my wobble and remind myself, it is okay, wobbles happen and are normal in recovery.

A relapse however means a complete return to old behaviours, following a lapse you continue engaging in the behaviours without being able to pick yourself up. You continue to lapse over and over; a relapse does not mean you have failed in recovery. It happens. What is incredibly vital is you reaching out for help to get back onto the recovery road. Engage with services and seek professional support.

Stopping A Lapse Becoming A Relapse

Being the incredibly stubborn person I am whilst also still holding on to that damaging belief that I was a healthy weight and my eating disorder was not really that serious, prevented me from reaching out. When I recognised I was struggling and unable to pick myself up, I really struggled to ask for help, as I always thought others in the service needed help more than me. I was reminded time after time that all eating disorders are dangerous, and my struggles were just as valid and important as others. My main advice is be as honest as possible with your treatment team. If you are in that mind-set then speak up. Every time I did when I was struggling we were able to prevent a relapse by stopping the snowballing when I was lapsing.

One example being six months into treatment, I had been discharged from day programme. It had been

Christmas, I had just recovered form a major lapse thanks to the constant diet culture bombardment of New Year's resolutions. I had gotten back on track however my mind started to wander, I was not in day programme anymore, and no one would know if I did not have my morning and afternoon snacks, no one was watching me anymore. I started to skip my snacks, then in therapy one day, I was asked how my meals and snacks were going. I paused and reflected. I admitted I had not been having snacks and was struggling with this element in my meal plan. They were extra and I was going to gain weight, I was a healthy weight already. I was adamant I did not need them; well the ED voice was adamant I did not need them, my metabolism suggested otherwise. As I was talking through what was happening, I looked up and noticed my therapist had cocked his head to the side, which I knew meant I was somewhat in trouble.

We talked about why I was skipping them and it was decided I needed a little nudge to remind me why it is important to have my snacks. So we set up a community support appointment for me to share my morning snack with a staff member and discuss the thoughts and feelings, and remind me of how the metabolism works and needs fuelling properly in order for it to work.

This example was not a relapse; it was a slip, a lapse. I engaged temporarily in behaviours, realised what I was doing and we came up with a solution so I did not spiral further.

That I feel is the absolute key when you recognise a slip or a temporary lapse in behaviours - create a plan. Write down what behaviour you have engaged in, remind yourself why this is unhelpful, dig out evidence you may have been given in therapy or old journaling you have wrote, and write down an action plan. What are you going to do differently tomorrow? How this will help you in recovery? Here is an example of my action plan for getting back on track with my snacks:

Lapse behaviour – I have been missing snacks on purpose, they will make me fat, I am already overweight I do not need the extras.

What led to the lapse? – Still a little wobbly after Christmas, surrounded by people dieting and I have always dieted after Christmas, it is hard to break the cycle.

What could I do differently? – Acknowledge it is a difficult time; understand why it is a trigger. Practice self-care and distraction techniques when the thoughts are intrusive and read back dietician info, into why snacks are important to keep or metabolism working.

What do I need to do to get back on track? – Revisit meal plans and stick to them 100%. Remember why you are recovering and your long-term goals, read through dietician information to help rationalise the thoughts.

Every time I noticed a lapse in behaviours I would write an action plan and give myself a goal for the following day to help get myself back on track. I often had to repeat my action plan, or do a more gradual approach, such as repeating the step ladder technique, but it did not matter as long as I was still working towards recovery and recognising the slips upon reflection.

One thing I did notice, I was not always aware of my lapses, so weekly reflections and check-ins were vital to keep me on track with my recovery and prevent relapses. Especially after I had been discharged from the service, as my weekly check-in was normally with my psychologist, now that was gone, I needed to ensure I still 'checked-in' with myself and kept track of my recovery.

At the end of every week, I would write in a journal, and think honestly about how the week had gone. I would reflect on my meal plan for the week and think about what

I had eaten and make sure it was challenging and balanced, not all safe foods. I would reflect on what went well and recognise where I struggled, which elements may need work and look at the following week. I thought about what exercises I had engaged in and thought honestly about my checking and compensatory behaviours.

Setting time aside each week to 'check in' with my recovery and also spending some time checking in with my feelings, were vital. How had the week gone overall, how was I feeling, was I avoiding any thoughts or feelings? Was there anything on my mind, bothering me that could lead to me lapsing or engaging with eating disorder behaviours? It felt like an ending to each week, that week had finished, and I could start the new week fresh. After reflecting I would also make sure I still set myself a goal for the following week. If upon reflection I noticed a lapse of behaviours throughout the week and could not turn it around, then that would become my goal for the following week. If I did not recognise any lapses, or I had been able to stop the lapse in its tracks and I was on track and things went quite well during the week, I would challenge and push the ED and set myself a new food goal, or try a new fear food. Constantly moving forward, constantly working towards becoming fully recovered.

Relapses

First thing to remember is you have not failed. Recovery is a complete rollercoaster and relapses can happen. Do seek support at this point to ensure long term damage is not being done. Again, this was always such a big issue for me; once again the whole weight stigma associated with atypical anorexia prevented me from doing this, which only led to me spiralling more. The sooner someone receives help the better chance of making a full recovery. It does not mean you will have to start all over again with treatment, it just means you need, and deserve, a reminder of all you have learnt so far, or a little extra help and support.

Be kind to yourself and try not to let the negative voices take full control, once again practicing self-care and being compassionate with yourself, reminding yourself it is okay and not the end. Going through old plans, goals and materials whilst waiting for treatment to commence will help you keep in a recovery mindset.

For me every time I relapsed it was because of some sort of major life event or trauma that was out of my control. If I was upset or anxious about something I would find myself returning to the ED ways to get back that control. Eventually I realised this was the case and I was able to plan in advance. Plan for scenarios which may trigger my eating disorder to trick me in returning to old behaviours to cope. Before I was discharged, I created a relapse prevention plan. I recognised events in my life where I knew I might struggle and planned for them in advance.

The first thing I listed on my prevention plan was warning signs, what sort of behaviours might I be engaging in, what thoughts might I be having. The next column was to recognise if it was a thought I may have or a behaviour, separating the two. The third column was to challenge that behaviour or thought, what is a more realistic way of looking at this, what information have I learnt that would argue this thought or behaviour, evidence it. Finally, the fourth column is plan! What I could do to ensure I was working on that behaviour.

Very similar to the lapse plan, however this is already filled out, already organised for, so if you find yourself in the situation where you are struggling to fight the voice and getting drawn into behaviours, you already have a plan on what to do and help on specific goals that you have already achieved.

On my plan, I referred to handouts and leaflets I had been given and any useful information I was handed and shown throughout treatment, to back up my rational thoughts. Every time I noticed myself lapsing and I could not seem to slow down or think of ways to stop the lapses, I would turn to this plan, as all the information I knew I needed was there, a handy guide personalised to me. This plan stayed out and was in a folder in our bedroom, in fact it still is (you never know when it might be needed). Also stated at the top of the plan are the areas of times where I may be high risk to lapsing or relapsing.

The most important thing I did with this plan was to share it with my loved ones. James knew the plan inside out, more than I did, and throughout my recovery journey he has referred to it when he has noticed me lapsing. He can question my behaviours and help me come up with ways to get me back on track. When needed he can look at the plan and find the relevant information and simply leave it out, a discreet way of highlighting that he noticed my behaviours but felt he could not approach me as the voice was too strong at the time.

One example of him doing this was after a meal out with friends. For some reason I just snapped and I needed to purge, I needed to get rid of the food, now. No thought challenging, no distractions, I just went with the voice, it was like I was possessed. After I had finished, I went into the bedroom to get changed into my nightwear and on the bed was my relapse prevention plan, and a leaflet I had been given on self-induced vomiting and the behaviours. Straight away I knew what I had done and reflected, I re-read the leaflet, logged my thoughts and feelings and tried to figure out what else was going on. Was there any other reason I could have purged? I journaled all my thoughts and feelings, I felt much better and recognised the lapse.

Support from loved ones is vital, he was not being pushy but simply nudging me towards the correct behaviours and reminding me of the materials that were available to me.

Chapter 15
Maintenance Plan

As well as my lapse planning and relapse prevention plan, I also created a maintenance plan. Ways to keep me focused.

This is an ongoing process, one that I still use today. Along the top of the plan is my rough set point weight, and a reminder that I need to accept my set point and focus on living my life, instead of wasting time trying to manipulate my body. I should be counting memories, not calories and remembering my self-worth is not a number on the scale.

I list the techniques and strategies that I have found beneficial during my recovery journey. What works for me, such as my resource box and distraction jar, a selection of worksheets that I have found particularly useful, information on radical acceptance and reminders on different thought challenging techniques. Any strategy that I have learnt and found helpful is listed here.

A reminder that these things have worked well for me in the past and not to forget about them.

I then compiled a list of good habits, the thoughts and behaviours I have found helpful and I wish to maintain, such as practicing mindfulness, creating video logs to record my feelings; the pausing and thinking of what I would say to a friend in this situation, to be kinder to myself. All the things that help me along the way and ease the detrimental thoughts.

The final section of my maintenance plan is the healthy eating habits I have adapted and want to keep up. My examples, being able to meet friends for a coffee and snack, enjoying a Sunday roast with the family and being able to host BBQs in the summer without them being perfect and my house looking like a show home. The things that I have achieved and am proud of and therefore want to keep doing.

A reminder of how far I have come and that these things can be enjoyable.

With all three plans in place, a lapse plan, relapse prevention plan and maintenance plan, I have been able to overcome many possible relapses in my recovery. Whether it's just looking over my maintenance plan from time to time, ensuring I am doing everything I should be and not forgetting anything that worked well, to writing out a lapse plan. I have found each of these extremely beneficial and would encourage you to do the same.

One other note I will add, is to leave these resources handy. I kept putting everything away thinking I was fine, and then having to dig it all back out each time I needed it.

I now keep my resource box out, full of all my flash cards, and also my distraction jar, they are currently in our bedroom, easily accessible. I also kept the Post-it notes around my mirror, as a constant reminder that I am already enough. And finally, all my relapse prevention planning, lapse worksheets and maintenance plans are in a separate folder on top of everything else. Not stashed away somewhere, but again easily accessible for both me and James. One day I hope they can go fully away, however this will not be until I am fully recovered. I don't care how long that takes, or if they are on my bookshelf forever, they need to stay where I can access them.

Self-Care

Be kind to yourself.

Recovery is exhausting and self-care plays such a vital and important role in maintaining good mental health. Lapses and relapses can knock our confidence and make us question if recovery is worth it. Take it from me, recovery is possible, recovery is hard, no doubt about that, but my gosh it is so worth it.

I developed a spider diagram of ways to practice self-care, what I enjoyed doing. I made sure every day, even just for ten minutes, I did something just for me. It was sometimes only something small, such as sitting with a cup of tea and doing a puzzle, just for ten minutes at the start or end of the day, but I made sure I did it.

Self-care does not have to be all about baths and face masks (although I would totally recommend this, it is one of my favourites, especially with all the bubbles in the world including a glass of bubbles too!) Self-care can be engaging in anything which you find relaxing. Taking any amount of time out of the day to unwind and rest your racing thoughts. What works for one person may not work for you, it is very personal and I often felt I was doing it wrong, as my version of self-care looked different to those around me. Finding time for self-care used to be impossible, however I recognised it was very much needed to ensure I did not relapse.

When I recognised that I was struggling with my eating disorder and beginning to lapse, I needed to ensure I set more time aside to practice self-care. It is important to practice self-care anyway, but even more so when you are struggling. I would find it hard to set time aside, as I was always too busy, however by recognising when I am feeling stressed and out of control, engaging in self-care activities and learning to recharge my batteries, I have avoided relapses.

The distraction jar I made for my compensatory behaviours became my self-care jar. I added more lollipop sticks into it, with things written on them I really love doing and find relaxing. So, when I do have a little time, and I'm unsure what to do, I can pull out a stick and engage with whatever it is telling me, such as:

- watching a film
- painting my nails
- playing a game

- reading a few chapters of a book

The self-care jar is personalised to me, and I fill it with activities that take different amounts of time so I can find one to fit my schedule.

Doing your weekly check-ins and setting time aside each week just for you is also a great self-care practice. I have already talked about how important it is to check-in with how you are feeling each week and reflect on the week that has passed to keep working towards recovery. Journaling and writing is a perfect example of getting in touch with your feelings and spending time recognising what you need.

Music was a big outlet for me, I sometimes struggled to explain how I felt and write down my feelings, but found it easier to express them through the arts. Painting, colouring and crafts were a perfect way to channel that emotion.

I love playing the flute, I also started learning ukulele in my recovery to give me another focus. Whenever I do have a little free time this tends to be my go-to. Playing my feelings and forgiving myself for mistakes, learning to be in the present moment and enjoying the sounds. Not just playing music but listening to music too, music is the soundtrack to my life; I have so many different playlists for my moods and will play the music to match my mood to help me feel the emotions. I had a 'go for it' playlist for when I would be battling the ED voice; full of motivational songs like, '*Fight Song*' by Rachel Platten, and '*This Is Me*', from The Greatest Showman. All music that helped me in my fight and pushed me along the way. My creativity has played a huge part in my recovery.

It does not matter what your form of self-care looks like, as long as you find a little time each day to keep your batteries charged. By letting them run too low and getting worn out, you cannot fight that ED voice and you will start to fall. This is such an easy way to help avoid a relapse, by keeping yourself well and mentally charged you will feel stronger and it will help you keep that rational brain.

Mindfulness

Mindfulness is a brilliant example of quick and easy self-care throughout the day, it can take very little time and keep you feeling well throughout the chaos of day-to-day life.

Admittedly I initially cringed at mindfulness practices; I always giggled during them in group sessions and could not take them seriously. However, with more and more practice, I can now honestly say, for me they have been a game changer. There are so many different free apps that now do guided meditations and in the evening if I am struggling to sleep, I will participate them.

Mindfulness does not always have to be about meditating though, it can just be about noticing the feeling and sensations around you. For example when washing up after eating a meal, instead of my mind wondering to unhelpful thoughts, I would bring myself to the present moment. *What does the temperature of the water feel like on my skin? What do the bubbles feel like? Can I hear them popping and what other sounds can I hear?* Keeping myself in the moment with what I was doing, instead of allowing thoughts to flood me.

I found mindfulness practice extremely useful to help me stay calm in stressful situations and stop me acting on eating disorder thoughts, whilst also helping me to actually recognise my emotions and allow me to feel them.

I now start every morning with a simple mindfulness technique. The first thing I do is check in with my mind: *What is going through my mind right now? What thoughts am I having?* I simply acknowledge them. The second thing I do is check in with my body: *How am I feeling in my body?* I do a quick body scan, *Am I feeling tense anywhere? Is there any part of my body that feels sore*? The third check-in is with my spirit: *How am I feeling*? Truthfully, being honest with myself and acknowledging and allowing myself to feel the emotions.

Remember, check in with your mind, body and spirit. A simple bit of mindfulness every morning and can be classed as self-care.

Also, throughout the day I do a quick deep breathing exercise. Every time I wash my hands, I pause and take a really big deep breath in through my nose for four seconds, hold it for four, then exhale though my mouth again for four. I then reboot by reminding myself, everything that has happened so far today is already in the past. Focus and recognise what I am feeling, then allow my mind to clear and carry on with my day. This technique is called the twenty second reboot, and I must say, I use it all the time when I am feeling stressed. It helps calm me down and manage my stress; it stops my thoughts turning towards unhelpful ways to deal with it.

I also practice rectangular breathing; I find this another easy and simple way to calm my stress levels.

Everywhere in the world around you there are rectangles, even this book is a rectangle, your phone, a window or a door. They can be found anywhere, so, when I recognise I am feeling stressed and getting overwhelmed I practice rectangular breathing. I find a rectangle, breath in as I follow the shape up, hold my breath and follow it across, release as I follow it down and then reset along the bottom of the rectangle.

I find myself doing this when I'm stuck in traffic, getting stressed and worked up that I am going to be late. I pause follow my front window screen around, then on the reset remind myself there is simply nothing I can do about this situation, it is beyond my control and getting worked up is not going to help me.

Overall, I have shared many tips with you to help prevent a relapse, by planning for scenarios to keeping your batteries charged through self-care. Also, what to do if you find you have relapsed. Remember to seek professional support to help you get back on track if your lapses are snowballing.

Here are my top tips to prevent relapsing and maintain your recovery:

- Do not try and recover independently, use your support network, whether it is friends, family or even online friends. Seek professional support and be as honest as possible with your team. They are there to support and help you. You do not need to be 'sick enough'.

- Keep in contact with your support system, unfollow people that encourage your checking behaviours and halt your recovery. Make sure you stay in contact with those who are your cheerleaders and want to see you well.

- Write it down, journal your thoughts and feelings, reflect on the week and take time to 'check-in' with your thoughts and feelings.

- Establish and maintain a regular eating schedule. Refer to old meal plans for ideas if needed and revisit dietician information, remember three healthy meals a day and three snacks is the key for a working metabolism.

- Maintaining your weight should not be hard work, work with professionals to determine what is healthy for you, remembering information about set point theory. You should not be engaging in behaviours to keep weight below its set point.

- Exercise for pleasure not punishment, it is key to remember that exercise is not a punishment for what we have eaten, but a celebration of how our bodies can move. Engage in exercise that makes you feel good and you enjoy.

- Distraction is key; when you find your thoughts drifting to food and weight related issues, distract yourself to redirect your thoughts.

- Know what makes you tick, recognise your triggers and plan in advance things that may cause your eating disorder mindset to play louder. Know that you will face your triggers one day, however, remember you are prepared for them.
- Help others, join in with the moderated chat rooms on BEAT's website, share ideas and share tips with others. What has worked for you may be able to help someone else which will give you a boost.
- Finally, be kind to yourself. It's not always possible to stop lapses or relapses from happening, no recovery journey can be perfect, so be gentle with yourself when hiccups happen, it really can make such a difference. Practice self-care and recharge your batteries.

Please remember relapse can be a normal part of eating disorder recovery, it does not mean you have failed, or you are weak. You have managed to get through it before and you will again, give yourself the same compassion as you would give to others.

Practice self-care and when you are ready, try again. No matter how many times I have fallen there is always a small part of me that whispers, you are not done yet, get back up. Look back at all you have achieved and learnt. There is no shame in repeating the recovery process, keep fighting.

Recover-ED

Is it possible to live a life completely free from all eating disorder thoughts?

There have been many arguments around this, a lot of people I have spoken to have very different views on whether this is possible. Some people believe you can live your life freely however, eating disorder thoughts will occur, but you can fight them easily remembering all you have learnt and been taught. Whereas other warriors and even my community support worker states they are fully recovered. Not a single eating disorder thought passes through their minds, they are able to eat intuitively and freely, and engage in no compensatory or checking behaviours.

Sounds incredible right? My community support worker is still one of my biggest inspirations, he has fully recovered, he is living proof it is possible. I will one day be able to say I am fully recovered.

There are of course, many different stages of recovery before reaching being fully recovered. Each stage takes a great deal of time and effort and you encounter different difficulties in each stage, as ED is losing power and will try anything to pull you back in. By being aware, and continuing to challenge that voice, you will get there!

Precontemplation Stage

The first stage of recovery is the precontemplation stage. You may be unaware you have a problem; however, others may be picking up on your behaviours. People may be gently trying to nudge you to seek help. Being a healthy weight, it was not my weight that gave my eating disorder away, my husband noticed my checking behaviours, restriction and exercise addiction. I was losing weight however, no one knew. James lived with me, it was impossible to hide all of my behaviours from him. He knew I had an issue long before I did, and I am thankful to him for speaking up.

Contemplation Stage

This stage means you are willing to admit you may have a problem. You may feel you are ready to receive help and support. The fear of facing this is intense and terrifying but the fear of long-term effects outweighs this. Seeking professional support is vital. You can start working on the roots of the ED and figure out where it stemmed from. For me landing in hospital time after time made me realise I needed help, I was not living my life, I was existing. I realised this was becoming serious, even though I was a healthy weight; I had to listen to what my body was trying to tell me and accept I was ill enough for help.

Preparation Stage

Brilliant, you are finally ready to change, but not quite sure how to do so. You have started to develop coping strategies and have learnt ways to deal with the exhausting ED voice. You have learnt more about the disorder itself and explored your thoughts and beliefs around food, weight and shape. You can identify potential barriers to change and recognise where you may fall and plan for this.

I worked hard with my team and worked through my own personal barriers, one being fear of weight gain. We discussed that body image is part of the ED and as we progress in treatment, this will ease. I had to trust the process, and I am so glad I did, it really did ease the more I engaged with my treatment team.

Action Stage

You got this! You are ready to implement all the strategies you have learnt in order to confront that pesky voice. You are trying different things, ideas and behaviours and facing those many fears. To do this well, you need to trust your treatment team. You have removed triggers from your home, maybe got rid of the scales or stopped buying diet foods, and really trying to fight this hard!

Getting rid of the scales for me was a massive turning point, I did not want to, but knew I needed to. It was time to take action and start tackling the illness head on.

Maintenance Stage

Professionals state you are required to have been in the action stage for around six months or longer before moving onto this stage. During the maintenance stage you are actively practicing new behaviours and trying to alter your thinking styles. You are practicing self-care and using the coping skills well, however you are also aware of triggers and are slowly revisiting them in order to face them and prevent a possible relapse.

You may have established new areas of interest and recognising your life has meaning. You may still have wobbles, that is completely normal, but you can pick yourself back up and refocus. This stage is where my personality changed a little. I became more confident, found a new career in public speaking and discovered just how vital self-care is to remain well.

Possible Relapse

Not everyone will experience relapses, however if you do, remember it does not mean failure. Revisit the stages of change and remind yourself of the techniques you have learnt and take some time out to refocus. Consider re-entering treatment if you have been discharged, just to get some support and figure out what may have caused the relapse.

I have had a few relapses along the way; however, I have reached out for help and support when I have needed it and managed to quickly get back on my feet. I remind myself; I have fought this once; I can do it again.

One other thing to be very aware of is that the body may heal a lot quicker than the mind. Mine certainly did, psychologists believe there are also three areas of recovery that tie into the stages, and each of these areas needs to heal properly to ensure long term stable recovery:

1. Physical recovery

The physical effects of ED have eased, your weight has reached its set point and your hormone levels have balanced out, meaning if you are female your menstruation cycle may have returned. Your blood levels are normal as your body continues to heal. However, some health issues may unfortunately be irreversible, due to the long-term damage that may have occurred, but your body has physically healed as much as it possibly can.

2. Behavioural recovery

All of ED behaviours you once engaged with have been tackled through the stages of recovery. You have addressed restriction, exercise and other compensatory behaviours. This will look different for every sufferer, as we all experience different behaviours and rules around food.

3. Psychological recovery

You have now also addressed the cognitive and emotional elements of what contributed to your eating disorder. This may include your body image, personality traits, rules created around food, emotional regulation and managing depression and anxiety.

Once you have addressed the different areas and completed the different stages of recovery, it starts to ease. You have learnt better ways of coping and can regulate your emotions in a healthier way. You are living with the voice, but you can challenge it and continue to do so daily.

I truly believe you can be fully recovered from this illness; I will never stop challenging that ED voice, I will never stop fighting and rebelling against the dieting culture until I reach this stage. The second I let my guard down, believe that voice, I notice I start to fall. By continuing every day to fight, I believe full recovery is possible, where I can live my life without a single eating disorder thought. However I can only reach this by never giving up and continuing to engage in the opposite action, doing the complete opposite to whatever that voice may be telling me to do, for as long as it takes.

Finally

My heart goes out to all of my fellow eating disorder warriors, trying to heal their relationship with food and body image in a world fixated with dieting culture. It is extremely difficult and made harder by the constant obsession others have and believe. I try my hardest to educate those I love, teaching them all I have learnt about set point theory and ways to love yourself. Practicing healthy behaviours and encouraging others to do the same.

I speak positively about my body when I hear people criticising theirs, leading by example. Vocalising what I have learnt about the metabolism and reminding people all food has nutritional value.

I encourage you all to do the same. Yes, I am met with backlash as people refuse to believe the truth but choose to believe the lies the dieting industry feeds them, and I understand and somewhat emphasise with them as they are victims of the dieting industry. I know what it is like to constantly be at war with yourself. I know for sure I will be teaching my child that their self-worth is not measured by a number on the scale, but by the size of their heart.

My main piece of advice to you is do not give up. Recovery is hard and unfortunately not linear, wobbles happen and that is okay, but recovery is possible.

Please do not lose hope; even hope can stand for 'Hold On Pain Ends'. Surround yourself with cheerleaders, people who want you to succeed and celebrate your achievements, no matter how small, celebrate with them. People who believe in you even when you may not believe in yourself. Remind yourself you are stronger than those mean voices in your head and have proven that just by even attempting to tackle this complex illness.

Keep going, it does not matter how long it takes or how many times you may fall, as long as you keep trying and tackling it.

Every time I have fallen, there is always a little piece of me that goes: N*o, you are not done yet, get back up. ED may be strong, but you are stronger."*

You are a warrior.

Chapter 16
Carers Guide

Self-Care For Carers

It can be truly exhausting trying to support someone living with an eating disorder. The arguments, battles and constant self-doubt and always thinking *am I doing the right thing here*? Can be completely overwhelming. It is so important to take time out for yourself if you are a carer, you cannot help others if you are feeling drained and exhausted. Try and schedule in some time away from the disorder and spend time re charging your batteries before going back into battle.

This does not have to just be baths and walks, but often meeting a friend for a drink. My husband was a member of a local darts team, so every Tuesday he would spend a few hours in the evening with his friends having a pint of Guinness, pretending he could actually play. That was his main recharge point and something he enjoyed doing but most importantly, it was a complete eating disorder-free zone.

Support Services

There is a lot of support out there for carers, it is just a case of finding one local, and if there are none local, finding a good resource or outlet online. BEAT have introduced a peer support group for carers, so people who have been through similar and have cared for someone with an eating disorder can listen and help those going through it now. It provides an ear and lets you know you are not alone in this battle. It is vital if you are supporting someone, to talk to others. It can be very stressful and by bottling up your emotions and not talking about them, you are at risk of developing a mental illness yourself.

If one-to-one peer support is not something you are comfortable with, BEAT also have other support services available, such as a web-based chat and a helpline. An advisor the other end of the phone or online, someone you can offload to when things are just a little much. Someone with training and who can offer practical tips and solutions for what you are experiencing. James often rang the helpline after arguments had escalated and he just felt so lost and unsure on what to do next.

There are also courses available; some NHS trusts offer courses for carers and again BEAT also run a course. If there is either option in your area, both me and James would recommend doing them. We were fortunate enough that our local NHS service offered a course, and this was offered to us when I entered treatment. James learnt so much about ED by participating. He was also able to learn about what should be on my meal plan so he could support me when planning the food shop at home, and also learnt different strategies and approaches when trying to help me battle. He was also in a group with others so was able to listen to other people's experiences and again it helped him feel less isolated.

James also learnt that some of the things he was doing was aiding ED, of course he had no idea. For example, he would never say if I had upset him when I chose a behaviour instead of spending time with him. If I chose to work out when actually he had planned a day out somewhere, he would not say that actually he was upset. He was scared of hurting my feelings, even though I was hurting his. He realised he was also aiding the disorder by helping me weigh out the ingredients at teatime. Again, he just wanted to please me and avoid the argument, but actually by helping me, he was encouraging that ED voice. James was able to see how often he was accidently aiding the disorder and learnt to say when it was being unreasonable. It was not intentional, he just did not want the arguments with me, but he soon learnt it was not me arguing back, it was the ED voice. We needed to have those boundaries and he needed to tell me when he was hurting, so I could see what that voice was doing to those I loved. Check with the treatment team if they offer family support, and if this is unavailable have a look at BEAT's website at the developing dolphins course.

Lone Carer

Do not try and tackle this alone, the more people your loved one can talk to the better. I was so convinced no one else needed to know about my disorder except my husband, I did not realise the strain and stress that put on him. I was encouraged to talk to others and by opening up to friends as well, it meant I had a bigger support network. It also meant James was not my only go to when I was struggling; I could message a friend and go for a cup of tea and talk things through, instead of waiting for James to come home from work, then exploding on him when he walked through the door. The more people I had in my support network the easier the battle became. James also knew that sometimes he might say something by accident that would trigger that voice, and if that was the case, I needed someone else to talk things through with. James was incredible throughout. However, asking him to be my only support was too much, for us both.

Research

Above all this, the most important thing you can do is do your research. Look up information on eating disorders from official sites, such as NHS and eating disorder charity sites. Familiarise yourself with the behaviours related to your loved one's illness. Learn what could be potential triggers and also read blogs written by those who have been through it. Remember that eating disorders do kill and do not be afraid of reminding your loved ones this.

Particularly with OSFED and atypical anorexia. Your loved one may not look ill, they may be functioning absolutely fine and it may be hard to believe how dangerous this disorder is. However, just because your loved one looks healthy does not mean they are. It is a mental disorder and the pain and torment going through their mind is enough alone for them to break. Also, just because they are a healthy weight remember that does not mean their body is healthy. Looking back throughout the whole of this book so far, none of my behaviours or thought processes were healthy, and my body was not healthy. It was malnourished and struggled to keep up with ED's demands. Do not be fooled by the stereotypes we are used to seeing.

Caring Styles & Responses, Animal Models

Eating disorder behaviours can often make a carer react in a certain way, which ultimately can lead to confrontations. Unfortunately, this may make your loved one feel insecure and stigmatised, resulting in the person you are caring for using their behaviours even more.

Below is a variety of 'animal' based caring metaphors devised by the Maudsley Hospital in South London, which is the largest mental health training institution in the UK. They developed the following analogies. Each animal analogy is an example of how a carer may react when helping battle those thoughts. It is not uncommon to swing from one approach to another during altercations. You may need to reflect on what your natural responses are and try different 'animal' approaches.

The Jellyfish – Too Much Emotion & Too Little Control

It can be extremely difficult to regulate emotions when caring for someone with an eating disorder. You can become very angry and distressed and therefore mirror the emotions of the loved one you are trying to help. When both parties are experiencing high emotions, it will strengthen the hold of the disorder, causing tears and pure exhaustion. The jellyfish can be quite common when you feel 'to blame' for the disorder, and perhaps have some perfectionistic views about your caring styles. It is so much harder to regulate your emotions when you are feeling stressed, tired or tense yourself. So self-care and self-compassion is vital.

Try asking yourself; what would you say to a friend looking in on your situation? Then try the following points:

- Take time to reflect – How do your jellyfish tendencies make you feel?
- What effects does your jellyfish sting have on your loved one?
- Are you burnt out? Do you need some time away to calm before trying to help?
- How can you further protect yourself from burning out?
- Do you have any negative core beliefs that need working on too?
- Too much emotion can be extremely overwhelming for both you and your loved one. Schedule in some self-care time and ensure you are not at risk of burnout yourself. Remember you cannot pour from an empty cup.

The Ostrich – Avoidance Of Emotion

If you find it hard to challenge the logic of the ED voice, struggle to cope when things get rough and choose to put your head in the sand and ignore it, you may well be an 'ostrich'. However, by avoiding a situation and avoiding your own emotions, you may come across accidently as uncaring and your loved one may feel unloved. It is so important to lead by example and demonstrate controlled emotions, showing your loved one it is okay if you are feeling frustrated at ED and expressing calmly how you are feeling. By dismissing your own feelings and ignoring what is going on, you are demonstrating emotional avoidance which may be a factor of your loved one's illness. Living with someone who can demonstrate ways of articulating emotions in a safe and healthy way can be a real aid to the sufferer.

If you find yourself burying your head in the sand, try asking yourself these questions. Remember self-compassion:

- Is ignoring this particular situation harmful and can it come across as uncaring?
- How can you express how a particular behaviour makes you feel?
- Is there someone you could perhaps practice with? Practice saying how you feel and talk through how to handle difficult situations?
- How do you regulate your own emotions, where could you demonstrate this more within the household?
- Can an ostrich sometimes be helpful? If so, when?

Changing your approach can be extremely challenging and speaking up about how you truly feel can be very uncomfortable. Try talking to a supportive friend about how you could express your feelings. Remember to try and demonstrate regulating your emotions in front of the loved one you are trying to support. Showing them how to handle those difficult emotions can be extremely beneficial.

The Kangaroo – Trying To Make Everything Right

This type of carer may try and over protect the sufferer and take on all aspects of their loved one's life. Putting them into their pouch so to speak, trying to avoid any discomfort, upset and stress. The downside to this is you are not letting your loved one learn how to handle life's challenges, and they may only feel safe when they are with you. This also means giving the ED voice what it wants to avoid hurting them and cocooning them trying to please them.

If you feel you may be overprotective to your loved one, try asking yourself these questions, once again being compassionate with yourself.

- Is being a kangaroo helpful to your loved one?
- What aspects of being a kangaroo can you experiment with?
- Think back to when you have been a kangaroo, how could you change that behaviour, even if it starts with a little step?
- Is being a kangaroo affecting you in any way?
- Is there any time when a kangaroo approach was helpful?

Taking a step back and allowing your loved one to be independent can be extremely difficult. By enabling safe risks and taking baby steps, you may find it more manageable.

The Rhinoceros – Uses Force & Logic To Win The Day

Having a rhino approach, can mean you are trying to tackle that eating disorder voice by confrontation, stress and being quite argumentative. Unfortunately, if your loved one backs down and agrees with the rhino, they struggle to build their own skills and again rely on you. They can become passive and even more anxious, or alternatively it can lead to more confrontations, as the ED voice screams back at the rhino and vice versa, resulting in the voice becoming more embedded.

If you find yourself being a rhino, ask yourself how you could calm yourself down in these situations, again remember to do this with self-compassion:

- Is being a rhino beneficial to yourself or your loved one?
- Could it be you are avoiding your own difficulties?
- What might be the positive and negative repercussions of being a rhino?
- What could you do to lower your own stress and anxiety levels, perhaps walking away when you feel rage building?
- Is there any time a rhino approach may be helpful?

Please try and remember that by arguing with that eating disorder voice you may well be strengthening it. It is also vital to allow the sufferers to develop their own reasons for wanting to change their behaviours, not just repeating yours.

The Terrier – Uses Persistence (often perceived as criticism)

Being a 'terrier' may involve you trying to wear out the ED voice. It may be perceived as 'nagging'. However, by constantly trying to chip away at the voice, the sufferer may switch off to what you are saying and you may become background noise. Also, by being persistent your loved one may think you are constantly 'on at them' and criticising them, making them feel not good enough and adding to their low self-esteem, therefore encouraging that eating disorder voice.

If you find yourself constantly picking at the voice, ask yourself the following using that compassionate voice:

- How may being a terrier effect your loved one?
- What effect has being a terrier had on you?
- Is there a way you could listen to your loved one more?
- What could you do to change this style of care, look back to when you may have had a terrier approach, what could you have said or done differently?
- Are there any times a terrier approach may be helpful?

ED could be described as a terrier, as it constantly criticises and nags your loved one. Active listening can be really helpful. Respond to what they are saying with compassion and encourage them to challenge the voice themselves. Try praising your loved one for trying and celebrate every small win.

James was of course my main carer throughout this time, and very often would flick between the rhino and the ostrich. At times he would ignore my excessive exercise, as he knew if he challenged it, there would be an argument as the ED voice was in the driving seat. This made me feel like he did not care, and then made that voice stronger as it would constantly pick up on it and reinforce the idea that my behaviours were normal.

However, there were times when he got so frustrated with the voice and flipped, so to speak. One evening I needed to go for a run, the voice was screaming and I had worked myself up into an anxious mess. I remember it was dark and heavy rain. James tried to talk to me and nudge me to make the correct decision, trying to make me see sense; however, that voice was too strong. He locked the door and took the keys away so I could not go out and exercise, locking me in the house. This was extreme however, he was so worried, I had not eaten in days, I was dizzy, it was dark and obviously heavily raining. I would have most likely collapsed, I realise that now however, not the best solution.

He was doing it to protect me and make sure nothing happened but by taking that rhino approach I felt trapped and even more anxious. I remember going to the bedroom, stropping like a teenager and doing sit ups until I fell asleep.

The next day we talked about what had happened and he had reflected using the questions above. He apologised and explained he did not want me to collapse and anything could have happened to me. He was so scared and worried he let his emotions take over, it was also dark and late at night. He then said he recognised he had turned into a rhino and he should have tried to keep calm himself. I also saw his point of view, it would have been foolish for me to go out, however at the time I could not hear my rational voice. There was no talking me down. We realised our mistakes, learned together and moved on.

There were also times he was a kangaroo, trying to protect me. However, by doing so he reinforced some of my behaviours by accident. He would let me weigh out all my foods, if it meant I would eat, and only cook specific meals which I deemed 'safe' again if it meant I would eat. He was trying to please me, although by doing so, he pleased the voice. It is so difficult to get the right balance and know what the right thing to do is. What can help your loved one to eat could be feeding another part of the ED by affirming unhealthy behaviours.

Inspirational Animals

The Dolphin – Just Enough Caring & Control

The dolphin carer is what many encourage you to try and become. The idea behind this is that a dolphin gently nudges the sufferer along. Not pushing or forcing, but nudging them in the right direction by demonstrating healthy behaviours and trying to remain compassionate and calm. Dolphin carers swim alongside their loved one offering encouragement but also know when to swim behind quietly and allow their loved ones to lead the way.

Try asking yourself the following to help become a dolphin:

- Are my own emotions influencing the situation?
- How could I find the balance to nudge but not push my loved one?
- What could be perceived as too much or too little for my loved one?

- Are there some cases I need to swim ahead and lead the way, by practicing healthy behaviours? Are all my behaviours helpful?
- Are there any times I have managed to be a dolphin? How did that help the specific situation and is there anything you could learn from that scenario?

Getting the right balance between what is being too pushy and not supportive enough can be extremely difficult. Reflect on times you were a dolphin and make notes to remember for the future. Remember you are learning, and it will take time to figure out what balance your loved one needs.

The St Bernard – Just Enough Compassion & Consistency

Another helpful caring approach is the St Bernard, filled with compassion warmth and calmness. This approach involves accepting the pain the ED is causing and developing ways to install hope into your loved one. Hope that they can change, that their future can be bright ED free. By responding consistently and becoming dependable in all circumstances the St Bernard attends to those who are lost by being calm warming and nurturing. The sufferer may be screaming in frustration and the St Bernard manages to stay calm and simply responds with warmth and by doing so, the sufferer may calm down too. Try asking these questions to help you develop a St Bernard approach:

- Has there been a time where you have been a St Bernard? How did my loved one react?
- If there was a time you were a St Bernard, how did it make you feel?
- Are there any phrases or particular responses your loved one reacts well to?
- How can you let your loved one know you are there for them when they are feeling lost?

- How can you find the balance of showing your loved one you care and being too overprotective?

Similar to the dolphin, finding the right balance between what is too much and too little can be tricky as everyone is different. Keep reflecting on what works for the individual.

Remember!

No one gets it right all of the time, take time each day, just five or ten minutes and reflect. What caring style has been used today? What could I have done to be more of a Dolphin or St Bernard? And remember to be self-compassionate; this is a tough journey for you too.

Things My Friends Did To Be A Dolphin/St Bernard

When I had started to be more open about my disorder, one of the things Emily did, who's story you read earlier, was that she had made me envelopes. On each envelope was an instruction such as, open me when you are feeling unloved, open me when you need a laugh. She had made 6 of them. Inside each envelope was a card and a photograph. The card contained a handwritten message, simply reminding me she was there and reminding me of a more positive time in my life. These little envelopes were very much a St Bernard approach. When I was raging war with myself, even though she was not there, the tone of her message resonated calmness and compassion. She was there and reminded me she loved and cared for me regardless of the ED voice. The envelopes calmed me down and made me feel loved and nurtured and gave me strength to fight another day.

I keep these envelopes in my resource box and re-read them, still to this day, and they still fill me with warmth and provide that encouragement, which may be needed.

An example of my friends using a dolphin's approach was when we were eating out together. They demonstrated healthy behaviours by not ordering low fat 'diet' foods and talking enthusiastically about food. No talks of calories just talk of what they 'fancied' eating. It felt they were leading the way.

Then after hearing they were all having starters, it made me question my ED voice, if they can do it why not me? What is the difference? So, I did. Then when the main came I started to feel a little overwhelmed. Everyone was talking about the food they had ordered and I remember my friend changing the subject, looking across at me and taking a deep breath in then out, almost signalling and reminding me to breath. Not drawing attention to me becoming agitated but subtly reminding me she was there. No pressure, no embarrassment, I just felt guided but not pushed. I copied their example by having and enjoying a starter, and when I started to panic, I was not criticised or wrapped in bubble wrap, I was simply nudged and reminded of a breathing technique to bring my anxiety back down on my own.

Times My Main Carer Used A St Bernard/Dolphin Approach

Moving on to my gorgeous husband. He too, managed to use the St Bernard and Dolphin caring models. One evening when I was fighting with my eating disorder voice, I became very distressed and upset and started shouting at him for help. I was lost and just felt so helpless. Instead of getting panicked on what to do, I remember he very calmly embraced me and went through a breathing exercise with me. Very quickly I felt soothed and calmer just because he was being so calm. He reminded me he loved me, and he was there regardless of what I did or said. Just having that reassuring calm voice defused the situation.

James became a brilliant dolphin, but my goodness it was a long process. He was learning too, and at times, yes, he did resort back to rhino and ostrich tendencies. These were his normal responses, so changing them took time, a lot of work and reflection.

One time he demonstrated the dolphin approach well was Christmas. We sat down and discussed my fears around Christmas Day together and planned several time outs throughout the day where I could just have some time to refocus. I explained what was worrying me and without judging he listened to my fears and we found ways around them. One of my big fears was of course Christmas dinner. However, he reminded me how many people in the country sit down and have Christmas dinner, and that he was looking forward to sitting down as a family and celebrating the day together. He did not push me but simply led the way reminding me, yes there is a lot of food on the table but, the focus will be on the family gathering. Without realising he encouraged me to think of alternative ways to tackle that lunch. During the day itself, James led by example, demonstrating normal portion sizes and allowed me to serve myself a good amount. This was difficult as I was unsure what I was doing, however he smiled at me and nodded when I looked at him for reassurance. A gentle nod reminding me I was doing well.

After lunch we took a walk just to settle down and have some time together, he praised me for lunch and for the rest of the day we talked about other things non-ED related. As tea approached, I felt a little panicked, I had eaten a big lunch, surely, I should skip tea?

I refused to get anything, so I did need a little nudge. He took me to one side and let me talk through my fears, then gently reminded me that even though I had a bigger lunch it did not mean I should not eat any tea, reminding me how the metabolism works. He then said he was going to get something, and he could help me get mine while he was there. I agreed, he did not force me, he just reminded me of the information I already knew and reminded me he would be by my side when at the buffet. A gentle nudge is all I needed and it worked. I was able to enjoy some cheese and crackers, however if he had forced me to do it, or given me a plate of food I had not chosen, I would have freaked out.

Making A Script

One thing I found myself constantly asking was for help. I remember looking at my husband with tears streaming down my face at mealtimes, knowing I had to eat but I couldn't. Begging him to help me somehow. This would make him freeze on the spot and unsure what to do. So, we developed a script for him, ways he could be a dolphin. We sat down together and looked back at our previous mealtimes, what had he said that worked, how could he respond to different scenarios. For example, I had a tendency to all of a sudden explode and need time away for a few minutes to let the anxiety come down a little. During this time, it was decided he could help by passing me a stress ball out of my resource box, letting me throw it around a little and let me have a few moments to blow off some steam.

Often if he followed me, I would feel pressured. We realised I needed time to calm, but he could help by making sure I had my coping mechanism handy. We also discussed things he could say, for example I had various handouts from the dietician reminding me what my body needed in a day. If I let the ED voice speak, I would often say things like, *I do not need this meal, and I ate loads earlier*. He could then gently remind me of what the dietician has said, instead of arguing back with his logical voice. Gentle nudges reminding me of what I had been taught.

James found it very difficult when he could see I was struggling, and would never know what to say or do, and instead look at me with puppy eyes, and say he felt useless. This made me feel guilty and not good enough for him, leading right into the disorder's hands. So, written on the script we also made a list of things he could do to help during these times. For example, talk about something else, distract me. Talk about his day at work, or whatever was on the news. Just to help me think of something else instead of letting those thoughts race. Another tip on his script was to ask if I needed anything from my resource box, flash cards or elastic bands etc?

Everyone is different so it is important to develop this script together with your loved one. What works for them, what does not? Our script was amended so many times, and it took a while for us to get it right, often what worked one day did not necessarily work the next. The point is if James froze and started to panic, he had his own little reminder of things he could do to help, taking that pressure off and easing the initial panic, so he could then feel confident in supporting me.

How can I ensure that my loved one knows I do love them?

I felt so unlovable during my recovery. I felt like a failure for having an eating disorder, constantly feeling not good enough. I cried so many times as James tried to help me and I constantly repeated the phrase, *you can do so much better than me. Why are you wasting your time with me? I do not deserve you.* It was suggested instead of repeating the normal phrases that we were both so used to hearing, he could be a little creative. So, he made a poster of reasons why he loved me. He included loads of pictures of times we were truly happy. Not one of the things he loved about me were to do with my appearance or weight, they were all to do with my personality, times where he looks back and giggles at something I may have said or done. We had this pinned up in the kitchen for ages, just a constant reminder that he does love me and more importantly why.

He also created a gratitude book, and every day he would write down a few things I might have done throughout the day to make him smile. It could be as simple as I text him during his lunch break to see how his day was going, or I gave him a kiss goodbye in the morning. Just little things that I do that make him feel loved.

He also included things I might have done for others that makes him love me, I am a kind natured person. I may have called a friend because they were feeling down themselves or spent time playing with my nieces. Reading these everyday helped me realise how much I do for him and actually I am not such a waste of space or horrible person, but someone who leaves Post-it notes on the pillow or bakes some cakes knowing he likes them.

I had no idea how much I did for others until I saw them listed each day. A daily reminder I am not this horrible monster my eating disorder has me to believe. But a kind loving wife, who cares for others and will do anything to make others smile.

Keep Talking & Learning Together

The final piece of advice for carers, is keep the conversations going. Keep talking about your feelings, do not bottle them up. Demonstrate and reinforce the idea that it is healthy to talk about emotions and feelings. Reflect daily on what has worked and not worked and remember your loved one is still there, somewhere. Just consumed by this illness. It is possible to recover from an eating disorder; however, it takes time and effort from both sides. Remember you will not get it right every time, caring for a loved one and watching them go through it is so difficult but on behalf of your loved one, we are grateful for your support.

Final Note From James

It is difficult to understand eating disorders and it is important to remember that behind the disorder your loved one is still there. What they do is not necessarily their choice but is because of the illness they have.

As I have discovered, there is no magic wand to make it better, but it is possible to recover from an eating disorder. Supporting someone with an eating disorder is not easy, but you just have to remember to be there for them when they need you and gently nudge them in the right direction.

Having an eating disorder is difficult and it is essential that people suffering from a disorder get the help they need, but it also has a massive effect on those around them and can put a strain on families and relationships. Support for carers is vital; make sure you are receiving support too. It helps to make you more aware by understand eating disorders but also helps you to know what you can do when your loved one is affected. Rest when needed and take some time out for you as it can be exhausting.

Chapter 17
New Life

I wanted a family of my own, more than anything. But years of disordered eating had left my reproductive system damaged. I had stopped having periods back when I was a teenager, and I had very irregular and strange cycles, but when the ED got a full grip of me, they completely stopped as my body was trying to preserve as much energy as possible. The thought of never being able to carry a child, never able to start a family was heart breaking. I knew if I wanted a family, if there was any chance at all I could possibly have my happily ever after, I had to recover. Throughout the whole of my recovery, the thought of having a family kept me going, it was my long-term goal. When the ED voice was too much and I wanted to use behaviours, I remembered my long-term goal: *Think of that family Zoe, if you want IVF or to adopt you need to be well.* It was my main reason for recovery and gave me strength to fight in the darkest of moments.

I must stress this before I explain what process we went through. Do not try and fall pregnant or look into fertility treatment until you are stable and have reached your set point. Once you have reached your weight's set point, and have maintained behaviour free, you may find your cycle naturally returning. Your body changes incredibly quickly during pregnancy and being able to mentally manage the change our bodies and minds go through during pregnancy is vital to maintain your wellbeing through this incredible journey into motherhood.

If you are in stable recovery and pregnant, communicate with your midwives and team, explain to them that you are in recovery for an eating disorder and do not be afraid to seek a little extra support if needed. They will not judge and are there to help you, whatever your struggles may be. Keep them updated on your thoughts, as your welfare and general wellbeing is in their best interest and working together honestly will help ensure you and little one are well looked after and are safe.

Fertility Issues

When I was well enough, eating regularly and nearly behaviour free, my partner and I agreed it was time to see a specialist to see what options we have available to us.

I had to go alone to the appointment and James was working away in London. I was terrified about what was going to be said, however once again I was extremely lucky and found myself with the most hilarious fertility specialist I could have asked for, from the second I walked in he made me feel completely at ease, as we discussed what had led to me having complications. I had also been previously diagnosed with polycystic ovary syndrome, so a double whammy of issues. He seemed confident that there were things he could do and explained IVF may be the best route.

We both had tests done to see what the best course of treatment could be. I felt so guilty, it was my fault, the reason we had to do all these tests, the reason we were having difficulties, the reason I could not give my husband a child. I was plagued with guilt, I had to remind myself constantly, *this was not my fault, it was due to an illness, and it was ED's fault*.

That said, I was amazed at the amount of options that were actually available to us, from fertility treatment to adoption. Even if I could not carry a child, that did not mean we couldn't have a family of our own, family is not always blood but those who care for you, love you and accept you for who you are. Love you unconditionally. Yes, carrying my own child had been a dream but the thought of giving a child in need a home, full of laughter and love, that I feel is just as important and also just as fulfilling.

The tests came back and we were lucky that there was hope, my body worked but it had seemed to have forgotten what to do, my body had simply stopped menstruating and was unable to start again. It needed a reboot if you like.

The fertility specialist told us I would be able to take tablets which would encourage my body to have a period, then the second tablets would help me ovulate. It was all very confusing and very overwhelming. Then once my body had kind of remembered what it should be doing, we could have the option to have IVF.

However, both sets of tablets had a side effect. Weight gain. I was in such a better frame of mind than I had ever been and as difficult as this was to accept, I knew it was the only way. I was desperate for my own family and been given a glimmer of hope, a chance that my body was indeed capable of carrying a child. Yes help was needed, but it was possible. I kept focused on this flicker of optimism and carried on with my recovery journey. I was discharged from the service in December, however in January I did have a set back and found myself in a relapse.

After Christmas is always a struggle. I was bombarded by diet culture and even though I was aware it could be a trigger and was prepared, I still fell. I found myself exercising more and severely restricting but was convinced it was just a post-Christmas diet. It was actually once again my husband that had noticed my behaviours and brought up the fact I was slowly relapsing. I was able to see sense and realise he was right, it was ED. I was struggling, I was quickly snowballing but even though I was aware, I was unable to pick myself back up.

I started to feel very tired and weak, I felt nauseous and just not very well. All the normal feelings I had when I was struggling with ED, according to my medication it was time for me to take my tablets to help me have a period that month, before taking them I had to do a pregnancy test to see if the last lot of medication had worked. I did one and put it down as I brushed my teeth. But something was different, not the normal blank negative symbol that had always appeared, but a blue cross.

Positive.

I looked down at it still brushing my teeth very confused. I remember thinking, well it must be wrong. I am not well enough to conceive at the minute and we have not started IVF. Then it hit me.

I am pregnant, I am carrying a child.

I felt overwhelmed with all emotions. Guilt for starters as I was currently relapsing, overjoyed that my body was carrying a child, and the thought of being a mum, this feeling I could not describe. I was absolutely over the moon. I went through to the bedroom where my husband was still dozing as it was a Sunday morning, opened the curtains and handed him the test. He had a very similar reaction to me, and said,

"But you can't be, we haven't started IVF."

We then both sat and discussed whether it could be a false positive, it could be wrong. So I did another test with a more expensive brand and this one too, said positive and I was 1-2 weeks pregnant. We both cried with happiness, overjoyed! But very aware this was going to be a difficult journey as I was in recovery, even though I had been doing very well, I was aware my body would change quicker than my mind may be able to handle.

I knew I needed to look after myself and my little miracle bean, and the news did pull me straight out of my relapse. The effort it took to get to this point, I could not risk anything, I could not risk losing our little bean.

Scare

I reached 6 weeks and I was at work and started to feel a little unwell. I went on my break, popped to the toilet before grabbing my lunch and noticed some blood. Gathering my rational mind, I reminded myself; *a bit of spotting is not uncommon during pregnancy, it is implantation bleeding, nothing to worry about. I will put a pad on just to remain clean.* I went on my lunch but was starting to get pains, period like pains and felt sick. I went to the toilet and I was bleeding, heavily. I had to change my pad within half an hour, I was convinced I was having a miscarriage.

I went downstairs to ring the midwife who advised me to go straight to A&E. I arranged cover and a colleague took me up to hospital where I met James. I was triaged within minutes and told I would have to have an ultrasound scan to see what was going on and check if my little bean had survived.

However, they could not do the scan that day and someone from the early pregnancy assessment unit would have to ring me for an appointment. It was Thursday afternoon so I would not be seen that day as it was 3pm and the department closed at 4pm. I went home convinced I had miscarried, waiting for a phone call.

I received a call on Friday morning. They were unable to see me until Monday. Four days. I felt hopeless, depressed and distraught. My husband tried to remain positive and kept telling me to wait and see, we would know for sure on Monday. I felt like all of this was my fault, I relapsed in January and I did not know I was pregnant, I believed I had lost my bean because of ED. I cannot truly express just how consumed in these negative emotions I felt. I tried to eat and keep to my meal plans, just in case little one was somehow okay, however the feelings were consuming me.

The whole weekend was a massive blur, I woke up on Monday morning after a terrible night's sleep, again pulling myself to bits, telling myself it was all my fault, because I had relapsed. I did not deserve a child. My husband drove me to the hospital, the drive was silent as I sat, tears trickling down my cheeks, preparing for the worst.

We were seen very quickly. I laid on the medical couch eyes closed, crying, holding my husband's hand, who at this point was starting to crack too. The lady carrying out the ultrasound explained what she was going to do and said she would then discuss with the midwife her findings. I braced myself, the sonographer then said,

"Looks okay."

She turned the screen to face us both and showed us, a tiny bean, with a strong heartbeat. I burst into tears, completely broken that somehow our little bean was okay. My husband also cried with me, in relief, and from that moment on, I vowed to look after this bean the best I could.

The sonographer continued her checks once I had calmed down and I looked at the screen in awe. How could something so tiny cause so much stress already? My heart swelled with unconditional love. We saw the midwife after the scan who explained sometimes a bleed can just happen, it was nothing to worry about, nothing to do with my relapse and everything looks completely normal.

After lots of reassurance and agreeing to be kinder to myself, we left the hospital and travelled home. I was clutching the picture of the scan, looking down at this tiny shape, overwhelmed with all these emotions.

First Trimester

The first few weeks of pregnancy very much reminded me of how I felt living with an eating disorder. The tiredness, the feeling sick and not quite with it. The first physical change I noticed was my chest. My boobs were getting very big! Initially I enjoyed them, my husband certainly was not complaining, but they did not stop, they kept growing and growing, I thought they would never stop! Then about 7 weeks into my pregnancy, I started to notice my clothes were getting tighter. However, instead of thinking, *Oh, it is because I am pregnant*, I automatically started analysing everything I had been eating, convinced it was too early for me to be showing and I was just getting fat.

I started to become obsessed with good and bad foods again. Every article I read on pregnancy and any advice I was given reminded me I should be eating my five a day and eating healthy. I found myself slipping into labelling foods good and bad, but I could not blame ED, it was masked by the pregnancy and me needing to look after our bean. I really struggled to eat anything that I did not class as healthy. I kept trying to remind myself that all food has nutritional value.

However, I became obsessed with ensuring I had my five a day and more! There are also certain foods you need to avoid and cut out during pregnancy, so, I found myself obsessing over food, but in a whole new way. I wasn't sure, was it due to pregnancy or was a little bit of it due to ED? It was so hard to tell the difference, it was exhausting.

For my own sanity, I let James become more involved with meal plans and I told him if there was something I had planned to eat that I could not, to save me constantly obsessing. Especially in restaurants, I would just double check, was this on the okay list? I trusted him more than I trusted myself. If I was not sure I would find an excuse to have a safer option, more healthy option or use it as an excuse to listen to ED. It was manageable but very tricky.

I also struggled with morning sickness, but that phrase drives me mad. It is not 'morning sickness' at all, but more like 'morning, mid-morning, lunch time, after lunch, afternoon, evening, middle of the night nausea'. Trying to eat when you feel constantly sick is hard enough without the ED thoughts piping up too. I found if I missed meals I would automatically think, well it won't do you any harm, you could do with losing a little weight, it is not good for you being overweight and pregnant. However, I found the odd occasion when I did not eat because I felt sick, it would actually make the nausea worse. Great! I felt sick if I did eat and sick if I didn't. I found myself constantly having to challenge the thoughts regarding sickness and reminding myself it was not food I was throwing up, but nutrients my baby may need.

I reached 10 weeks and one Saturday morning I was getting ready to go out. I reached for a pair of jeans and got them on but then I tried to do up the button - nope, not happening. My first thought was, *it is not baby, you are fat*, my body was getting bigger, but not just my stomach. I switched to a dress and noticed it was tight around the ribcage, nothing seemed to fit right, everything I tried on felt tight. I broke down in tears as my mind was racing, *was it the baby or was it me just getting fat? Surely it was too soon for all of these changes, it must be me, I am just fat all of a sudden*. It took me ages to calm down, I ended up messaging a few people I knew and asked their experiences, and when they noticed they could not fit into clothes, all the responses were different however everyone seemed to struggle from week ten onwards. It was not too early, it was indeed baby, but for the rest of the day, wearing something I felt un-comfy in, made the ED voice very loud and harder to ignore. I found every mealtime that day I had to challenge the thoughts and think hard about what I was doing, being pregnant is exhausting enough let alone having that to constantly battle too!

From week 11, I started to notice a little bump and it was impossible to hide my pregnancy at work. I wanted to keep it a secret until the 12-week scan, but I did have a visible bump. My bump, my miracle. Finally, week 12 arrived and we were due to have our 12-week scan, seeing the little bean on the screen was incredible, it had changed so much within the last six weeks. The bean was now a little person, moving and wriggling around, waving and stretching.

It really was phenomenal seeing how much it moved. We had now reached what is known as the safe week, the risk of miscarriage had dropped significantly and we were in awe of our baby. By the end of the week, my bump had gotten very noticeable. We announced our pregnancy, and we were bombarded with goodwill messages and support.

A lot of close friends did ask how I was doing in regard to ED, and I was honest, I told them,

"Yes, the thoughts are strong but my love for this bean is stronger, I just have to recognise what is me trying to be healthy and what is the ED trying to pull me in."

One thing I have learnt throughout the whole of my recovery, is being completely honest really is the best way.

My midwife was also very aware that I was in recovery and knew I may need extra support and we were able to plan for this. Again I felt like I had a safety net, I felt supported.

I was now 13 weeks, I was at work sat on the floor, and one of my colleagues made a perfectly innocent remark and said to me,

"Wow you are getting so big, look at your bump are you sure it is not twins?!"

At first of course the voice jumped in and tried to ruin this moment by saying; she has just called you fat, you should diet, you should restrict.

However, instead of running with the thoughts I rubbed my bump and smiled, yeah, I was big already. I had this beautiful life inside me, it was my job to nurture and care for this bean that was no longer a bean, but that is the nickname we had adopted. Every time someone commented on my size, I kept closing my eyes and remembered the scan pictures from our 12-week ultrasound. There is one picture where the baby looks like it is waving at us and I remembered I was growing a life. Everything was going to get bigger, my eating disorder might not like this, but it was happening anyway. And I would find new ways of adapting and tackling that ED voice.

Second Trimester

I found the second trimester a little easier to handle. The world knew I was pregnant, I had a visible bump and the morning sickness had eased off. Each stage of pregnancy had its own issues, and the thing I found most difficult in the second trimester was an increase of hunger.

I was getting peckish in between meals especially if I missed my snack and found I needed more fuel to keep me going all day. I began analysing everything that I was eating, instead of listening to my hunger signals. It got to about three o'clock in the afternoon, every day and I would find myself thinking of food and my stomach would be rumbling. I would grab an apple or a piece of fruit, but it just did not fill me. I needed something else, which flooded me with guilt and gave the ED an excuse to scream at me.

An apple should be enough, I was being greedy and I do not need anything else. But I did, I needed to listen to my hunger signals. I swapped my single piece of fruit for some berries and yogurt instead, which seemed to do the trick. However, I could not ignore the fact it was indeed more. I needed more, I had to listen to what my body required, and accept this. I kept reminding myself it was not just for me, I need to look after bean as well and it did work on easing some of the guilt around eating extra, whilst still trying to get all the vitamins which bean needed too.

It seemed impossible to balance everything, eating right without over doing it. I still did not trust my body enough to tell me to stop eating when I was full, the thoughts came flooding back: *what happens if I am never full and I just gain and gain and gain*? Unhelpful comments came flooding from all around me, when I found myself eating more, in particularly at snack times, I would be greeted with phrases like; "*You are eating for two*", and *"Is baby hungry today?"* These were comments from people who knew full well about my eating disorder too.

Every time these comments were made it made me doubt what I was doing, was this excessive? Was I doing the right thing? Eventually it all got too much and at my next midwife appointment, I spoke to her honestly about the fact I was struggling to know what was right. My midwife was able to be a sympathetic and understand my worries, we went through what I was eating daily and she was able to clarify that it was all completely fine and if anything I was overdoing it with the fruit. We agreed, I had become a little too obsessed with all the articles and websites telling me what I should and should not be eating.

I needed to relax a bit for the sake of my mental health. We agreed I would not look at any articles and just talk to her instead and let her help me with my meal planning from then on.

I reached 14 weeks into my pregnancy and that was it, nothing fitted right, I was uncomfortable, everything was tight and I was growing. I knew my stomach needed to grow; it made sense. What I severely struggled with was everything else growing. My legs and bum were now huge. Trying to squeeze into my normal clothes only made that voice scream: *your bum is getting fat, no excuse, and there is no baby in there!* Despite all the information on hormones and the fact everything grows in pregnancy, I believed that voice. I knew I needed some clothes that fitted right, so my husband and I bit the bullet and went shopping.

We knew it was going to cause many feelings, buying clothes bigger than normal, but I constantly reminded myself why. We entered the shopping centre and headed straight to a shop which I knew did maternity wear. I picked up a few things begrudgingly and went to try them on. I was going to look awful. However, when trying on these maternity leggings and a little green dress with daisies on, I did not feel huge, they fitted well and were comfy.

They were still my size but designed for pregnancy. They stretched with my growing body and made room for the baby and my other growing body parts. I did not buy loads as I simply could not afford them, just one of each of the essentials, work trousers, leggings, a dress, a pair of jeans and a few tops and of course, I got measured for some bras. I could not cope anymore with trying to squeeze mine into a bra that simply covered nothing anymore and left nothing for the imagination. I started to feel better now I was comfy, nothing was tight and I had room to grow.

I also found myself back to my old tricks with regards to comparing. I kept comparing my pregnant body to other mums to be. I did not have a nice neat little bump, I had grown everywhere and kept thinking I just looked fat instead of pregnant. I did it everywhere, just like before, and the worst thing was I didn't even realise. I would compare my bump to people in the hospital when I went for my scans. I adored how they all looked and they were glowing, what was wrong with me?

I did it online, I knew other women that were pregnant and when they posted pictures, once again found myself thinking, gosh they look amazing, they have such a lovely bump, they do not look like they have gained everywhere else, it is just me. I teamed up with someone from work who was just two weeks further along than I was. She knew about my history of eating disorders and somewhat understood. I remember one day at work we were remaking the displays, tidying them up, when I mentioned how lovely she looked.

She laughed out loud and said,

"*Are you kidding? My skin has broken out in spots, I cannot remember what my toes look like, I have ballooned everywhere, I keep knocking things over with my arse and I just feel pants all the time"*

I gasped, what? How could she think this way? She looked stunning to me. I then shared my own thoughts and we giggled, as we realised we thought the exact same thing. My insecurities were not so much ED related, but seemed to just be general pregnancy issues which many people have.

Through sharing them I no longer felt guilty or ashamed that I hated my body when this miracle was happening, it was a normal response. Not selfish of me at all, my mind was just adjusting slower to what my body was growing; my mind felt like it was constantly playing catch up.

I was now 18 weeks and I did feel better within myself. I had energy again and thought maybe it was safe to engage in more exercise than what I was doing. I wanted to keep fit.

At this point the country was in lockdown due to the Vovid-19 pandemic, so I was unable to do my weekly swim, what could I do instead? I was only allowed to leave the house once a day for a walk and being trapped at home with so much uncertainty and having no control over what was happening was having an impact. I needed to find safe workouts online, so I turned to prenatal yoga, courtesy of YouTube.

I tried to do this three times a week, however, it was not making my heart race as much as swimming did and it just did not feel like I was exercising. I was also rubbish at it, I had no balance and fell over a lot. I was beginning to get anxious about whether I was doing enough exercise, so I decided to fish out the Wii and my entire collection of Just Dance games. I set it all up and got dancing, I felt great, I was sweating and my heart was pumping, the calorie counter in the corner was flashing and I could not help but be drawn to it, praising myself for the calories I was burning.

After I had finished the workout I went for a shower and then grabbed lunch. After lunch I went to tidy up, but I was unable to move. I was in agony; my back had gone. I could barely walk, had I been sat funny? Did I pull something standing up? Not once did it occur it could have been the exercise.

I was then stuck on the sofa or in bed for four days, unable to move, unable to do anything, having to ask my husband to help me stand whenever I needed the toilet or needed a drink. I felt completely useless. After a few days' complete rest and constant hot water bottles on my back, it started to ease. The guilt of not being able to do anything started to bubble and I decided some gentle exercise would be a good idea, loosen me up again.

I found myself heading for the Wii again and setting up Just Dance. My husband questioned if it was a good idea, I explained I would take it slowly and I just needed to move a little, however within minutes, I was hooked again, going for it, and not able to take my eyes off the calorie counter. I got halfway through the workout before I had to stop. The pain was unbearable again. I could not do this sort of exercise while I was pregnant, I had to take it steady.

I found myself unable to move for a few days again and then when returning to exercise I stuck with yoga and gentle stretching exercises. Eventually I got better at prenatal yoga and started to enjoy it more, I just needed to give it time. I had to adapt my exercise pattern to accommodate pregnancy, I needed to look after myself and my back or I would be laid up again.

Finally, we reached 20 weeks and I was able to have my next scan. I was so excited, but the familiar nerves kicked in. Was everything going to be okay, what if something was wrong, had I done something wrong?

The nerves were unreal, I arrived at my scan and luckily was not waiting long. I went straight in and laid there for what seemed to be forever, panicking as the doctor doing the ultrasound checked little one over. She then turned the screen and showed me each of the baby's organs all working and functioning well.

I took a deep breath out and actually started to cry. The emotion just got too much, everything was going well, I just needed to trust my body and stop thinking of the worst-case scenario. I was then asked if I wanted to know the gender. I nodded, the lady then pointed it out on the screen, I was being blessed with a baby girl.

Once again, flooded with emotion, I cried. I have no idea why I was just so overwhelmed. A beautiful baby girl, there she was, thriving regardless of all my negative thoughts, regardless of my worries over if I was doing everything right, she was perfect.

Cravings

I had some of the strangest cravings throughout my first trimester. I craved grapes, mainly because I think my body was missing wine and grapes were as close to a glass of Shiraz I was going get for a very long time. I had no problem constantly snacking on grapes, it was not a problem for that voice, however in my second trimester I started craving something else, very intensely.

I craved peanut butter and cheese sandwiches and it really was at the most random times of the day. If I ignored the cravings and tried to carry on, I could not focus, I could not concentrate and it was all I could think about.

I tried to distract myself however, I could not. I ended up eating these weird but wonderful sandwiches at all hours of the day. The feeling of guilt that swamped me after was exhausting, I felt like I was binging and out of control with my eating.

Pregnancy cravings are completely normal. I reminded myself of set point theory and I did find if I had my cravings my hunger signals would compensate and I would feel less hungry later on. It is not the end of the world if you have a sandwich for a snack, and my goodness they were incredible.

I found if I tried to ignore my cravings and distracted myself, they would only come back stronger later on. I remember craving a sandwich in the middle of the afternoon. I had eaten dinner, had a snack and tea was in an hour or so. I talked myself out of it, I did not need it and it would go. I kept thinking about it but kept being stubborn and not giving in. We had tea, washed up and sat down to watch a film. I could not concentrate on the film, my craving was all I could think about and I cannot even tell you what film we had watched!

We went to bed, again I was denying myself my craving, telling myself I did not need it, and went to sleep. I then awoke at about three am. My craving had come back with vengeance, I tossed and turned getting angrier and angrier with the craving, until eventually James woke up. He asked me what the matter was, I admitted to my craving and he laughed at me, how dare he laugh! I was fuming.

He got out of bed and returned with one round of bread filed with cheese & peanut butter, I ate it and instantly felt calmed. We laughed about why this was my craving, would little one be peanut obsessed? When I woke up, I was a little concerned about my middle of the night snack, but instantly calmed again, reminding myself of set point theory, telling myself, one sandwich would not make a difference to my overall weight, nothing terrible happened and it did not mean I was losing control with food.

Just to confirm my thoughts, I messaged a few friends who had children who then shared some very similar stories about midnight trips to find salted crisps and sending out partners to find a specific type of ice cream. The different stories about cravings reassured me it was completely normal and was also very amusing to read, my 3am sandwich really was not such a big deal.

Third Trimester

Ah third trimester, the return of; how on earth can I be hungry again? What is this pain? And all the emotions possible in the space of half an hour.

Stretch Marks

My morning routine now consisted of showering and then covering my bump and top of my legs with stretchmark prevention creams, lotions and potions. I thought they were working, but there they were, taunting me at the top of my legs, deep purple in colour, a series of stretch marks. Heat rushed into my cheeks and I felt ashamed. My body was big; there is no doubt about that. Clouded by that eating disorder voice my mind turned to how I could get rid of these ugly scars marking my body. I kept thinking my husband would find me unattractive; he would want to leave me once our little girl was born. Swamped with insecurities, just because of some stretch marks. Convinced this meant I had gotten fat, and forgetting I had a miracle growing inside me.

I could not find my rational voice, negative emotions heightened by hormones swamped me and I fell to the floor in tears. My husband heard my little outburst and came to see what the matter was. I hid my ugly body from him, telling him to leave me alone, screaming I was hideous. He looked at me puzzled.

He then sat beside me on the bedroom floor and put his arms around me. Once I had calmed down a little, he took my hand in one of his and with his other cupped my chin, looking me straight in my tear stinging eyes he told me,

"How can you be hideous? You are carrying our baby girl, you are glowing and have never been more beautiful to me."

Great more emotions to deal with! I now could not stop crying because of what he said. I sobbed in his arms, covering him with snot and tears as the emotions all poured out. Eventually I calmed enough to tell him my problem, showing him the little purple marks on my skin, ashamed of them and once again I found myself in tears as I looked at them. I glanced up at James who looked completely puzzled, which I found strangely irritated by.

I said to him,

"Look they are horrible, it just means I am fat. You will detest them and will leave me."

To my utter annoyance he then burst out laughing. I was not impressed, how could he find this funny? He helped me off the floor and sat me on the bed, once again his arms around me, he then told me;

"Those little marks are a reminder of what an amazing job you have done carrying our little girl, how can I see them as ugly when they are part of the most beautiful thing we have created together?"

He was my rational voice during this time, all I could see was my body growing and my skin unable to cope. I saw them to begin with as such a shameful thing, wanting to hide them away and convinced my loved ones would view me differently. The whole situation was not helped by those raging hormones, filling my body with intensity, no middle ground. I decided I would continue to use my lotions and would learn ways to deal with them later, for now I needed to continue with my day.

Heart Burn

I started to struggle with heartburn at the beginning of my third trimester. Everyone is different and I had the occasional bout during my second trimester, but all of a sudden it hit me with force. Everyone seemed to be full of suggestions on avoiding heartburn, however all of them seemed to make my eating disorder voice excited. Someone suggested I avoid all foods that give me heartburn, so constantly watching and tracking my food. Obviously, ED would love this.

Someone suggested smaller portions. I had only just learnt what a normal portion was, making them small again would only confuse me. One person suggested I eat before 6.30pm so the food had time to settle, but I had just learnt how to unfollow this rule and by setting myself times again, I feared would instantly set me back in that frame of mind. Finally, my personal favourite, someone actually suggested that I lose weight to help with my heartburn. I was heavily pregnant, hormonal and recovering from an eating disorder, did you really just suggest I lose weight?

I decided to try the first option, to see if I could discover which foods triggered my heartburn, so I could avoid them in the future.

Here is a list of what gave me heartburn;

- spicy foods,
- anything tomato based or tomatoes themselves,
- anything cheese based and any cheese,
- garlic,
- citrus,
- fruit juice,
- certain fruits,
- chocolate,
- mint,
- tea,
- coffee,
- soda,
- onions,
- all red meat,
- bigger meals,
- and finally, milk.

So, what on earth could I eat which contained none of these things? There are of course many options, but for me one of my main meals is pasta with chicken in a tomato passata based sauce, full of onions, peppers, garlic and lots of spice. Basically, everything that could give me heartburn.

Another of my favourite foods is curry, another no go. My friends would often tease me about my love of spicy foods; I could eat a vindaloo and not be phased, now a korma triggered pain! It seemed all I could eat that did not cause me pain, were foods I used to eat when I was struggling - stir fry, fresh fish and vegetables. This seemed no issue, however, I found after a few weeks of cutting out all of my favourite food groups I was starting to fall back into old habits. I was constantly watching what I was eating; making sure it would be okay. This might not seem an issue, but limiting myself to only root veg and certain meats made me feel trapped again, not living.

I started to worry as I recognised my thoughts, I was scared to eat anything not made at home in case it had something in it that could trigger my heartburn. The familiar anxiety around social eating had returned, I felt like I had been catapulted backwards.

I felt so guilty, one evening we had some left-over pork from our Sunday roast and James and I decided we would make a Greek salad with it. It was a very warm day and I have some sort of weird love affair with olives. We made the salad, lots of fresh tomatoes, cucumber, lettuce, pork, spinach, feta, spring onion, radish and obviously olives. James made a salad dressing and we sat down for our meal. We enjoyed it thoroughly however about an hour later, I was in pain. Heartburn from a salad, are you for real? We talked about what was in it and remembered the spring onion, feta possibly pork and tomatoes. I suggested next time we just have the salad with cucumber, lettuce, pork and spinach, even as I said it, I laughed. That was not a meal, not really. I knew cutting out all of these foods from my diet was not good for my thoughts but what other options did I have? I had just learnt how to eat freely and intuitively, I felt broken.

There is good news though, I found a few other non-eating disorder suggestions that worked well for me, that could help ease that pesky pain.

- Not laying down after meals, keeping propped upright so the heart is above the stomach acid.
- Try and sleep slightly propped up too, perhaps a few extra pillows just to help.
- Carbonated drinks can have an impact, although this means watching what you drink a little, it can help.
- Talk openly to your midwife to find a medicine suited specifically for you and that is safe.
- Rest after meals, avoid exercising after eating except a gentle walk. Bending down and movement can send the acid into your oesophagus.
- Keep talking to your midwife and antenatal team, once again be honest with your triggers and remember that your mental health is just as important as your physical health. If something is going to trigger your thoughts, be honest with them and come up with alternatives.

Pelvic Girdle Pain

Oh, my goodness what was this agony?! I couldn't walk, move or even roll over in bed without pain taking over the lower half of my body. Very quickly I was diagnosed with pelvic girdle pain. (PGP) and it was explained to me that my hips were also misaligned. I was given physio and told to go easy. I had to rest, I had no choice, I couldn't physically do anything but rest. Even getting up from the sofa I needed assistance, which played right into ED's hands. One day after lunch I had completely seized up, and I had to ask my husband to give me a hand up, straight away that voice piped up. *It's because you are fat.* No. It is because I am heavily pregnant and have this medical condition. I was able to battle with the thoughts a little, but as time went on the thoughts got stronger.

It took a while for the physio to take effect and some days I couldn't even get out of bed, having to rely heavily on my partner to do everything. I felt swamped with guilt, I should be cleaning or exercising, I should be doing something! As I got angrier with myself for being unable to do things, the more the ED voice took over. My mind started to wonder how many calories I should be consuming if I was not burning as much, I started to question what I was eating and when my hunger cues kicked in I found myself questioning them. Did I need anything? Should I be eating if I couldn't move? All the thoughts I could normally challenge were flooding in but hidden.

Due to being in a large amount of pain, I also found it masked my hunger cues. I was so focused on what I was feeling in my legs and pelvis, I became unaware of when I felt naturally hungry. I also hated having to ask for things to be brought to me. I did not want to bother James by asking for a snack, so sometimes I didn't bother. To overcome this fear and the mind reading skill I was so obsessed with, I decided to actually talk to him instead. Turns out he did not mind one bit and would rather I ask for help than me be in constant pain.

Eventually the pain eased enough for me to be able to do things on my own. Very quickly I realised my eating had been off and I resorted back to a meal plan to kick start my hunger cues again.

On occasions I still needed help. I had such a hard time accepting that this was indeed okay. I was carrying a lot of extra weight, fluid and baby, and I wanted to be able to do everything on my own. Prove to everyone that I could be this super woman, dealing with pregnancy 'perfectly'. But this was just not feasible, perfect pregnancy does not exist.

Luckily, I had a wonderful physiotherapist, who when explaining my condition, reassured me it was not weight related and I did NOT need to diet. All I needed to do was rest, do my exercises and try a little walk daily. Then when I started to improve, I could do slightly longer walks and go back to my prenatal yoga. I was adamant this pain was because I was 'fat' however upon research it turns out that one in five pregnant people can struggle with PGP or SPD. So, it is actually quite common, and did not occur because I was 'fat'.

Weight Gain

I sat calmly as the midwife explained how much weight I may be gaining each week. I nodded and understood why this happens. ED on the other hand had different ideas. The second I left my appointment and was alone with my thoughts, there it was, that voice. *You cannot gain all that weight, not all of it is for baby, you need to start eating really healthy and exercising more to keep this weight gain to a minimum.*

Every time I tried to eat after that appointment, the reminder of weight gain was on my mind. I had no idea how much weight I was gaining, as I never looked when I got weighed for routine appointments and my midwife completely understood why. However, I started to grow curious, but actually it was the ED that was growing curious. I decided to try and focus on what my body was doing and growing as opposed to the weight gain. I continued not to look at the numbers on the scale and my chart.

The third trimester also meant once again, I was hungrier than before and needed to increase what I was eating. AGAIN!

Trying to do this whilst constantly thinking of weight gain felt exhausting. I desperately wanted to eat intuitively and had learnt how to do so well, but the idea of how much extra weight I may be carrying was exhausting.

I found my hormones overwhelming me and I remember getting very upset one evening about everything. Frustrated by my hunger cues, frustrated that my body was indeed growing still and frustrated at the ED voice. I knew I needed to keep up with my hunger cues and carry on intuitively eating if I was to stay focused on recovery.

It was hard, but I knew I had no choice but to keep pushing forward, not just for me, but for that little girl wriggling around inside me. Crying through some meals became the norm for a while, as I forced myself to follow what I knew was the right thing to do. Forced myself to shout back at the ED voice and do what was right for me, what was right for my body and for this little bean.

Am I Good Enough To Be A Mum?

Not exactly eating disorder related but it certainly played into the negative self-critic part of my brain I was still battling. So many new mums I have spoken to have had this fear and for me that fear was far too real. *What if I did the wrong thing? What if she grows up and hates me? How do I know I am doing right by this little girl?*

One evening I was doing a little research on bottle feeding, making sure I knew what I was doing and had everything we needed. I stopped, put my phone down and burst into full blown sobs. Hormones obviously not helping at this point either, but I was terrified. My husband straight away took me in his arms and asked what on earth had happened to make me suddenly explode like this. I started to tell him what was going through my mind, and then as I started, I could not seem to stop.

It came flooding out, everything I was fearful of and everything worrying me about the next chapter of our journey together, all my insecurities. I could not stop. After what felt like an eternity of irrational thought sharing, he simply asked,

"Is that all?"

Somewhat annoyed at his response I shouted back,

"What do you mean is that all! I am going to be a crap mum!"

He then reminded me these thoughts are common and I couldn't be the perfect mum, reminding me of that perfectionistic trait I have. We will get it wrong sometimes but that is ok, we are learning and have never done this before.

He encouraged me to make a list of everything that was bothering me and I did. We then made a plan to look into each one a bit at a time and to break it all up. All of a sudden, things felt clearer, I had so much to learn but could not learn it all at once. I needed to focus on one area at a time.

We tackled bottle feeding that night, I already knew what I was meant to do, as I had been over it with the midwife, it was just making sure I was confident. The next night we tackled sleeping, again going through the information from the midwife and researching any gaps we had. By the end of the week, I felt much calmer and could not understand why I had got so wound up. The insecurities were still there, however, I also understood these were common for all new mums and I was not alone in this.

I started talking to friends who had children, to help me make sense of my worries and spoke openly to my midwife who again, was able to help.

One of my biggest worries was: *what if she inherits my eating disorder? What if she grows up hating her body too and I do not recognise it? What if she suffers and struggles like I have, and I miss it?*

Even though I am in solid recovery I still find myself talking negatively about my body sometimes, and I still catch myself talking about food groups. Yes, I correct myself, and also talk and encourage others to talk to themselves like they would a friend and remind them that no food is bad, but I still thought: *will it be enough to counteract? How do I know that I will do the right thing?*

Having an eating disorder has actually equipped me with more knowledge and understanding about food. It has educated me in ways I could never have imagined and opened up my eyes to how our bodies work. I have all this knowledge, which I will be sharing with this little girl. If I had not gone through treatment and ED programme, I would still be believing diet culture and possibly inflicting that on my child. This is much more dangerous. Just because I have had an eating disorder does not mean my child will develop one too, and if she does, I am aware of the signs, symptoms and warning signals, and understand where to go to seek help and support early on.

What's Next?

I simply cannot protect her from everything in the world, as much as we want to wrap our little ones in cotton wool, we cannot. I know I need to let her live and be her own person, but I can guide her in the right direction regarding how to respect her body and celebrate all it can do.

Pregnancy was not easy to navigate through; it is hard enough without still having that little gremlin in your head trying to twist every little thing into a negative. My midwife was incredible throughout the whole of my pregnancy and they are there to answer any questions you may have. They are not eating disorder specialists though, if you do need specific help, do not wait. Not nourishing your body properly can have serious consequences on yourself and your new-born and should not be left undealt with.

I was fortunate enough to be nearly fully recovered when I was pregnant. Yes, I had lots of wobbles throughout as that voice did twist everything, but I was very quick to act, realising what was going on and dealing with it. I stayed healthy throughout pregnancy, and now I cannot wait for our next chapter to begin. It will not be easy, I know, but I have tackled this, I have tackled the ED head on, I can tackle anything.

Post-Baby

Just when I thought this whirlwind was settling down, a whole host of emotions hits you. The second I gave birth to our little girl I cried. I have been unable to stop since. I have always struggled to cry openly and this no longer seems an issue. I keep looking at our daughter in awe, how did we create such a beautiful gift? Overwhelmed with emotions, and incredibly happy. However, looming over me was my new body, softness where there use to be muscle, roundness where it was once flat and stretch marks where my skin was once flawless. Of course, at first it was impossible to get in the mind frame of body neutrality. My eating disorder voice started to scream at me, I knew I could lose my baby weight quickly, I had lost weight quickly before once, I could do it again right?

I was also asked constantly how I planned on getting my post-baby body back. I wanted to scream at people that yes, my body has changed but can we just appreciate what it has been through, what it has done? I remember just before Rosie was born, a woman stopped me in Tesco and asked

"How are you planning to get back in shape, I bet you cannot wait to get all slimmed down."

I was absolutely gob smacked that a complete stranger had assumed that is what I wanted to do straight after birth!

At the time all I wanted was to spend time with my new-born once she had arrived, but unfortunately it is just the world we live in, consumed with diet culture. I politely explained to this woman that I was trying to accept my body and would not be crash dieting once I had given birth; the look she gave me was atrocious. It was like I was speaking a different language. She continued to go on about the franchise she used and how it had helped her, I did end up snapping when she said for the thousand time, "*get your body back.*"

I shamelessly lost my temper. My body has not gone anywhere! I do not need it back, it is still here; I am not nor never was a floating head. However, the damage had been done, it had started to reawaken that voice. How would I get my body back? Did I look that awful? If a complete stranger thought this way surely that is what everyone thinks?

These constant comments excited that voice and the response used this to try and entice me back, trying everything to draw me into all the post-baby diets that were advertised all over social media. Thanks to algorithms my media platforms knew I had just had a child and therefore generated adverts that they thought I may be interested in.

They were of course all dieting ads, in particular intermittent fasting. I knew what would happen if I engaged in this behaviour, I would snowball very quickly. However, they were there, constantly, and that voice kept saying, I could do it differently this time, I know where I went wrong, I would stop before it turned into ED again. I remembered thinking back to times where I had thought like that before, and knew deep down, it would never be enough.

Tiredness kicked in around day five, the baby pinks vanished and I was hit hard by the baby blues. Terrified I would fail this little one somehow, terrified I would not be enough. These thoughts, the constant bombardment from dieting ads and looking at my new body all seemed to get too much. I found myself restricting, but once again making excuses for it. Little one needed feeding when I was due to eat, she needed changing or playing with, there was always something that needed doing, between keeping up with Rosie's demands, to making sure the washing and day-to-day chores were still being done. I found it too easy to distract myself from nourishing my body. I felt guilty if I rested, the voice saying: *you should be doing this, or how can you rest when there are some bottles that need washing and sterilizing? You are failing as a mum by not doing everything.*

I managed to stay well whilst James was off work, we could share the night feeds, share the jobs around the house and tag team when needed. We made sure we both ate well and would take turns in eating breakfast and dinner if needed. However, when he returned to work, I started to fall, struggling to get meals and snacks due to being busy. It was the Coronavirus pandemic as well, so I could not really go anywhere and support was limited. So, loneliness started to creep in. I felt so guilty if I reached out, services were already stretched, I should be able to cope.

Anxiety around another lockdown and feelings of everyone else was coping; I should just get on with it. Add those feelings to the thoughts around my new body and this is where I started to really struggle. Too many negative thoughts in my head started to spin and eventually it all got a little too much.

The constant need to do things, I was manic. However, very quickly I felt weak, my body was still recovering from childbirth and could not cope with missing meals and eating little whilst trying to do everything else. I could not exercise at all due to me needing stitches, but I felt I had to do something about my body. I started to get headaches, and just did not feel well. My husband picked up on my behaviours very swiftly and was quick to act. He pointed out my headaches could be linked to restriction and I would not be so tired if I fuelled my body.

Of course, he was right, however once I started to fall, I found it very hard to bring myself back out of ED's grasp. Behaviours became sneaky and almost too easy. When James returned to work, I knew I had two options. Carry on down this path that ED was trying to entice me with. Yes, lose my baby weight and run away from the feelings I was trying to avoid, run away from the feeling I was not good enough, run away from feeling scared I would fail. Exist once more and not live fully, not experiencing my little one grow up. **Or** recognise what was happening, realise I was being hard on myself and give myself a little break. Learn to ignore the housework, it could wait. Accept these feelings are normal for a new mum and remember help is always available.

I desperately wanted to choose option two, I wanted to continue living my life fully and there was a fear my daughter would pick up on my behaviours and struggle just like I have done. I needed to accept my emotions and accept my new body. After all, without my body changing I would not have this beautiful gift. This was just another part of my recovery journey I needed to tackle head on before it spiralled out of control. I ended up seeking a little extra support from a counsellor and private dietician after the birth, I knew what I needed to be doing, I had all my resources still. I just needed a nudge and someone to talk through all these feelings with. Help regulate my emotions and untangle some of my thoughts. I went back on guided meal plans to rebuild my strength and ensure my cognitive functions were back to normal.

I stayed in maternity clothes for months after giving birth. A few comments were made to me, such as "oh I fitted back in my jeans in four weeks." I wanted to scream, well good for you! What do you want a medal? But bit my sarcastic tongue and resisted. I knew I would not fit back into my pre-baby clothes, and if I tried it would just anger the voice and my mind would be flooded with ED thoughts. So, instead I allowed myself extra time and focused on being comfy. Baggy tops and leggings were my go to. Then one day, when I was in a good frame of mind, feeling well and ED thoughts nowhere to be seen, I tried on my old jeans.

They did not fit; I laughed as I looked in the mirror and reflected on what my body had done for me. I stroked the roundness and smiled down at Rosie, who was asleep in her Moses basket. How could I hate my body? Look at what it had done for me? Did it matter that these jeans no longer fit? What was more important to me? Getting back into these jeans or continuing to spend my time and energy on this little miracle?

That weekend my husband and I went shopping and I was able to buy some new jeans that were comfortable and fitted well, and a few new jumpers. I was not going to attempt to squeeze into my old jeans and walk around uncomfy making that ED voice scream. Remembering and reminding myself that the label and size mean nothing. Reminding myself of all the body image work I had previously done, revisiting it all.

My set point has changed, my size altered, and my heart is now full.

Full of unconditional love for this little one and amazed at just how incredible my body is, in awe with what it can do, my Rosie lines (stretch marks) a constant reminder of what my body once did. It carried and grew my little girl. To me, they are simply my daughter's first artwork and like a tattoo, I display them proudly.

Accepting my new body whole heartedly and remembering what is truly important. I look in the mirror and find myself giving thanks to my body.

Thank you body, for all you have done.

You have done an amazing job and produced something so beautiful.

I refuse to hate you.

Chapter 18
Letter To Rosie

I cannot describe the feeling I had when I first held your tiny body in my arms. Completely overwhelmed with a love and affection for someone I had only just met. A love that was unconditional and indescribable yet very real. My beautiful Rosie, you will never know just how much you were wanted and just how much you are truly loved.

The journey to get you here has been long, and at times seemed impossible. Yet here you are, despite everything. I will continue to fight this eating disorder to stay well for you and continue to fight that voice every day.

I will try and shield those behaviours from you and pray you never know this pain.

I will do my absolute best to raise you to be a strong individual and teach you all the skills I have only just learnt myself. I will encourage you to see people's inner beauty and guide you to look carefully at how we judge others.

I will try my absolute hardest to let you grow and flourish independently, but will always encourage you to love yourself and hopefully radiate kindness.

I will allow you to make mistakes and learn from them, however, still protect you and care for you ensuring you come to no harm.

I know I cannot completely shield you, but hopefully you will know the balance between emotional resilience and that it is ok to show and share your emotions, especially and always with me.

I pray you know you can always come and talk to me about anything and I will listen. I may not get it right, this is new for me too, but I will try my absolute hardest to be the mum you deserve.

I know one thing for sure little one. I will encourage all your hopes and dreams no matter what they may be, encourage you to explore the beautiful world where we live and love you unconditionally, now and always.

Chapter 19
Myths Busted.

The following is a genuine list of things that have actually been said to me throughout my diagnosis and recovery journey. If you know someone struggling, no matter how well meaning, please don't ever say anything like this to them.

- "You do not look like you have an eating disorder." – This one in particular is the worst, eating disorders do not have a 'look', anyone can struggle. You do not need to be a certain size, gender, race or age to struggle with an eating disorder. The stereotypical image we have of an eating disorder is dangerous.

- "It is your choice to have this illness" – I am sorry what? I choose to be in constant pain? My thoughts obsessing with food and my weight, my body shutting down and the fear of not being ill enough to get help, you think I chose this! It is a serious mental health disorder, never a personal choice. I did not just wake up one day and think, oh I am going to starve myself and exercise till I pass out now.

- "It is your parent's fault" – No, it is not, every person suffering is different. Eating disorders develop differently and there are no specific guidelines to prevent this from happening. I did not know what I was doing to myself, how should they.

- "It is just attention seeking" – Similar to it is a choice, I would rather dress up as a penguin to receive attention than this. Also suffers go to great lengths in hiding their behaviours, keeping it a secret is a big element.

- "You just took this diet a bit too far" – Some eating disorders may be triggered by dieting, but the number of times I was told it was just a diet "gone wrong" was painful. Again, it is a very serious mental illness that has catastrophic consequences.

- "Eating disorders are just about people not eating" – If only it was that simple, that was just a result from poor body image, negative self-talk, severe low self-esteem, emotional avoidance, trying to feel in control. As well as checking behaviours, exercise addiction that can be just as dangerous as other addictions, combined with all the other severe medical complications. But if all you see is me not eating, that must be all that is going on.

- "Atypical anorexia is not that serious" – The BMI chart may say healthy, but what about the other complications of atypical anorexia such as; irregular heart rhythm that can lead to heart disease and heart attacks, osteoporosis, loss of muscle mass, amenorrhea, as well as the mental complications, depression, anxiety, preoccupation with food, body image, low self-esteem and of course, death? Atypical anorexia is just as serious as anorexia.

- "I wish I had your will power" – This is not will power, this is mental torture. I wish I had the ability to live my life freely; no part of this illness is impressive.

- "I wish I had your figure" – Similar to willpower, this figure is impossible to maintain without slowly killing myself, do not wish for this, I would not wish this on my worst enemy.

- "Oh, so you just don't like food? Like a really bad fussy eater" – No, quite the opposite actually, I love food. It is torment how much I was denying myself things that I actually adore over and over again, as a way to punish myself.

- "Is it just a control thing? You cannot control everything you know" – It is not just about having a sense of control, a part of it may be yes, but once again, eating disorders are complex and are made up from a variety of factors.

Recovery Myths

- *You can recover by following a diet scheme which encourages healthy eating.* – The number of times people tried to encourage me to join Weight Watchers or Slimming World to teach me about food was embarrassing. I needed to completely step away from the diet culture and these companies have you watching what you eat. I needed to learn intuitive eating and accept my body, not be encouraged to shrink and obsess with my figure.
- *You are eating now; I am pleased you are better again.* – Just because I am eating does not mean I am well, it takes years of hard work, and eating disorders are so much more than food restriction. Just because I am eating does not mean my thoughts are not still entwined.
- *Just eat healthy and make sure you exercise.* – I am pretty sure this is what got me into this mess in the first place; concentrating too much on 'good' and 'bad' foods, forgetting all food has nutritional value, and making sure I exercised, *having* to exercise, *needing* to.
- *You just need to learn self-discipline.* – I am very self-disciplined, you have no idea just how self-disciplined you need to be to maintain an eating disorder, this is just not helpful at all.
- *I know some great exercises that will help you lose weight well.* – I can lose weight, too well. I need to step away from seeing exercise as a weight loss aid and more about enjoying moving my body. I do not want to be encouraged to lose weight when that is the very damaging thing I am trying to quit.
- *If you wanted to lose weight, I have some great tips.* – Good for you, keep them to yourself, I do not need or want to lose weight, I am trying to step away from the dieting world and love myself.
- *You will always have an eating disorder, you can never*

fully recover. – Full recovery is possible, yes it takes a long time, but with the right help and support it can be done.

Chapter 20
The End?

I know my struggle is far from over, however everything I have learnt so far will equip me for any future wobbles.

I finally understand how important it is to actually allow myself time for self-care. You really cannot pour from an empty cup, I will say it one last time: self-care is not selfish. It is a necessity.

Now I am physically healed and my metabolism works, I have started my relationship with intuitive eating and really tune into what my body is telling me. I eat when I am hungry, stop when I am full and trust myself to create my meal plans, ensuring all food is included. If ED does pipe up, I still engage in the opposite action, I know if I do not continue to challenge it, let my guard down, then it will take hold of me again.

I am about to embark on a new challenge and start training to become a counsellor, which I hope to do alongside my career as a public speaker. Helping those who are struggling with mental health, this is something a few years ago I would have never thought would have been possible. I have discovered a new passion during recovery and also developed a new personality. A more confident and outgoing individual with a love of life.

I am unsure if I will ever get rid of my ED voice, however I have learnt to treat the voice with love, kindness and compassion instead. For I understand now it was just trying to protect me from emotions so big and hard to face; however, I have learnt to embrace those emotions and feel them, instead of running away. When ED thoughts appear, I recognise it as just that, it is a thought, I do not have to do anything with it. Simply acknowledge it and move on with my day.

I have spent too much of my life in a war. A war I raged within my own mind and took it out on my body. Enough. I refuse to spend another day on the battlefield.

I am experiencing what my life could be like fully recovered and I am hungry for that life.

A life free of numbers, feeling the highs and lows. Being present with loved ones and accepting myself, wholeheartedly. Having energy to enjoy life's little moments that add up. Simply living.

I have been labelled as mentally unwell for so long I forgot who I was. Who I really am. I am actually a surfer, a TEDx speaker, musician and author. A wife, a mother and a friend. Yes, I live alongside mental illnesses, they are part of me, but they are not who I am.

Life really is too short to spend another day at war with yourself.

You are destined for much greater things.

More Information

As I am writing this, eating disorder services are severely underfunded and trying to access treatment in some parts of the country is impossible. If you are one of those fighting to get the help and support you deserve, please do not give up, please reach out to these charities and services and speak to them about what could be done and what they could offer.

For more information regarding eating disorders in the UK:

BEAT: www.beateatingdisorders.org.uk

National centre for eating disorders: www.eating-disorders.org.uk

First steps ED: www.firststepsed.co.uk

SEED: www.seedeatingdisorders.org.uk

Anorexia and Bulimia Care: www.anorexiabulimiacare.org.uk

Somerset and Wessex Eating disorder Association: www.swedauk.org

Wednesday's child: www.wednesdayschild.co.uk

ORRI: www.orri-uk.com

FEAST: www.feast-ed.org

FREED from ED: www.freedfromed.co.uk

For further information or to follow Zoe:

Twitter: @RebelBarefoot
Instagram: @Barefootrebel1

Chronos Publishing
Life Stories

We sincerely hope you enjoyed this book.

If you'd like to know more about our forthcoming titles, authors and special events, or to be notified of early releases then follow us:

on Facebook @ChronosPublishing

on Twitter @ChronosPublish

or come find us on the web at:

www.chronospublishing.com

We love what we do and we'd like you to be part of a thriving community of people who enjoy books and the very best reading experiences.

Taryn Johnston
Creative Director
The FCM Group